The Medieval Translator

II

WESTFIELD PUBLICATIONS
IN
MEDIEVAL STUDIES

Volume 5

CENTRE FOR MEDIEVAL STUDIES
QUEEN MARY AND WESTFIELD COLLEGE
UNIVERSITY OF LONDON
1991

The Medieval Translator

II

Edited by Roger Ellis

CENTRE FOR MEDIEVAL STUDIES
QUEEN MARY AND WESTFIELD COLLEGE
UNIVERSITY OF LONDON
1991

© 1991 Centre for Medieval Studies,
Queen Mary and Westfield College, University of London,
Hampstead Campus, London NW3 7ST

ISBN 1–870059–04–2
ISSN 0269–9699

This volume was prepared using facilities provided by the
Computing Services, Queen Mary and Westfield College,
University of London.

Typeset at the University of London Computer Centre.

Printed and bound by Short Run Press Limited, Exeter,
England.

Contents

vi

Acknowledgments

THIS volume could not have appeared without the encouragement and help of Mrs Marie Denley and other members of the Editorial Board of Westfield Medieval Publications, particularly Drs Felicity Rash and Peter Denley. I take this occasion, on behalf of the contributors, to thank them for their very kind offices. The volume also depends on financial support from the British Academy and the Isobel Thornley Bequest, and it is a pleasure as well as a duty to express thanks to those bodies and, in particular, Miss Pat Crimmin, secretary of the latter.

Introduction

ROGER ELLIS

THIS volume of papers heard in 1987 at the first Cardiff Conference on the Theory and Practice of Translation in the Middle Ages — as it has since become known — is designed to complement an earlier volume of papers from the same Conference.[1] Not surprisingly, a degree of overlap exists between the two volumes. Thus

(i) Translation into Middle English of French romance figured prominently in vol. 1, and reappears here in the papers of Hosington, on the M.E. translation of *Partonopeu de Blois*, and Mills, on M.E. versions of *Gui de Warewic*. The similar prominence accorded in vol. 1 to M.E. translations of (mainly Latin) religious works finds an echo here in the papers of Wollin and Pezzini, on translations into Latin, and thence, separately, into Middle English and medieval Swedish, of the revelations of St. Bridget of Sweden, and in the paper of Easting, on M.E. translations of the *Tractatus de Purgatorio Sancti Patricii*.

(ii) Chaucer's importance in the field is again underlined, as it was in vol. 1, by a paper on *Troilus and Criseyde* by

---

[1] *The Medieval Translator. The Theory and Practice of Translation in the Middle Ages*, ed. by R. Ellis et al. (Cambridge, 1989).

Thompson. (In general, as in vol. 1, and by interesting contrast
with the volume edited by Jeanette Beer,[2] named translators
are thin on the ground in this volume: apart from Chaucer, we
have only Jean de Meun, whose translation of the Abelard-
Heloise correspondence is the subject of a paper by Brook.)
(iii) Overlap also exists in Pratt's use, in her paper on 'the
translation practices of some German ... poets' (p. 2), of the
pronouncements of classical and patristic writings on the
subject of translation to provide a theoretical frame for her
discussion — as, indeed, for the whole volume.[3]
(iv) The contributors to this volume also make common cause
with their counterparts in vol. 1 in their detailed accounts of
translational techniques and practices, for example, the
problems of translating into rhyme (the papers of Easting and
Mills, cf. Hosington p. 236). Not all of the features described
here were also noted in vol. 1, but they are readily paralleled
in other translations.[4]

[2] *Medieval Translators and their Craft*, ed. by J. Beer, Studies in
Medieval Culture XXV (Kalamazoo, 1989); see also my review, *Allegorica*,
12 (1991), 53–68.

[3] Papers in vol. 1 which similarly use this material are those of Burnley,
Machan and, above all, Copeland.

[4] Consider, for example, Jean de Meun's distinctive doublet 'es vins et
es vainnes'. Brook speculates that this results from Jean's inability to decide
whether the Latin of his original 'should be "vinis" or "venis"' (p. 121). The
feature has parallels in the BL Claudius B I translation of St. Bridget's
Liber Celestis (noted in my study of the M.E. translation of *Benjamin
Minor*, in *The Medieval Mystical Tradition in England 1992*, ed. by M.
Glasscoe (Exeter, forthcoming); see further n. 10 below. For a second
example, consider the translation of two elements in a phrase in reverse
order, observable in the anonymous M.E. translations of the *Liber* studied
by Pezzini (pp. 186 n. 17, 199 n. 25), and characteristic of both the M.E.
Benjamin Minor and the Claudius *Liber* (the practice also occurs as a
feature of scribal practice in Latin manuscripts: in copies of the Latin *Liber*,
for instance).

For all that, this volume breaks ground not turned in the previous volume, and genuinely complements the latter in a number of ways. Most obviously, by contrast with vol. 1, which was restricted almost entirely to M.E. translations of French and Latin, vol. 2, though continuing to feature M.E., also includes papers on translations into Middle High German and Middle Dutch (Pratt), medieval Swedish (Wollin), Old French (Brook, Beer) and medieval Welsh (Lloyd-Morgan). Similarly, the classical and patristic models discussed in vol. 1 are extended by reference to the pronouncements of the twelfth century rhetoricians (Pratt) and to Dante, Petrarch and Seneca (Thompson).

A more important difference lies in the fact that several papers in this volume consider the circumstances in which translations were produced, whether monastic (Wollin on the Vadstena scriptorium) or courtly (Foz on the court of Alphonse X), and introduce us to the individual figures for whom, or at whose direction, the translations were produced: Raymond, Archbishop of Toledo, Alphonse X of Castile (Foz), Philip II of France (Beer). Two papers in particular (those of Foz and Lloyd-Morgan) provide an overview of translation activity in a specific area — for Foz, Toledo; for Lloyd-Morgan, Wales — during periods of 150 and 300 years respectively, involving translation from Arabic on the one hand and French and Latin on the other,[5] and permit us to conclude, for example, that later translations were characterised by greater literalness than earlier ones (p. 40, cf p. 51). The contributors' sense that translation exists in a specific time and place, as a medium of communication

[5] The latter focusses mainly on French. For a complete picture of the state of translation in medieval Wales, translations into medieval Welsh out of Middle English could also have been considered (a point kindly communicated to me by Mr Andrew Breeze).

serving specific purposes, is obviously easiest to document
when we are not dealing with anonymous translations. Thus
Pratt is able to hypothesise, from the cases of 'two of the
earliest [named] courtly adaptors', that clerical translators
would naturally start with religious translation, and then move
to translate secular material (p. 14). Yet even when the
translations are anonymous, careful reading of their evidence
can yield results. Thus texts produced for a specialised
readership — the aristocracy, the cloister — may undergo
comparable simplifications when redirected to a wider
audience: we might compare Hosington, p. 232, on the
bourgeois readership of a work originally produced for an
aristocratic audience, and Easting, on adaptations for lay
audiences of a text 'compiled in a Cistercian milieu for
monastic consumption ... to prompt meditation on ... the
rewards of the monastic life' (pp. 171–2).[6] (Easting's paper
also, by implication, addresses the question of the temporal
dimension of translation in that it considers three M.E.
versions of the *Tractatus* produced over a hundred and fifty
years, and even, p. 173 n. 40, refers to later developments in
the translation of the *Tractatus*).

This greater contextualisation of translation, if I may so
call it, accompanies a subtle change in the image of the
translator. Many of the papers of vol. 1 envisaged translation
as a solitary activity, the translator working by himself with a
single text in front of him: two of the named translators may
even have worked in prison, that ultimate image of scribal
subjection to higher (originary) authority.[7] In the papers of
the present volume translation appears most often as a process

[6] Cf. comments by Pezzini on the adaptation of *Liber* VI.lxv for a
'feminine audience, probably secular' (pp. 191–2).

[7] I.e. Malory and Usk, the subjects of papers in vol. 1 by Batt and
Medcalf.

of collaboration: with other translators (Foz, p. 37, draws attention to the specialisation that could accompany such collaboration); with readers (Foz, cf. Lloyd-Morgan p. 52); with other translations (Pratt, Foz: sometimes translators worked with an existing translation of the same text); and with other texts (Beer, Easting, Mills). These differences in emphasis explain the different arrangements of papers in the present volume. If we except the framing opening and concluding papers, the papers are arranged not generically, as was the case in vol. 1, but so as to lead the reader from accounts of translation in Toledo and Wales, by way of translation at the monastery of Vadstena and the court of Philip II, to the named translators Jean de Meun and Chaucer, and thence to anonymous translators — first those who produced different versions of the same text, and then those who worked alone.

On two points, of course, the contributors to this volume are in complete agreement both with the contributors to vol. 1 and with the translators themselves. The first concerns the difficulty of producing a translation. A notable difficulty, barely touched on in vol. 1, is the translation of tone, and especially irony and humour.[8] This is central to the papers of Beer and Hosington: the latter's paper, which concentrates, like Thompson's, on the changing role of the narrator in the translated text, has the added interest of drawing on the *Troilus* for some of its details. Another, as we saw, is the translation of prose or verse into rhyme. Underlying all such difficulties is the sheer difficulty of mastering a foreign language, well dramatised in the story of the translators who

[8] A notable exception to this generalisation in vol. 1 was provided by Field's paper. It is noteworthy that detailed comparisons of originals and translations in respect of style — a project as risky as it is seductive — are more regularly represented in this than in the earlier volume.

drank infusions of plants thought to facilitate the retention of
Arab words, or ate almonds on which had been traced
abbreviated versions of Arab words (Foz, p. 42).

Comparable difficulties, it must be admitted, also attend
the modern study of translation, and explain the tentative or
paradoxical conclusions often advanced (eg 'the co-existence
of freedom and fidelity' in the translation of *Partonopeu de
Blois*, p. 240, cf. p. 252). As I have noted elsewhere, 'every
instance of practice that we may be tempted to erect into a
principle has its answering opposite, sometimes in the same
work'.[9] One reason for this diffidence is quite simply the
problematic status of both original and translated texts. In
general the contributors to vol. 1 took for granted the status of
their texts; by contrast, several of the papers in this volume
address that question directly by considering the complex
textual relationships existing between originals and translation:
even when reliable editions exist of both, the interpretation of
their evidence is far from straightforward. Hence the final
essay in this volume, by Marx, demonstrates the pitfalls that
accompany the attempted production of a critical edition of a
translation by citing the complex relations between three M.E.
manuscript copies of a translation from an Anglo-Norman text
and the two manuscript copies in which the latter is
preserved.[10] Hence too, as a way of shortcircuiting some of

---

[9] *Allegorica* 12, 65–6. Another difficulty, partly of the critic's own
making, concerns the identification of a distinctive style of translation which
would enable us to link it, as by the same writer, with other original or
translated work (p. 206).

[10] Marx's caveats impose caution even when the translator appears to be
self-evidently and self-consciously operating, as in the earlier-noted instance
(n. 4 above) of doublets of visually similar words, which Brook saw as a
feature of Jean de Meun's translation practice. Such doublets might have
first appeared in the copy of the Latin de Meun was using for his
translation; comparable doublets do occur, for instance, in manuscripts of

the difficulties, the comparative analyses here offered of different translations into the same vernacular, or closely related vernaculars, of the same text, whether the latter is preserved in a single version (Pezzini, Pratt) or in different versions (Easting, Mills): a comparative study of translation practices, best undertaken when the same text is being translated, allows firmer conclusions to be drawn about the practices of each version.[11]

Nevertheless, this volume shares with its predecessor a spirited rejection of the common assumption that translation is inferior to 'original' writing (pp. 46, 68, 91), and reacts in very similar ways against the equally common distinction, regularly forced and frequently unhelpful for the study of medieval translation, between translation and adaptation (p. 95), since 'authors, translators and scribes were frequently one and the same' (pp. 266–7).[12] (Admittedly, I should not wish entirely to collapse the distinction, notional though it is and unstable though the boundary that it represents may be.) The contributors' understanding of the importance of translation can be supported in any number of ways from the assembled evidence: for example, translation into the vernacular can be part of a programme of creating national identity (hence the choice not of Latin but of Castilian to translate Arabic texts in

the Latin of St. Bridget's *Liber* (and cf. the speculations of Marx, pp. 262–3, on a parallel doublet in the M.E. *Complaint of our Lady*, though his argument there can be turned on its head as readily as that of Brooks).

[11] As Pratt argued in her contribution to *Medieval Translators* (Beer, p. 220), different versions of the same text probably represent different attitudes towards translation.

[12] Pratt's observation that the term *diuten* 'seems to cover a range of meanings from translation to interpretation' (p. 24), though repeating a point made in her earlier article (Beer, *Medieval Translators* p. 222), bears centrally on this point.

the thirteenth century, p. 32);[13] or it can assist powerfully in the creation of a standardised written vernacular (pp. 40, 66).[14] In Beer's words, translation (and, one might add, writing about translation) 'remains a dangerously vital process' (p. 97).

---

[13] Cf. remarks by Chaucer on the status of English as a medium for scientific translation, and as an expression of national identity, in the prologue to his *Treatise on the Astrolabe* (*The Riverside Chaucer*, ed. L. D. Benson et al. (Oxford, New York, Toronto, 1988), p. 662, especially ll. 50–59.

[14] Conversely, if a 'unified and standardised literary language' were already in existence, it might well exert a centripetal pull on texts translated from another language (p. 58).

Medieval Attitudes to Translation and Adaptation: the Rhetorical Theory and the Poetic Practice

KAREN PRATT

ALTHOUGH *remaniement*, the reworking of given subject-matter, was a craft widely practised by vernacular poets in the Middle Ages and translation formed a major sub-category of the genre, there is a dearth of precise theoretical pronouncements on this activity in the vernacular literature of the twelfth and early thirteenth centuries. Apart from the very brief references to aims and methods which appear in some prologues and epilogues, there is little material with which a modern critic might arrive at criteria for judging the success or failure of a medieval adaptation on its own terms.

For medieval theories of translation one has recourse to the statements of the translators and commentators of Sacred texts: notably Jerome, Augustine and Boethius, or to the widely-studied classical rhetoricians Horace, Cicero and Quintilian. The latter served as important sources for the medieval *artes poeticae*, and it is in this later medieval form that vernacular authors probably became acquainted with classical poetic doctrine on the art of rewriting. Although we have no proof that the major German adaptors of the late

twelfth and early thirteenth centuries had read the treatises of
Matthew of Vendôme, Geoffrey of Vinsauf, Eberhard the
German, John of Garland, and so on, it is clear from their
works that some had received rhetorical training in the schools
and were familiar with a range of precepts codified in the
extant *artes*.[1]

One of the aims of this paper is to discuss the relevance
and usefulness of these two sets of theoretical material (the
rhetorical and the biblical) for an assessment of the German
adaptor's task. In so doing, I hope to reexamine and elucidate
the meaning of key terms which are vital to our understanding
of medieval translation — namely fidelity, literality,
subject-matter and sense (Chrétien's *matière* and *sen*). In
particular, I shall examine the extent to which the Latin theory
may have influenced statements about adaptation made by
German authors in their prologues. Finally, the vernacular
theory will be compared with the translation practices of some
German (or Germanic) poets, and explanations offered for the
differences between theory and practice.

In early medieval translation theory, fidelity to a source
was equated with literal translation.[2] This seems to have
involved the use of direct formal equivalents and the retention
as far as possible of the original word order and syntax.
Literality was especially important when translating the Bible,
for the word of God was authoritative and needed to be

---

[1] See my article 'The Rhetoric of Adaptation: The Middle Dutch and
Middle High German Versions of *Floire et Blancheflor*', in *Courtly
Literature: Culture and Context*, edited by Keith Busby and Erik Kooper
(Amsterdam, Philadelphia, 1990), pp. 483–97.

[2] See Louis G. Kelly, *The True Interpreter: A History of Translation
Theory and Practice in the West* (Oxford, 1979).

preserved as completely as possible.[3] Even Jerome, who generally argues that the translator should avoid word-for-word rendering and concentrate instead on conveying the sense of the model ('non verbum e verbo, sed sensum exprimere de sensu'), concedes that he translated Holy Scripture literally because the order of words was an integral part of the mystery: 'et verborum ordo mysterium est'.[4]

However, for the translation of non-biblical texts, Jerome points out the artificiality of the literal method ('Si ad verbum interpretor, absurde resonant' — If I translate them word for word, they sound ridiculous — complains Jerome to Pammachius). This highlights the dangers of using verbal equivalents which are not functional equivalents in the two languages, or of employing etymologically related words which, as a result of semantic change, no longer have the same range of meaning or connotative value.[5] In order to avoid these pitfalls the *interpres* must proceed not word by word, but sense unit by sense unit: 'per cola et commata' says Jerome in his preface to Ezechiel, using Cicero's terminolgy found in his *Brutus*, 162 and *Orator*, 211. Furthermore, he must adapt the source language to the needs of the target language. This method of dynamic equivalence was, however, seen by its critics as a means of adding meanings to the model, hence the need for Jerome's spirited defence of this approach in his famous letter to Pammachius. Although he has

---

[3] See Augustine's *De doctrina christiana*, II, 19–20 and III, 2–3, edited by Migne, *Patrologia Latina*, 34, cols. 43 and 65, in which he recommends literal translation even to the detriment of style, since God's word has multiple meanings, none of which should be forfeited.

[4] Jerome, *Ad Pammachium* (Ep. 57), edited by Migne, *Patrologia Latina*, 22, col. 571.

[5] The problems of shifting verbal usage and semantic change are discussed by John of Salisbury in his *Metalogicon*, Book III, Chapter 4.

avoided literality, he nevertheless claims here not to have
changed the sense of the original nor to have added anything:
'nihil mutatum esse de sensu, nec res additas, nec aliquod
dogma confictum'. This is still, therefore, a conservative
approach to translation.

Interestingly, in arguing his case, Jerome invokes as
authorities two classical rhetoricians, thus appearing to place
himself in the camp of literary translators. He first chooses to
quote Cicero's *De optimo genere oratorum*, V, 14 (which
clearly influenced the title of Jerome's letter: *De optimo
genere interpretandi*):

> nec converti ut interpres, sed ut orator, sententiis isdem et
> earum   formis   tamquam   figuris,   verbis   ad   nostram
> consuetudinem aptis. In quibus non verbum pro verbo necesse
> habui reddere, sed genus omne verborum vimque servavi.
> [And I did not translate them as an interpreter, but as an
> orator, keeping the same ideas and forms, or as one might
> say, the 'figures' of thought, but in language which conforms
> to our usage. And in so doing, I did not hold it necessary to
> render word for word, but I preserved the general style and
> force of the language.][6]

Then Jerome repeats Horace's famous words from *Ars poetica*,
133–34: 'Nec verbum verbo curabis reddere fidus | Interpres',
thus seeming to align himself with those who saw fidelity in
negative terms as the attribute of clumsy, inexperienced
translators.[7]

---

[6] Since Jerome's text differs little from Cicero, quotations are taken
from Cicero's *De optimo genere oratorum*, translated by H.M. Hubbell,
Loeb Classical Library (London, 1949), pp. 364–65. I would prefer,
however, to render *interpres* by 'translator'.

[7] Cf. Cicero, *De finibus bonorum et malorum*, III, 4, 15, translated by
H. Rackham, Loeb Classical Library (London, 1914), pp. 230–33:
> Nec tamen exprimi verbum e verbo necesse erit, ut interpretes
> indiserti solent, cum sit verbum quod idem declaret magis usitatum;

Jerome was not the only medieval theoretician to cite
Horace. Matthew of Vendôme, in his *Ars versificatoria* (circa
1175), criticises 'ill-taught persons ... who paraphrase the
fables of the poets word for word', saying that they must be
encouraged to 'imitate wonted events, so that they utter truths
or verisimilitudes. Nor should anyone propose to render word
for word like an overly faithful translator' — 'Nec etiam
aliquis verbo verbum proponat reddere fidus interpres'(IV,
1).[8] Similarly, Horace's advice to poets to treat again
traditional material already in poetic form: 'Difficile est
proprie communia dicere'(128) is echoed by Geoffrey of
Vinsauf in his *Documentum de modo et arte dictandi et
versificandi* (early thirteenth century):

equidem soleo etiam, quod uno Graeci, si aliter non possum, idem
pluribus verbis exponere.
[Though all the same it need not be a hard and fast rule that every
word shall be represented by its exact counterpart, when there is a
more familiar word conveying the same meaning. That is the way of
a clumsy translator. Indeed my own practice is to use several words
to give what is expressed in Greek by one, if I cannot convey the
sense otherwise.]
The *Ad Pammachium* is a highly polemical work, in which Jerome uses his
powers of rhetoric and chooses his quotations carefully from classical
treatises in order to defend his practice in this particular case. His attitude
to translation is not, however, to be equated in all respects with that of his
authorities. In general, Jerome was much more conservative than his Roman
predecessors, varying his approach according to the nature of the material
to be rendered into Latin.

[8] Matthew's *Ars versificatoria* is quoted from Edmond Faral's edition:
*Les Arts poétiques du XIIe et du XIIIe siècle. Recherches et documents sur
la technique littéraire du moyen âge*, Bibliothèque de l'Ecole des Hautes
Etudes, No. 28 (Paris, 1924) and in the translation by Ernest Gallo,
'Matthew of Vendôme: Introductory Treatise on the Art of Poetry',
Proceedings of the American Philosophical Society, 118, No. 1 (1974),
51–92, here pp. 180 and 84 respectively.

Et quanto difficilius tanto laudabilius est bene tractare materiam talem, scilicet communem et usitatam, quam materiam aliam, scilicet novam et inusitatam. (II, 3, item 132)[9]
[And just as it is more difficult, so it is more praiseworthy to treat well such material, that is well known and familiar, than to treat the other sort of material, which is new and unfamiliar.]

The aim of Geoffrey's work, like that of Matthew, was to train schoolboys in the craft of versification. The boys were expected to produce new compositions using old subject-matter, often imitating the style of the great masters. Although this activity did not necessarily involve translation, it seems likely that translators drew on the skills acquired in this way. German adaptors of the *Blütezeit* (late 12th and early 13th centuries) can thus be viewed as the inheritors of a fairly continuous tradition of rewriting (*imitatio* or *aemulatio* as a means of learning the poetic craft), a tradition stretching from Cicero (see *De oratore*, II, 22, 90–93), Horace, Quintilian (who suggests paraphrasing a text in order to analyse it and to experiment with structures)[10] and Longinus (who presents *imitatio* as a path to the sublime)[11] down to the school exercises described by Matthew and Geoffrey. However, in this classical, rhetorical tradition, unlike that of Bible translation, fidelity is considered a negative feature, especially of course if the rewriting occurs in the same language. Thus, in order to avoid possible charges of plagiarism Geoffrey advises the *remanieur*:

[9] The *Documentum* is also quoted from Faral's edition.
[10] See *Institutio oratoria*, X, 2, on imitation.
[11] See Longinus, *On the Sublime*, Chapter 13.

1.   not to delay where others have done so, but to treat briefly the fully developed descriptions and digressions of the source:

> non debemus ibidem immorari circa digressiones vel descriptiones, sed breviter locum illum materiae transilire. (*Documentum*, II, 3, item 133)

2.   and not to be tied to the pattern of words of his model, nor retain them in the same order:

> ne sequamur vestigia verborum ... Ibi dicamus aliquid ubi dixerunt nihil, et ubi dixerunt aliquid, nos nihil. (II, 3, item 134).

However, innovation and originality are placed within strict boundaries, and his pupils are warned not to depart from the *materia* in such a way that they are unable to return to it:

> ut de materia non transeamus ad talem articulum unde reverti nesciamus ad materiam. (II, 3, item 135).

Although Geoffrey probably exerted no direct influence on the German adaptors discussed below, these strategies can be illustrated from their works.

Matthew of Vendôme in his *Ars versificatoria* also gives advice on the reworking of existing material, which requires differing treatment depending on whether it is already in verse (*materia exsecuta* or *pertractata*) or not yet versified (*materia illibata*). The former is considered the more difficult to rework, and the master suggests his pupils might eliminate from it deficiencies in grammar, vocabulary, metre and logic, while deleting superfluous elements and supplying what is wanting:

> Sunt enim quaedam verba quae, quasi damnata, debent in serie tractatus praetermitti ... Debent enim minus dicta suppleri, et inconcinna in melius permutari, superflua penitus aboleri. (IV, 2, Faral, p. 180)

[Indeed, there are certain expressions which, though condemned, ought to be omitted from the course of the work ... Hence what is not fully expressed must be filled in, what is awkward must be improved, and what is superfluous must be entirely done away with. (Gallo, pp. 84–85).]

Here we seem to have the theoretical justification for the emendations, additions and deletions which German adaptors make to their *materia exsecuta*: the Old French verse narratives which serve as their sources. Matthew concludes though that the ideas or content of the original must be followed, while changes in vocabulary and syntax are necessary in order to avoid plagiarism:

> Igitur materiae pertractatae sententiis erit a modernis collateraliter insistendum, verbis permutatis et variato dictionum matrimonio, ne, si verba authentica et easdem juncturas aliquis sibi in proprium velit vendicare, penuriae sensus possit deputari. (IV, 15, Faral, p. 184)
> [Hence moderns must follow closely the meanings of material already treated. Change the words and wed them in a varied manner, lest, in wishing to arrogate to yourself the original words and in the same order, you be thought to lack judgment. (Gallo, p. 87)[12]]

This emphasis on the preservation of the ideas (*sententiae*) of the model echoes Jerome's contention that the content or meaning of a non-biblical source text is more important than its formal characteristics. Moreover, Matthew seems to be singling out for innovatory treatment only the formal

[12] Gallo here translates *insistendum* by 'must follow' (p. 87). I have preferred this reading to Douglas Kelly's more tendentious 'must be emphasized' in 'The Scope and Treatment of Composition in the Twelfth- and Thirteenth-Century Arts of Poetry', *Speculum*, 41 (1966), 261–78 (p. 267). However, Kelly's interpretation of this passage is more in keeping with Carl Lofmark's view of adaptation with its insistence on the authority of the source, which is discussed below.

characteristics of the model (*verba* and *dictio*). However, comparison of vernacular translations with their sources reveals that the sense of the original, in other words the interpretation which the earlier author had placed on the subject-matter, is not always preserved intact. As Louis Kelly rightly observes, there is always an element of subjectivity in translation: 'The essential variable is what the translator sees in the original, and what he wishes to pass on' (p. 227). Likewise, Claude Buridant, discussing the two approaches to the *materia* outlined in the *artes*, namely *amplificatio* and *abbreviatio*, makes the important point that *materia* is not 'matière, mais ... ce qui doit être dit'.[13] Again, a subjective process of selection and judgement is implied. It seems therefore that mature poets and adaptors went further in practice than the rhetorical manuals designed for schoolboys allowed. Indeed, Geoffrey of Vinsauf's more sophisticated *Poetria nova* does not give such constraining advice on the reworking of material, but concentrates instead on the whole process of literary creation: *inventio, dispositio, elocutio, memoria* and *actio*.

The creative independence and selectivity of a medieval author are important features in Douglas Kelly's helpful elucidation of the relationship between *matière* and *sen*. He describes how a medieval poet trained in rhetoric would employ topical invention in order to 'express *san* in a given *matiere*'.[14] Beginning with a mental picture of the work he

[13] Claude Buridant, 'Translatio medievalis. Théorie et pratique de la traduction médiévale', *Travaux de linguistique et de littérature*, 21 (1983), 81–136 (p. 119).

[14] Douglas Kelly, 'The Art of Description', in *The Legacy of Chrétien de Troyes*, edited by Norris Lacy, Douglas Kelly and Keith Busby (Amsterdam, 1987), vol. I, pp. 191–221 (p. 192). What follows is a summary of Kelly's definition of topical invention. See 'Topical Invention in Medieval French Literature', in *Medieval Eloquence*, edited by James J.

wished to produce, he would adapt the material to this picture by identifying in it places (*loci*) which were susceptible to elaboration using topoi. The result would be *materia propinqua*, which he describes as a 'combination of *materia*, topical additions and links that eliminate lacunae'. The *materia propinqua* 'contains ideas the author wishes to show forth' i.e. his own conception of the subject. Moreover, *sen* is also a product of context, hence of *conjointure*. The example Kelly gives of this process is 'Thomas's adaptation of the Tristan legend to his own conception of courtly love'.

It is probable, therefore, that German adaptors, like the French *remanieurs* and translators of Latin models who preceded them, were practised in the art of amplification and would quite naturally elaborate on their source material during rewriting. Not tied to literal translation as were scriptural translators, they could, if they wished, employ amplificatory devices and topical invention in order to confer on their original a new *sen*. By adopting a rhetorical mode of rewriting, they differed fundamentally even from the Jerome of the *Ad Pammachium*, for in spite of the latter's citation of Horace, his approach to the content and doctrine of his models was conservative even in his non-literal translations.

Before turning to the German poets' own statements in their prologues, with a view to assessing the influence on them of the translation models discussed thus far, it is worth looking briefly at John of Salisbury's comments on the translation of Aristotle's works in his *Metalogicon*, dated 1159. In Book III, Chapter 4, on *De Interpretatione*, John maintains that twelfth-century teachers of the liberal arts could sometimes explain the doctrine of the ancients more simply and effectively than the original masters. Their method, he says, was to add details drawn from other sources,

Murphy (Los Angeles, London, 1974), pp. 231–51.

supplementing the original and explaining it in comprehensible terms. Yet the words of the ancients were nevertheless to be preserved since 'they contain tremendous hidden as well as apparent power'.[15] He concludes though that 'if possible, both the words of the arts and their sense should be preserved; but ... if we cannot save them both, the words should be dropped without losing their sense' (p. 170).

John's words demonstrate that the debate concerning source fidelity was alive in the twelfth-century schools, where the authority of Aristotle's own words was still jealously guarded, but could ultimately be sacrificed to sense. The medieval teachers mentioned by John who supplement their sources from elsewhere reflect a tendency observable in much medieval translation and will be illustrated below by Meister Otte's *Eraclius*.[16]

Turning now to vernacular translators' own statements about their task, we find that the most common themes expressed in the prologues are:

1.   That the translator's chosen source is authoritative, being older and truer than the possible alternatives.
2.   That the translator has rendered it faithfully, adding and omitting nothing.

[15] Quotations from John of Salisbury, *Metalogicon*, translated by Daniel D. McGarry (Berkeley and Los Angeles, 1955). Here p. 168.

[16] Paul Chavy, 'Les Premiers Translateurs Français', *The French Review*, 47 (1974), 557–65, notes that 'il sera légitime de supprimer le superflu et d'ajouter le profitable' (p. 559) if the poet's aim is didactic, and Geoffrey of Waterford in his translation of the *Secret des Secrets* clearly feels justified in exploiting other authoritative sources:

Souvent i metterai autres bonnes paroles, les ques tot ne soient mie en cel livre, al mains sunt en autre livres d'autoritei, et ne sunt pas mains profitable ke celles qui en cel livre sunt escrites. (B.N. fr. 1822) (Quoted by Buridant, p. 116).

3. That his aim has been to render it in an intelligible form
for the edification or moral instruction of his readers/listeners
who do not speak the language of the original.

4. That the translation has been carried out either to the
glory of God, in order that the poet's talents be put to good
use, or at the behest of a patron (the *Auftragstopos*).

It is clear that remarks concerning fidelity to an
authoritative source are reminiscent of the tradition of biblical
translation. Pfaffe Konrad, in his epilogue to the *Rolandslied*,
claims that he translated his French model first into Latin, then
into German, adding and omitting nothing:

> danne in di tûtiske gekêret.
> ich nehân der niht an gemêret.
> ich nehân der niht uberhaben.   9083–85[17]

> [then turned into German. I have added nothing to it.
> I have omitted nothing from it.]

His words echo not only Jerome's '*res additas*' (*Ad
Pammachium*, quoted above), but also St. John the Divine's
warning at the end of Revelations against adding or
subtracting anything from the word of God:

> Si quis apposuerit ad haec, apponet Deus super illum plagas
> scriptas in libro isto. Et si quis diminuerit de verbis libri
> prophetiae huius, auferet Deus partem eius de libro vitae, et
> de civitate sancta, et de his quae scripta sunt in libro isto.[18]
> [If any man shall add unto these things, God shall add unto
> him the plagues that are written in this book. And if any man

---

[17] Quoted by Carl Lofmark, *The Authority of the Source in Middle High
German Narrative Poetry*, Bithell Series of Dissertations, No. 5 (London,
1981), p. 48.

[18] Quoted from Apocalipsis 22, 18–19 in *Biblia vulgata*, edited by A.
Colunga and L. Turrado (Madrid, 1977).

shall take away from the words of the book of this prophecy,
God shall take away his part out of the book of life, and out
of the holy city, and from the things which are written in this
book.]

Wolfram too claims to have '*volsprochen*' his story of
Parzival (*Parzival*, 827, 28), a term which implies that nothing
has been left out.

Similarly, when German adaptors state that their written
sources contain the truth, as do Pfaffe Konrad, Wolfram
(*Willehalm*, 5, 15), the author of the *Ezzolied* and many
others,[19] they are following either Jerome, who identified
truth with the authentic text ('*Hebraica veritas*') or Augustine,
who equated truth with preserving content.[20]

Finally, the scribe who produced the epilogue to
Veldeke's *Eneit* likewise echoes the concerns of biblical
translators not to alter the meaning of their models:

heme ne was ter reden nit so ga
dat he dore sine scolde
den sin verderwen solde,
sint dat he sich's underwant,
want alse he't geschreven vant,
also hevet he't vore getogen,
dat'er anders nit hevet gelogen
dan alse'r ane den buken las.   13516–23[21]

[He was not so hasty with his words that he might
distort the meaning, since he undertook to select only
what he found written there and did not lie apart from
preserving those lies he already found in the books he
read.]

---

[19] For examples, see Lofmark, p. 24.

[20] See L. Kelly, p. 206.

[21] Quoted by Lofmark, p. 41.

It is not surprising that one finds reminiscences of the theory of biblical translation in the prologues of Middle High German adaptations, since, as Carl Lofmark demonstrates, translation in Germany began with clerics rendering into the vernacular Latin texts on religious subjects. It is significant that two of the earliest courtly adaptors, Veldeke and Pfaffe Lamprecht, first treated religious, then secular material: Saints' Lives concerning Servatius and Tobias, followed by the *Eneit* and *Alexanderlied* respectively. No doubt they wished to confer the same credentials on their courtly romances as they did on their more edifying works.

However, although the clerical tradition of translating Christian subject-matter has clearly influenced the vernacular theory of translation as expressed in prologues, it is questionable that these pronouncements offer the key to the adaptor's activity in practice. Lofmark, in emphasising the authority of the source in German translation practice of the High Middle Ages appears to ally himself with the group of French scholars headed by Jean Fourquet and Michel Huby who have defined '*adaptation courtoise*' — the translation of French courtly literature into German — in such a way as to minimise the innovation and originality of the German texts.[22] However, a comparison of most Middle High German adaptations with their models reveals discrepancies and innovation at all levels of the work and suggests that

---

[22] See Michel Huby, *L'Adaptation des romans courtois en Allemagne au XIIe et au XIIIe siècle* (Paris, 1968) and Jean Fourquet, *Hartmann d'Aue, Erec. Iwein. Extraits accompagnés des textes correspondants de Chrétien de Troyes avec Introduction, Notes et Glossaires* (Paris, 1944). Taking these exordial professions of fidelity to the model at face value, this group of critics argues that the German translators strove to preserve the content and meaning of their sources and their only scope for novel intervention was in the verbal presentation of the material. In other words, only at the level of *forme* (including structure) not *fond*.

translators in practice rarely adhered to their avowed aims. James Schultz, in his review of Lofmark's book, emphasises the conventional nature of exordial veracity claims supported by written sources,[23] and Claude Buridant, having noted that 'si l'on confronte en effet certaines déclarations d'intention à leur mise en pratique, on observe des distorsions' (p. 107), concludes that source fidelity is a topos common in French, English and German literature. Indeed, though sometimes sincere, it often functions as part of the *ab adversariorum* type of *captatio benevolentiae*, by which adaptors, in order to recommend to their audience their own version of a story, castigate their rivals, ostensibly for basing their works on inauthentic sources.[24]

It seems therefore that biblical translation theory is something of a red herring when applied to the translation of courtly romances in the vernacular. My contention is that the poetic, rhetorical tradition of rewriting provides a much more useful key to the understanding of *adaptation courtoise* in practice. Unfortunately, few Germanic translators working in the late twelfth and early thirteenth centuries make statements about their task which link them with the rhetorical tradition. Exceptions though are Gottfried von Straßburg and Diederic van Assenede. The latter, who rendered *Floire et Blancheflor (version aristocratique)* into Middle Dutch around 1260, emphasises the difficulty of translating into verse, then seems to refer to the two rhetorical processes taught in the schools,

[23] See James Schultz, *Germanic Review*, 57 (1982), 164–66 and Jeanette M.A. Beer, *Narrative Conventions of Truth in the Middle Ages* (Geneva, 1981).

[24] See *Rhetorica ad Herennium*, I, 4, 8 and Tony Hunt, 'The Rhetorical Background to the Arthurian Prologue: Tradition and the Old French Vernacular Prologues', *Forum for Modern Language Studies*, 6 (1970), 1–23 for a discussion of this strategy.

namely *amplificatio* and *abbreviatio*:

> Men moet corten ende linghen
> Die tale, sal mense te rime bringhen,
> Ende te redenen die aventure.   19–21[25]

> [One must shorten and lengthen the tale, if one wishes
> to versify it and put the story into words.]

Gottfried's famous literary *excursus* in his *Tristan*, in which he describes Hartmann's poetic talents, constitutes a second allusion to rhetorical procedures:

> Hartmann der Ouwaere,
> ahî, wie der diu maere
> beid'ûzen unde innen
> mit worten und mit sinnen
> durchvärwet und durchzieret!
> wie er mit rede figieret
> der âventiure meine!   4619–25[26]

> [Hartmann von Aue, ah, how he colours and
> ornaments the story thoroughly, both externally and
> internally, with words and ideas! How he uses the art
> of diction to bring out the meaning of the story.]

Werner Fechter has shown the similarities between this terminology and the sections of Geoffrey of Vinsauf's *Poetria nova* which treat of stylistic ornament:[27]

Sit brevis aut longus, se semper sermo coloret

---

[25] Quoted from Diederic van Assenede, *Floris ende Blancefloer*, edited by J.J. Mak (Zwolle, 1960).

[26] Quoted from Gottfried von Straßburg, *Tristan*, edited by Peter Ganz, 2 vols (Wiesbaden, 1978).

[27] Werner Fechter, *Lateinische Dichtkunst und deutsches Mittelalter: Forschungen über Ausdrucksmittel, poetische Technik und Stil mittelhochdeutscher Dichtungen* (Berlin, 1964).

Intus et exterius ...   742–43

... sed intus et extra
Sit color et pingat manus artis utrumque colorem.

                                                           1886–87

[Whether it be brief or long, a discourse should always have
both internal and external adornment...]

[rather, see that there is both internal and external adornment.
Let the hand of artistic skill provide colours of both
kinds.][28]

Geoffrey and Gottfried are here stressing the importance
of harmonising meaning with expression, of choosing
ornament appropriate to sense.[29] According to the latter,
Hartmann has, by means of his abundant rhetorical skills,
presented with admirable clarity ('*kristallîniu wortelîn*', 4227)
the meaning he found in, or decided to impose upon, his
subject-matter.[30] Similarly, Gottfried himself has given us his

---

[28] Quoted from Ernest Gallo, *The 'Poetria Nova' and its Sources in
Early Rhetorical Doctrine* (The Hague, Paris, 1971) and Margaret F. Nims's
translation (Toronto, 1967).

[29] See my discussion of these passages in *Meister Otte's 'Eraclius' as
an Adaptation of 'Eracle' by Gautier d'Arras*, Göppinger Arbeiten zur
Germanistik, No. 932 (Göppingen, 1987), pp. 124–27. My interpretation
differs from that of Lofmark, who says of the phrase 'mit worten und mit
sinnen' that Gottfried 'does not give the adaptor licence to invent
significance, but expects him to apply his wits and sensitivity to the story'
(p. 73). This statement fits in with Lofmark's insistence that Hartmann has
merely made more explicit the meaning inherent in his source 'der âventiure
meine'. I prefer to see in Gottfried's words a reflection of the process of
topical invention as outlined above.

[30] See Paul Salmon, 'The Works of Hartmann von Aue in the Light of
Medieval Poetics' (unpublished Ph.D. dissertation, London, 1957) for a
discussion of Hartmann's use of rhetoric.

own version of the Tristan story, the subjective element in this process hinted at by the words '*mîn lesen*':

> waz aber mîn lesen dô waere
> von disem senemaere:
> daz lege ich mîner willekür
> allen edelen herzen vür.   167–70.

> [The fruits of my reading of this love story I lay willingly before all noble hearts.[31]]

Having attempted to show that the discrepancies between the theory and the practice in the Middle Ages are often attributable to the differences between the biblical and rhetorical traditions (the former in general influencing vernacular theory: the latter, practice), it is now necessary to examine more closely the different methods employed by vernacular translators. In order to illustrate this diversity in translation practice the following material will be discussed. First, Meister Otte's *Eraclius* as an instance of an adaptation which combines additional, chronicle material with its main source, and whose author represents the historical approach to translation (the adaptor as *compilator*). Second, Diederic van Assenede's *Floris ende Blancefloer* as an example of a translated version which draws on two literary sources. Third, the Middle High German *Flore und Blanscheflur*, whose author Konrad Fleck, along with Hartmann von Aue and others, exemplifies the didactic, moralising approach to translation. Finally, to broaden the scope of this enquiry, the English, Dutch and German versions of *Floire et Blancheflor*

---

[31] Again, Lofmark's interpretation of these lines endows them with a meaning which suits his thesis, but which may not be consonant with Gottfried's intention: 'Gottfried has found the proper source and reports its substance' (p. 49). This reading in no way reflects the pride in authorship so evident in the master of Straßburg's words.

will be contrasted in order to illustrate dissimilar treatments of
the same subject-matter by different translators all working in
the thirteenth century.

The prologue to Otte's *Eraclius*, a romance composed
around 1210, affords us some insight into the German's
attitude towards translation. Having declared that he has not
in the past used his God-given talents wisely (a familiar
exordial topos[32]), he expresses the hope that the present work
will atone for his sins of omission. The subject-matter is
particularly appropriate, being the life of the emperor
Heraclius, who won back the Holy Cross from the pagan
Persians in the seventh century. The eponymous hero is thus
introduced as an instrument of God and Otte claims to tell the
true story about him:

> deste gewisser sult ir wesen,
> daz ich iu niht wil missesagen   88–89[33]

> [You should therefore be all the more certain that I
> am not going to tell you lies.]

However, the truth according to Otte (who proudly presents
himself as a '*gelêrter man*' (136) in his *exordium*) turns out to
be the historical truth about the emperor. While Gautier
d'Arras produces a flattering account of Heraclius's life — a
positive *exemplum* for all to emulate — and shows his hero
dying triumphant, the German adaptor has compared Gautier's

---

[32] See in particular the prologues to the *Roman de Thèbes* and the
Roman de Troie with their references to the parable of the talents as the
author's *causa scribendi*.

[33] Quoted from *Eraclius. Deutsches Gedicht des dreizehnten
Jahrhunderts*, edited by Harald Graef (Straßburg, 1883). Cf. lines 108–12.
There exists a more recent synoptic edition by Winfried Frey, G.A.G., No.
348 (Göppingen, 1983).

Eracle with chronicle evidence and found it wanting.[34] He consequently chooses to depict the historically authenticated events of Heraclius's later life: his adoption of heresies, his incest and his ignominious death from dropsy, even though in so doing he ruins Gautier d'Arras's moral conception of his material and produces an ultimately negative rather than positive *exemplum* in his hero.

Otte's scholarly approach to translation is reminiscent of the methods used by teachers in twelfth-century schools as described by John of Salisbury and can readily be compared with other medieval translators such as Pfaffe Lamprecht and Veldeke, who both use additional sources with which to correct or supplement their main French one. Veldeke draws on Virgil's *Aeneid* and the writings of Dictys and Ovid; Lamprecht on the *Historia de Preliis*; Otte includes information from the Middle High German *Kaiserchronik* and from Otto von Freising's Latin *Chronicon*. Furthermore, both Veldeke and Otte add material which sets their stories more firmly in their historical contexts and indeed within the history of salvation.

Despite Otte's emphasis on historical truth, this German adaptor also seemed concerned to produce a well crafted work. Hence his use of terminology reminiscent of Gottfried when he speaks in his *procemium* of:

> dirre wârheit, mit rîme,
> die ich zesamen lîme
> mit den geziugen, die ich hân.   119–21[35]

---

[34] For a fuller discussion of Otte's additional sources see my *Meister Otte's 'Eraclius'*, Chapter 14.

[35] Cf. Gottfried's *Tristan*, 4713–14 and Geoffrey's *Poetria nova*, 1247. I am aware that *lima* in Latin and *lîmen* in Middle High German have different meanings, but it is nevertheless significant that they occur in similar contexts. Cf. *Eracle*, 47–48.

[This truth, which I am versifying and putting
together with the tools which I possess.]

The adaptation itself shows some signs of rhetorical
influence and amplification, but whereas the majority of
German translations of courtly romances are much longer than
the originals, Otte, like Herbort von Fritzlar in his *Liet von
Troye*, has preferred *abbreviatio* to *amplificatio*. Thus although
Otte has preserved the main lines of the original plot, apart
from its ending, and although he does sometimes translate
very literally, numerous minor alterations at the level of
characterisation, theme, rhetorical embellishment, use of direct
speech and so on have resulted in a much abbreviated, more
historical account of the life of Heraclius and a version of the
story rather different from that envisaged by Gautier d'Arras.

While Otte illustrates the practice of using a more
authoritative Latin text (Otto's *Chronicon*) in order to correct
one's primary model, Diederic van Assenede seems to have
had recourse to a German translation of the French *Floire et
Blancheflor* so as to facilitate the translating of the same
source into Middle Dutch. This phenomenon is discussed by
Buridant, who says, 'la pratique de la compilation est telle que
l'on n'hésitera pas, à l'occasion, à utiliser ouvertement une
version préexistante, ce qui peut être une solution de secours
et de facilité' (p. 132). He reminds us of Curt Wittlin's
observation that some Spanish translations of St. Augustine's
De Civitate Dei were produced with the aid of
second-generation Italian versions.[36] Some of the innovations
to the French model which Diederic's and Fleck's versions
share are not attributable to a common source, for there is too
much stemmatic evidence against this. I have therefore argued

[36] Curt Wittlin, 'Traductions et commentaires médiévaux de la Cité de
Dieu de saint Augustin', (*Mélanges Rychner*), *Travaux de linguistique et de
littérature*, 16 (1978), 531–41.

elsewhere that Diederic, who composed his poem around
1260, knew Fleck's romance, dated circa 1220, and drew on
it both for some fairly insignificant details and for some
substantial additions to the model.[37] These include elements
in the rhetorical descriptions of Blancheflor's cenotaph and
Flore's palfrey (Died., 922-29, Fleck, 1994-2004 and Died.,
1484 ff., Fleck, 2735 ff.), and Blancheflor's conversation with
the emir and prayer to God, which have no counterpart in the
French original (Died., 703 ff., Fleck 1687 ff., especially the
metaphor in Died., 739, Fleck, 1734). In fact the Fleming
seems to be admitting that he used more than one source when
he says:

> Dat was al waer, ons en bedrieghe
> Dese boec ende andre, daer wi inne
> Al vinden ghescreven haer minne   282–84.

> [This was all true, unless we are deceived by this
> book and others in which we have found a complete
> account of their love.]

Since the detail just related by Diederic is not present in his
main source — 'dese boec'— but is suggested by Fleck's
account of events (see Fleck, 599–609), the words 'ende
andre' may well be a veiled reference to the Middle High
German version.

Diederic's use of the German romance is however fairly
restricted and most of the time the Fleming provides a very
close, literal rendering of his French model. Nevertheless, he
complains in his prologue that he found the task of translation
difficult. This may be a humility topos, but it may also explain
Diederic's need to use a Germanic version to help him to

---

[37] This thesis was presented in an unpublished paper given at a meeting
of the British Branch of the International Courtly Literature Society in
January, 1982.

understand the French original. Indeed, at one point he appears totally to misunderstand the *Conte*, translating the Old French '*s'ante*' (his aunt) as if it were a name '*Vrouwe Sante*' (433), then being forced to invent a daughter for her '*Joncfrouwe Sibilie*' (438) when he comes across the aunt's name in the model. This seems to be taking the desire to omit nothing to ridiculous lengths. Another section of Diederic's *Floris ende Blancefloer* which may have been influenced by Fleck is the *exordium*. Diederic, like the German but not quite so thoroughly, has imposed a *sen* on his *matière*, by emphasising the moral message inherent in it. Consequently, his prologue introduces the story of Floris and Blancefloer as one of steadfast love '*ghestadegher minnen*' (14) which eventually triumphs over all opposition, yet which brings with it joy and suffering '*rouwe*', '*toren*' and '*vro*' (44–47). In the poem proper, this *sen* is elaborated through direct speech[38] and other rhetorical *loci* by means of the types of amplification taught in the schools.

This procedure is best exemplified, however, by Fleck's *Flore und Blanscheflur*, which not only contains verbal parallels to Hartmann von Aue's works, but also illustrates the same approach to source material as its illustrious predecessor.[39] Both Germans have carried out an *explication de texte* on their models and have woven their interpretation into their own version of the story. Instead of employing the methods of biblical translators, they use the approach of biblical exegesis — hence the term *diuten*, which occurs

---

[38] See my 'Direct Speech — A Key to the German Adaptor's Art?' in *Medieval Translators and their Craft*, edited by Jeanette Beer, Studies in Medieval Culture, XXV (Kalamazoo, Michigan, 1989), pp. 213–46.

[39] For verbal parallels see *Bruchstücke von Konrad Flecks 'Floire und Blanscheflur' nach den Handschriften F und P unter Heranziehung von BH*, edited by Carl Rischen (Heidelberg, 1913), pp. 101–30.

frequently in German prologues to describe the adaptor's task and which seems to cover a range of meanings from translation to interpretation.[40] Like Hartmann, who begins with a *sententia* announcing the ethical values which provide the framework for his version of the Yvain story:

> Swer an rehte güete
> wendet sîn gemüete,
> dem volget saelde und êre   1–3[41]

> [He who turns his mind to true goodness will be accorded good fortune and honour.]

Konrad Fleck commences his prologue with a moralising generalisation in praise of virtue, and introduces his audience to his major themes: '*rehte hôhiu minne*', '*tugent*', '*triuwe*' '*kumber*' and '*froude*' (true love, virtue, loyalty, pain and joy). It is the amplification of these themes that contributes substantially to a translated version over twice the length of the French original. The other major impulses which bring about an extension of the source are the desire to explain, motivate and render explicit events and actions in the model and a concern to ornament the material with rhetorical figures.[42]

I have already suggested ways in which Konrad Fleck's translation of *Floire et Blancheflor* differs from that of Diederic. The latter is a more faithful rendering, the former

---

[40] For references, see Lofmark, pp. 48–51.

[41] Quoted from Hartmann von Aue, *Iwein*, edited by G.F. Benecke and K. Lachmann, revised by Ludwig Wolff, 7th edition (Berlin, 1968).

[42] See my 'The Rhetoric of Adaptation'. The edition of Fleck's poem used here is that of Emil Sommer, *Flore und Blanscheflur: eine Erzählung von Konrad Fleck*, Bibliothek der gesammten deutschen National-Literatur, No. 12 (Quedlinburg and Leipzig, 1846) supplemented by Rischen's fragmentary edition mentioned in note 39.

more rhetorically elaborate. The latter author extends his source by a quotient of 1.2, the former by 2.5.[43] In this respect comparison proves instructive with the Middle English *Floris*, which was composed during the thirteenth century by a poet from the South-East Midlands and is a much abridged version of the French source, displaying little rhetorical elaboration.[44] The English poet concentrates on plot and action, retains dialogue in shortened form, suppresses or drastically reduces rhetorical descriptions (cf. Geoffrey's *Documentum*, II, 3, item 133) and avoids repetition, sometimes by telescoping parallel episodes. He does not offer a new moral conception of the material. For him the story of Floris and Blauncheflur is a straightforward, exemplary tale of constant love, and as such requires little authorial comment.

Konrad Fleck, on the other hand, emphasises the religious message implicit in his source. His version makes it clear that it is Blanscheflur's deep Christian faith and trust in God which eventually converts the pagan Flore to the true faith. And this conversion is vital for world history, since the lovers will produce a child who was to be the mother of Charlemagne. In order to stress further the difference between pagan and Christian lovers, Fleck is willing to modify the plot with regard to the character of the pagan emir. Whereas the French poet allows the emir to abandon his barbaric custom of killing each new virgin bride after one year of marriage to him (the emir having been converted to more humane behaviour by the example of the innocent young lovers), Fleck omits this detail

---

[43] These quotients were arrived at by averaging quotients based on the length of the *Conte* in each of the two fairly complete extant manuscripts.

[44] See *Floris und Blaunchfleur, a Middle English Romance*, edited by F.C. de Vries (Groningen, 1966). Despite the fragmentary nature of the surviving manuscripts, it is clear that the adaptor's intention was to shorten his source and indeed abbreviation is a common feature of the Middle English romances.

and his emir remains cruelly grotesque, a representative of false love.

Another modification in his treatment of the subject-matter concerns the love theme. In the Old French *Conte* the lovers are presented as victims of a type of Ovidian love which matures on reading pagan erotic literature. The German version, while containing Ovidian elements, stresses the courtly nature of their love. From an early age they practise '*hôhiu minne*' and Fleck is careful to stress that they do not consummate their love until after they are married. The sensual link between *amour* and *clergie* forged by the French poet is thus erased.

In contrast, Diederic, while following Fleck in his courtly portrayal of the lovers, does not emphasise the religious elements of the model or the conversion theme. Clearly reluctant to change details of plot in his primary source, the Fleming has retained the more humane picture of the emir he found in the *Conte*.

In conclusion, the aims of the German, English and Dutch adaptors of *Floire et Blancheflor* were evidently not to emulate scriptural translation by providing a literal, faithful version of the original in a new language. Despite the somewhat conservative statements found in the prologues and epilogues of many translators, in practice they indulged in the type of rhetorical rewriting recommended by the classical and medieval *artes*. While claiming that the content and meaning of their model was paramount, the meaning which they actually elaborated rhetorically was often the new *sen* which the translator subjectively found (or perhaps one should say invented) in his source. In spite of the general tendency in the Middle Ages to assert with the Preacher that there is 'nothing new under the sun' and in spite of the negative attitude towards novelty expressed by several medieval poets,[45] it was possible for an adaptor to endow his model with one or more of the many basic truths which had existed since the creation, but which his French predecessor had not necessarily associated with nor written into the adaptor's source material. It was in this spirit of rhetorical rewriting that Wolfram could say 'ein maere wil i'u niuwen' (*Parzival*, 4, 9) and in this way that the tension between tradition and originality in medieval literature could become a productive source of poetic creativity.[46]

---

[45] Lofmark sums up this attitude with the words: 'Not plagiary, but innovation is a sin' (p. 11) and quotes *Aiol*, 7 and the *Chanson d'Antioche*, 8, where the expressions 'novel jongleur' and 'nouvel jogleor' are obviously pejorative. Yet it is worth noting that by the thirteenth century, notably in Guillaume de Lorris's *Roman de la Rose*, a poet could boast of totally novel subject-matter: 'La matire est et bone et nueve' (39), 'et la matire en est novele' (2064). Quotations from the edition by Felix Lecoy, C.F.M.A., 3 vols (Paris, 1970).

[46] I should like to thank my colleagues Peter Christian and Cyril Edwards for checking my translations of the German authors quoted here.

Pratique de la traduction en Espagne au Moyen Age: les travaux tolédans

CLARA FOZ

IL EST courant, depuis de nombreuses années, d'englober sous l'appellation d'École de Tolède l'ensemble des travaux de traduction de l'arabe en latin et en roman castillan réalisés au douzième et au treizième siècles en Espagne, à Tolède ou à Barcelone et à Tarazona. A cette époque les Espagnols avaient repris aux Arabes une partie du territoire que ces derniers occupaient depuis plusieurs siècles et, sur le plan culturel, la reconquête de Tolède fut capitale, cette ville et sa région comptant un certain nombre de caractéristiques qui allaient favoriser l'émergence d'un mouvement de traduction: d'une part, la population tolédane, composée d'autochtones, d'Arabes et de juifs, présentait un pluralisme linguistique puisque le roman castillan, l'arabe et l'hébreu se côtoyaient sur un même territoire. A ces trois langues qui coexistèrent dans la Péninsule ibérique pendant plusieurs siècles, vint s'ajouter, peu après la conquête de la ville par Alphonse VI, le latin, alors employé par les moines clunisiens chargés par le roi de remettre sur pied l'Église tolédane. D'autre part, Tolède, après la chute du califat de Cordoue en 1031, avait hérité d'une partie des ouvrages rassemblés par le calife Al Hakan; à ces trésors étaient venus s'ajouter d'autres manuscrits venus d'Orient et réunis par de riches bibliophiles tolédans durant la période des royaumes indépendants qui suivit la fin du califat de Cordoue. Ainsi, Tolède, grand centre de la culture arabe, devint, avec la reconquête du territoire par les chrétiens en 1085, le point de rencontre de deux civilisations, le lieu d'échanges entre l'Orient et l'Occident, celui-ci accusant un retard culturel et scientifique énorme par rapport à celui-là. En fait, les Occidentaux ne tardèrent pas à s'apercevoir des limites de leur savoir et des possibilités de l'élargir qui s'offraient à eux par le biais de la traduction des écrits philosophiques et scientifiques hérités des Arabes. C'est donc une quarantaine d'années seulement après la reconquête qu'une vaste entreprise de traduction, connue plus tard sous le nom d'École de Tolède, prit naissance dans cette ville. Mentionnons, pour clore ce rapide aperçu des conditions historiques dans lesquelles s'inscrit ce mouvement de traduction, que les travaux de Tolède constituent en fait le prolongement d'une activité amorcée en Espagne dès le dixième siècle: la culture arabe parvint en effet à certains lettrés européens de cette époque par divers intermédiaires comme le moine Gerbert d'Aurillac (devenu plus tard pape sous le nom de Sylvestre II) qui voyagea et étudia en Espagne entre 967 et 970, Mosé Sefardi, un lettré juif qui à la fin du onzième siècle traduisit en latin des oeuvres rédigées en arabe et en hébreu, ou, à la même époque, les étudiants de l'École de Chartres qui se rendirent dans la région de l'Ebre et réalisèrent quelques traductions de l'arabe vers le latin.

Ce qui distingue les travaux tolédans de ces différentes initiatives, c'est l'ampleur des réalisations attribuées à l'École de Tolède, appellation sous laquelle il convient de voir une vaste entreprise de transfert culturel reposant sur la traduction, mais dont l'objet n'est ni l'apprentissage de l'opération de traduction proprement dite ni l'élaboration d'une théorie générale de la traduction. Sans entrer dans le détail des réflexions[1] suscitées par l'attribution du terme d'école à cette entreprise, mentionnons que l'idée d'un mouvement ayant pris naissance entre 1126 et 1130 pour s'achever à la fin du treizième siècle vers 1287 mérite d'être nuancée: en effet, certains facteurs permettent de différencier l'oeuvre des traducteurs du douzième siècle (qu'il convient de situer entre 1130 et 1187 environ) de celle des traducteurs du treizième (1252–87), les deux étant en outre séparées par une période d'un demi-siècle pendant laquelle l'activité traduisante fut assez limitée.

En ce qui concerne par exemple les conditions dans lesquelles furent menés les travaux, il est clair que le patronage exercé par l'Église tolédane au douzième siècle en

[1] C'est Amable Jourdain qui fut le premier, en 1819, à désigner les travaux de Tolède comme un tout organisé: 'nous l'avouons avec une jouissance que l'homme de lettres peut apprécier, la découverte de ce collége [sic] de traducteurs nous a dédommagé des épines sans nombre dont est semée la route que nous avons parcourue.' *Recherches critiques sur l'âge et l'origine des traductions latines d'Aristote et sur des commentaires grecs ou arabes employés par les docteurs scolastiques.* Nouvelle édition revue et augmentée par Charles Jourdain (New York, 1960), p. 108. Suivit l'article de Valentin Rose 'Ptolemaeus und die Schule von Toledo' publié dans la revue *Hermes* en 1874, article sur lequel D.M. Dunlop devait plus tard se fonder pour écrire 'Toledo was a real teaching centre', 'The Work of Translation at Toledo', *Babel*, vol. 6, n° 2 (juin 1960), p. 55. En fait, dès 1927, C.H. Haskins avait pris quelque distance par rapport à l'emploi du terme d'école pour décrire les travaux tolédans: 'Of a formal school the sources tell us very little, but the succession of translators is clear for more than a century, beginning about 1135 and continuing until the time of Alfonso X (1252–84)', *Studies in the History of Mediaeval Science* (New York, 1967), pp. 12–13. En 1963, l'arabisant Richard Lemay alla même jusqu'à qualifier la notion d''École des traducteurs de Tolède' de 'légende', 'Dans l'Espagne du XIIᵉ siècle, les traductions de l'arabe au latin', *Annales ESC*, 18, p. 639. A ce point de vue se rallie d'ailleurs la majorité de ceux qui, à l'heure actuelle, s'intéressent à cette question.

Clara Foz

la personne de Raymond,[2] archevêque de Tolède de 1125 à
1152, se compare difficilement au rôle de mécène qui fut celui
du roi de Castille et de León, Alphonse X,[3] au siècle suivant:
il reste en effet peu de traces tangibles de l'intervention du
prélat alors qu'au treizième siècle la figure du souverain, passé
à l'histoire sous le nom de *Rey Sabio* (Roi Savant), domine les
travaux; il est cité dans les prologues comme le responsable
des réalisations qui sont commandées par lui, puis, le plus
souvent, revues et corrigées par ses propres soins. Le poids
exercé par Alphonse X sur l'entreprise de traduction du
treizième siècle apparaît également dans la nature des ouvrages
traduits — ils étaient presque exclusivement consacrés à
l'astronomie et à l'astrologie, les deux domaines de
prédilection du roi — dans l'organisation du travail — les
prologues indiquent que le souverain lui-même répartissait le
travail entre ses divers collaborateurs en fonction des
compétences de chacun[4] — de même que dans l'adoption du
roman castillan comme langue cible de la grande majorité des
travaux — on passait ainsi du latin, employé au siècle
précédent, à la langue vernaculaire d'Espagne, désignée par le
souverain comme *el nuestro lenguage de Castilla*.[5] Enfin,
sous le patronage du souverain, les travaux sont beaucoup plus
'organisés' qu'au douzième siècle puisqu'aux traducteurs
viennent s'ajouter l'*emendador* (c'est-à-dire le correcteur), le

---

[2] Sur l'archevêque Raymond voir A. Gonzalez Palencia, *El arzobispo Don Raimundo de Toledo* (Barcelona, 1942), et J.F. Rivera Recio, *La Iglesia de Toledo en el siglo XII (1086–1208)* (Roma, 1966).

[3] Sur Alphonse X voir E. Procter, *Alfonso X of Castile* (Westport, Connecticut, 1980).

[4] Voir à cet égard N. Roth, 'Jewish Translators at the Court of Alfonso X', *Thought*, vol. 60, n° 239 (December), 1985.

[5] C'est-à-dire 'notre langue castillane', désignation qui témoigne du poids qu'Alphonse X accordait à la langue nationale.

capitulador (c'est-à-dire celui qui divise la matière en chapitres) et le *glosador* (c'est-à-dire le glosateur ou commentateur).

Qui étaient les traducteurs du douzième et du treizième siècle? D'où venaient-ils? A quel milieu appartenaient-ils? Quelle était leur formation? Les réponses que nous apporterons à ces questions nous permettront de dégager un certain nombre de caractéristiques propres aux activités de traduction de chaque époque.

Les principaux traducteurs du douzième siècle — disons ceux qui ont laissé quelque trace car d'autres oeuvrèrent sans doute dans l'anonymat — forment un total de treize personnes réparties entre deux groupes principaux, les Espagnols et les étrangers. Le premier groupe, formé de six personnes, compte un nombre égal de chrétiens (Domingo Gonzalez, Hughes de Santalla et Marc de Todède[6]) et de juifs (Abraham Bar Hiyya, Abraham B. 'Ezra et Jean de Séville). Deux d'entre eux jouèrent le rôle de traducteurs intermédiaires oraux en roman castillan, permettant ainsi à un autre traducteur connaissant peu l'arabe de traduire de cette langue en latin. Le deuxième groupe réunit sept personnes soit deux Italiens (Platon de Tivoli et Gérard de Crémone), trois Anglais (Adélard de Bath, Robert de Chester et Daniel de Morley) un Dalmate (Hermann le Dalmate) et un Flamand (Rodolphe de Bruges). Tous

---

[6] Selon José Gil, *Los colaboradores judíos en la escuela de traductores de Toledo* (Washington, 1974), pp. 65–66, Marc de Todède appartient à la période de transition qui fait le lien entre les traducteurs du douzième et ceux qui travaillèrent pour Alphonse X au siècle suivant. Pourtant, bien que ses activités soient postérieures à 1187, c'est-à-dire à la fin de la période d'activités du douzième siècle, il vivait à Tolède à l'époque où les traducteurs tolédans y travaillèrent et certains facteurs — utilisation du latin comme langue de la traduction, patronage des travaux par l'Église et voyage à Tolède dans le but de s'y procurer des manuscrits — permettent de le rattacher à ces derniers.

n'eurent pas le même poids dans l'entreprise de traduction: dans le groupe formé par les Espagnols, Jean de Séville apparaît comme la figure de proue du mouvement en raison de ses capacités — il connaissait l'arabe, le roman castillan ainsi que l'hébreu et un peu de latin et s'intéressait aux sciences aussi bien qu'à la philosophie[7] — mais également parce qu'il était connu de plusieurs autres traducteurs qui lui dédièrent des travaux ou qui étaient en contact avec lui. Dans le groupe formé par les étrangers c'est Gérard de Crémone qui se présente comme le chef de file de l'entreprise dans sa deuxième phase, amorcée vers le milieu du douzième siècle après la disparition de l'archevêque Raymond; cet Italien, qui eut certainement autour de lui plusieurs collaborateurs, signa en effet entre soixante-dix et quatre-vingts traductions arabo-latines touchant aussi bien aux mathématiques, à l'astronomie, qu'à la médecine ou à la philosophie.

La première remarque qui s'impose à propos de ce groupe de traducteurs est la place occupée par les non Espagnols, la majorité des lettrés étant originaires de terres étrangères, principalement l'Italie et les Iles britanniques. Ce fait s'explique si l'on considère deux facteurs observables à cette époque, à savoir d'une part l'existence d'une langue écrite 'universelle', le latin, commune à tous les lettrés européens, et d'autre part la nécessité pour ces derniers de se déplacer pour accéder au savoir contenu dans les manuscrits que les Espagnols avaient hérités des Arabes. En ce qui concerne le milieu d'origine des traducteurs, une bonne partie d'entre eux exercèrent des fonctions au sein de l'Église: c'est le cas de Domingo Gonzalez, de Gérard de Crémone ou de Robert de Chester par exemple, et ceux qui n'y exercèrent aucune fonction précise ne formèrent pas un groupe

---

[7] José Gil, pp. 30-35, présente une liste exhaustive et détaillée des traductions de Jean de Séville ainsi que de ses compositions.

parfaitement distinct; ainsi, Hermann le Dalmate étudia-t-il en France, sous la direction de Thierry de Chartres, dans le cadre de l'école épiscopale du même nom.

Ces hommes qui s'attachèrent, au douzième siècle, à traduire en latin des ouvrages de science et de philosophie hérités des Arabes possédaient-ils une formation particulière qui les préparât à la traduction? La question est vaste et ne saurait être tranchée en quelques lignes, d'autant que tous ceux qui participèrent aux travaux n'étaient pas du même niveau. Cependant, si l'on s'en tient aux conditions préalables à toute entreprise de traduction à savoir la connaissance de la langue de départ, celle de la langue d'arrivée et celle, enfin, de la matière, il apparaît que certains lettrés latins connaissaient imparfaitement ou ignoraient la langue source à savoir l'arabe; les juifs, eux, n'étaient généralement pas des latinistes, mais ils connaissaient l'arabe. Quant aux sujets, il convient de souligner que les lettrés latins découvrirent, par la traduction, des idées scientifiques et philosophiques nouvelles pour eux, alors que leurs confrères juifs avaient vécu en contact avec la culture arabe, ce qui leur donnait un avantage évident pour en comprendre les oeuvres. Nous analyserons maintenant les répercussions que ces caractéristiques eurent sur la manière dont furent menés les travaux de traduction.

Le fait que les lettrés chrétiens aient eu en commun la langue latine, langue de l'Église et du savoir à cette époque, favorisa sans aucun doute les échanges entre les divers intervenants, comme en témoigne la collaboration de Robert de Chester et Hermann le Dalmate, ou les liens ayant existé entre ce dernier et Rodolphe de Bruges.[8] Plus important fut l'impact que le milieu dont la plupart des traducteurs étaient issus, à savoir l'Église, eut sur la manière d'aborder la traduction. Ces lettrés, dont la culture était très biblique,

---

[8] Voir à cet égard le prologue mis au jour par A. Jourdain, p. 104.

devaient, en raison de leur appartenance à l'Église, servir la foi; très significative, à cet égard, est l'attitude d'un homme comme Daniel de Morley: la lettre,[9] destinée à l'évêque de Norwich, dans laquelle cet Anglais affirme que s'il s'intéresse aux 'philosophes païens' plutôt qu'aux 'Pères de l'Église' c'est par souci de tirer profit d'un savoir émanant d'infidèles, permet de relier l'intérêt de ce lettré latin pour la philosophie et la science des Arabes à l'obligation dans laquelle il se trouve de servir l'Église. Sous sa plume, l'entreprise de traduction du douzième siècle apparaît d'ailleurs comme une vaste opération de récupération devant profiter aux chrétiens. Dès lors, il n'est guère étonnant que la manière de traduire ait subi à cette époque l'influence de deux facteurs apparemment contradictoires à savoir d'une part le respect de la lettre, inspiré chez les lettrés latins par la doctrine théologique chrétienne du Verbe, parole de Dieu, et d'autre part la tendance à transformer, à adapter ou même à supprimer certains passages ou mots jugés peu conformes à l'esprit catholique: c'est en effet ce qui ressort de divers travaux[10] consacrés aux traductions de cette époque.

Enfin, les différents degrés de connaissance que ces hommes avaient des langues et des sujets de la traduction eurent aussi des répercussions sur leur travail de traducteur. On usa en effet de divers procédés pour surmonter les difficultés résultant d'une méconnaissance totale ou partielle de l'arabe, langue dans laquelle les oeuvres étaient rédigées; au plus courant de ces moyens, l'utilisation d'un traducteur

---

[9] Citée par Jacques Le Goff, *Les intellectuels au Moyen Age* (Paris, 1985), p. 24.

[10] Voir, en particulier, Richard Lemay, 'Fautes et contresens dans les traductions arabo-latines médiévales: l'Introductorium in astronomiam d'Abou Ma'shar de Balk', *Revue de Synthèse*, III série, n°[s] 49–52, Centre international de synthèse, 1968, pp. 101–23.

intermédiaire juif ou mozarabe qui disait le texte arabe en roman castillan, moyen auquel un bon nombre de lettrés latins eurent recours, vint s'ajouter la collaboration et l'échange de traductions entre divers traducteurs ainsi que la consultation et parfois la copie de traductions latines existantes. Pour ce qui est des difficultés d'interprétation auxquelles les lettrés latins firent face du fait qu'ils ne possédaient pas toujours une bonne connaissance des sujets traités dans les ouvrages arabes, il est permis de croire que ceux qui leur permirent par leurs connaissances de la langue arabe d'accéder à ces textes les aidèrent également à en comprendre le contenu. Il faut également mentionner à cet égard que si les activités de traduction du douzième siècle présentent une grande variété thématique — les textes touchant à l'astronomie, à l'astrologie, aux mathématiques, à l'alchimie, à la médecine ou à la philosophie — le repérage des sujets abordés par chaque traducteur indique que hormis Jean de Séville et Gérard de Crémone les Tolédans n'abordèrent pas l'ensemble de ces disciplines. On observe chez eux une certaine spécialisation: Hughes de Santalla se consacra à l'astrologie et aux sciences occultes, Platon de Tivoli aux mathématiques, à l'astronomie et à l'astrologie; Rodolphe de Bruges, lui, s'intéressa principalement à l'astronomie.

Les traducteurs du douzième siècle formèrent donc deux groupes: le plus important en nombre regroupait des lettrés avides de connaissances dont la principale activité était l'étude et la traduction — parfois doublée de fonctions au sein de l'Église — activité pour laquelle certains quittèrent leur pays d'origine pour se rendre en Espagne. Le deuxième groupe était formé de lettrés juifs qui possédaient deux avantages au moins sur leurs confrères chrétiens: d'une part, ils connaissaient plusieurs langues et d'autre part ils avaient vécu en contact avec la culture arabe. Ceux-là, plus que les lettrés latins, étaient aptes à la traduction et les chrétiens qui les firent travailler comme traducteurs intermédiaires à l'oral ne s'y trompèrent pas. Voyons maintenant quelle était la situation au siècle suivant.

Les traducteurs du treizième siècle forment un total de quinze personnes, réparties entre deux groupes principaux, les Espagnols et les étrangers. Le premier groupe, formé de dix personnes, compte six chrétiens (Alvaro D'Oviedo, Bernard l'Arabe, Fernando de Tolède, Garci Pérez, Guillem Arremon Daspa et Jean Daspa) et quatre juifs (Judas B. Mosé, Ishâq B. Sîd, Samuel Levi et Abraham Alfaquin). Le deuxième groupe réunit cinq Italiens (Bonaventure de Sienne, Egidius de Thebaldis de Parma, Petrus de Regium, Jean de Crémone et Jean de Messine), eux aussi chrétiens. Tous n'eurent pas le même poids dans l'entreprise de traduction patronnée par Alphonse X: ainsi, les collaborateurs d'origine italienne formaient un tiers des effectifs mais eurent une influence bien moindre que celle exercée par les traducteurs d'origine juive qui n'étaient que quatre mais furent particulièrement actifs: en fait, deux d'entre eux, Judas B. Mosé et Ishâq B. Sîd, constituèrent les 'piliers' de l'entreprise de traduction patronnée par Alphonse X: ils apparaissent dans les prologues des traductions comme les véritables responsables du travail, les chrétiens espagnols leur servant plutôt d'aides et les Italiens traduisant en d'autres langues (le français ou le latin) les versions espagnoles d'ouvrages arabes précédemment produites à l'instigation du souverain.

Au treizième siècle, les deux tiers des effectifs étaient donc originaires de la Péninsule ibérique. Si les nationalités sont moins diversifiées qu'au douzième siècle, le milieu d'origine des traducteurs par contre, est plus varié: les Italiens étaient des partisans de l'empereur,[11] et leur présence en Espagne aux côtés d'Alphonse X qui assuma les fonctions de

---

[11] Voir à cet égard les renseignements fournis par E. Procter, pp. 129–30.

chef du Saint Empire romain germanique durant quelques années (1267–72), témoigne du caractère plus politique que culturel de leur appui. Parmi les chrétiens espagnols, seuls Guillem Arremon Daspa et Garci Pérez exercèrent des fonctions au sein de l'Église; plusieurs traducteurs, par contre, sont désignés par l'appellation de *maestre* c'est-à-dire de maître, signe que ces lettrés avaient dû étudier pendant un certain nombre d'années pour devenir enseignants. Quant aux traducteurs d'origine hébraïque, deux d'entre eux exercèrent des fonctions à la synagogue de Tolède et les deux autres provenaient de grandes familles juives dont certains membres exerçaient leurs activités à la cour des rois d'Espagne à qui ils servaient de médecins par exemple. Du point de vue 'formation', ces lettrés juifs parlaient et écrivaient l'arabe, la langue de départ des traductions commandées par Alphonse X, ce qui n'était pas le cas d'une grande partie de leurs collègues chrétiens: parmi ces derniers en effet, Italiens et Espagnols réunis, seuls Bernard l'Arabe et Fernando de Tolède connaissaient suffisamment l'arabe pour être en mesure de travailler seuls à partir de cette langue. En matière de connaissance des sujets enfin, il faut mentionner que le travail de traduction patronné par Alphonse X s'inscrivit dans un milieu pénétré depuis longtemps par des apports arabes et que de plus les réalisations touchèrent à un nombre limité de textes d'astronomie et d'astrologie principalement, ce qui réduisit considérablement les difficultés par rapport au siècle précédent. Pour les matières, les intervenants d'origine juive furent sans aucun doute les plus compétents: la preuve en est qu'outre leurs traductions, ils furent chargés par le roi de 'créer' un certain nombre d'ouvrages à partir de modèles arabes.

L'entreprise de traduction du treizième siècle se présente donc comme une entreprise essentiellement espagnole et le choix opéré par Alphonse X d'adopter, à une époque où le latin avait pratiquement l'exclusivité en Occident en matière de communication écrite et d'enseignement, le roman castillan comme langue cible de la plupart des travaux, témoigne d'une volonté d'inscrire ces réalisations dans un cadre national.

D'instrument oral intermédiaire qu'elle était au siècle précédent, la langue espagnole, commune à l'ensemble des intervenants du treizième siècle, acquit, par la traduction, un statut de langue écrite et cet état de fait, marqué en outre par le poids des traducteurs d'origine hébraïque, véritables spécialistes de l'arabe et des matières, eut des répercussions considérables sur la manière d'aborder la traduction: conformément à la longue tradition observable chez les traducteurs juifs depuis Philo Iudaeus, l'oeuvre de traduction du treizième siècle fut marquée par une littéralité extrême qui se doubla d'un travail lexicographique considérable ayant pour objectifs de forger une langue écrite et de définir les termes nouvellement créés pour exprimer les concepts techniques et scientifiques contenus dans les originaux arabes. Les indications figurant dans les prologues de divers travaux de traduction de cette époque le montrent, c'est bien autour des traducteurs d'origine juive et en particulier de Judas B. Mosé que s'organisa le travail, celui-ci apparaissant comme le traducteur en chef auquel furent adjoints, selon les travaux, différents collaborateurs chrétiens: pour la traduction du *Lapidaire*, oeuvre mêlant l'astrologie et l'alchimie, ce fut Garci Pérez et pour d'autres travaux, Guillem Arremon Daspa ou Jean Daspa.

En fait, au treizième siècle, la collaboration ne s'arrêtait pas une fois la traduction établie puisque les oeuvres traduites devaient, avant de pouvoir être intégrées aux livres du roi, subir une étape de correction au cours de laquelle intervenait l'*emendador* c'est-à-dire le correcteur et parfois même le roi qui, lui, avait bien entendu tous les droits: le prologue au

Libro de las estrellas[12] dans lequel il est mentionné qu'Alphonse X a supprimé ce qui lui paraissait superflu, répété ou écrit en mauvais castillan, permet de mesurer le poids du souverain dans les travaux.

On peut donc dire que les traducteurs du treizième siècle se présentent comme un groupe organisé au sein duquel les tâches sont partagées en fonction des compétences de chacun, tous bénéficiant de la protection du roi. Le terme de groupe s'applique de manière plus incertaine aux intervenants du douzième siècle puisque à cette époque c'est davantage à un réseau de traducteurs travaillant à une vaste entreprise de récupération du savoir scientifique et philosophique hérité des Arabes que l'on a affaire. De fait, leur souci premier étant de récupérer le plus rapidement possible un savoir qui allait s'avérer capital pour l'évolution de la pensée occidentale, il n'est guère étonnant que les traducteurs du douzième siècle n'aient pas exposé par écrit leur manière de concevoir la langue ou la traduction. De cette époque, en effet, il n'existe, à notre connaissance, aucun traité grammatical, lexicographique ou 'linguistique' émanant des traducteurs eux-mêmes. Dans les prologues, les réflexions des traducteurs se limitent en général à une comparaison entre les langues, comparaison dont l'objet est de relever l'inaptitude du latin à exprimer les concepts scientifiques et philosophiques contenus dans les textes arabes. Au treizième siècle, malgré toute l'importance accordée à la définition de termes et à leur création, aucun ouvrage consacré aux langues ou à la traduction ne vit le jour. On devine cependant, grâce en particulier à divers articles figurant dans le recueil de lois des *Siete Partidas* et grâce aussi à la nature des consignes données par le roi à ses collaborateurs, l'importance que le souverain

---

[12] En partie présenté par Antonio Solalinde, 'Intervención de Alfonso X en la redacción de sus obras', *Revista de filología española*, 2, 1915, p. 287.

accordait à la langue: elle différencie l'homme de l'animal et doit être bien employée pour être bien comprise et non pas utilisée sans discernement.

En l'absence de textes présentant des réflexions théoriques sous-jacentes à l'acte de traduire tel que les traducteurs le concevaient au douzième et au treizième siècles, ce que l'on sait des difficultés rencontrées par les traducteurs et des solutions qu'ils envisagèrent est révélateur: au coeur d'une grande partie des problèmes auxquels ils se heurtèrent se trouve le mot. Les traducteurs prirent des infusions de plantes — classées par langue — qui, selon eux, avaient le pouvoir de faciliter la rétention de mots arabes; ils avalèrent, sous forme de pilules, la cendre de ces mêmes végétaux brûlés, ou, plus intéressant encore, mangèrent des amandes sur lesquelles étaient tracés en abrégé des mots arabes. Les mots, comme en témoigne la légende selon laquelle un traducteur d'origine juive, après qu'un moustique eut vidé son cerveau de tous les mots hébreux qu'il contenait, perdit l'usage de cette langue, étaient comme empreints d'une matérialité. En fait, ils avaient non seulement une place à eux dans le cerveau, mais ils étaient doués d'un pouvoir extraordinaire puisqu'ils provoquaient parfois, chez ceux qui se trouvaient en contact avec eux, des réactions curieuses: c'est du moins ce que raconte une autre légende selon laquelle les lettrés qui entreprirent de lire et de traduire l'ouvrage astronomique de Ptolémée l'*Almageste* se mirent, au moment où ils abordèrent le mouvement des astres, à léviter et à se déplacer suivant le mouvement des planètes étudiées.

Aussi étonnants que ces récits[13] puissent paraître — ils relèvent bien entendu d'une représentation de la réalité quelque peu déformée et amplifiée par l'imagination — ils

---

[13] Rapportés par Alvaro Cunqueiro, *Tertulia de boticas y escuela de curanderos* (Barcelona, 1976).

témoignent, comme toute légende, des idées partagées par ceux qui, à cette époque, s'attachèrent à traduire en latin ou en roman castillan des oeuvres arabes. Ces croyances sont bien entendu d'un intérêt évident par ce qu'elles révèlent de la valeur attribuée au signe linguistique: pour ces hommes, il partageait la nature de la chose et participait de la substance elle-même. C'est en tenant compte de cette attitude envers la langue qu'il convient d'analyser la question de la traduction à Tolède au douzième et au treizième siècle. Ainsi se trouve motivée la littéralité dont sont empreintes les traductions latines ou espagnoles des Tolédans. Ainsi leurs réalisations s'inscrivent-elles dans une longue tradition antérieure à toute tentative de penser la traduction comme une opération *sui generis* et par là même antérieure à toute véritable théorisation entourant l'acte de traduire.

French Texts, Welsh Translators

CERIDWEN LLOYD-MORGAN

Dysgais yr eang Ffrangeg —
doeth yw ei dysg, da iaith deg.[1]

SO BOASTED the Welsh poet Ieuan ap Rhydderch in the
fifteenth century: he had mastered the fair French tongue, he
said, which opened the door to wisdom and learning. And
although such explicit avowals are not frequently encountered
in the written sources of medieval Wales, it is clear that Ieuan
ap Rhydderch was not alone in acquiring this skill. For if the
archival evidence for the acquisition of a knowledge of
French, whether spoken or written, is scanty, there is no lack
of concrete testimony as to the results of Welsh people
learning that 'fair tongue'.[2]

---

[1] Henry Lewis, Thomas Roberts and Ifor Williams (eds), *Cywyddau Iolo
Goch ac Eraill*, second edition (Cardiff, 1937), p. 228.

[2] For general surveys of the evidence see e.g. Marie Surridge, 'Romance
Linguistic Influence on Middle Welsh', *Studia Celtica* 1 (1966), 63–92;
Llinos Beverley Smith, 'Pwnc yr Iaith yng Nghymru, 1282–1536', in *Cof
Cenedl. Ysgrifau ar Hanes Cymru*, edited by Geraint H. Jenkins (Llandysul,
1986), pp. 3–33.

Until comparatively recently romanticism, sentimentality or political partiality, or even a potent cocktail of all three, has encouraged scholars, both inside and outside Wales, to cherish the image of a medieval Wales whose culture was divorced from the rest of Europe. Too often it has been assumed that Wales was an island of primitive Celtic culture, where oral tradition reigned supreme, unsullied by booklearning, and where, presumably, bardic xenophobia kept the door firmly closed against the infiltration of alien material.

Nothing, of course, could be further from the truth, and recent research demonstrates beyond doubt that Welsh literature began to absorb material from other cultures at a very early date. Dr Marged Haycock, for example, in a recent article on three early medieval poems from the Book of Taliesin (MS Peniarth 2 in the National Library of Wales) has shown that, already in poetry originally composed perhaps between the ninth and eleventh centuries, there is unambiguous evidence that Welsh poets had quite detailed knowledge of narrative traditions from the continent.[3] The three poems she discusses reveal close familiarity with the tales of Hercules and Alexander and may indeed be, as she suggests, 'the earliest vernacular poems on Alexander and Hercules in western Europe'. Yet, as Dr Haycock stresses, 'the emphasis of modern Welsh scholarship has been on those poems which are generally considered to be ''pure'' or ''uncontaminated'' reflexes of archaic Celtic or even Indo-European genres'.[4] In other words, the evidence for the assimilation of foreign material into medieval Welsh literature

---

[3] Marged Haycock, ' ''Some talk of Alexander and some of Hercules'': three early medieval poems from the Book of Taliesin', *Cambridge Medieval Celtic Studies*, 13 (1987), 7–38.

[4] Haycock, p. 8.

is there if only we are prepared to recognize it rather than ignore it.

The amount of borrowing during the early Middle Ages should not, however, be exaggerated. Three out of some sixty poems in the fourteenth century Book of Taliesin, plus a sprinkling of French loan words here and there in the earliest Welsh prose tales[5], can scarcely permit us to go as far as certain scholars who have seen French sources lurking behind virtually every Middle Welsh text. It should be stressed, however, that, even in the early Middle Ages, literature from outside Wales, from continental Europe as well as from England, was filtering in, and the oral transmitters of literature were not always averse to incorporating into their stock-in-trade elements of narrative material derived from the written, learned, traditions.

Nevertheless, it is not until the early thirteenth century that large-scale borrowing became common. By that period, contacts with other countries had become closer and more numerous, and French culture in particular had begun to leave its mark on Welsh literary tradition. Contacts between Wales and France, either directly or via England, increased rapidly from the time of the Norman conquest of Wales, and have been well documented.[6] It is understandable, therefore, not to say inevitable, that French texts should make their presence felt in Wales. The powerful influence of French culture during the twelfth, thirteenth and fourteenth centuries was also an important factor, for the French language became something of an international language as Latin had been,[7] and even as

[5] e.g. Ifor Williams (ed.), *Pedeir Keinc y Mabinogi* (Cardiff, 1930), p. xxxiv.

[6] See Marie Surridge, 'Romance Linguistic Influence', passim.

[7] Bernard Bischoff, 'Foreign Languages in the Middle Ages', *Speculum* 26 (1961), 209 ff.

late as the end of the sixteenth century business correspondence between merchants of the Low Countries and Italian bankers in London was still conducted in French.[8] French literature too became fashionable, as witness the surge of translations of French tales and romances into most of the vernaculars of Western Europe; medieval Welsh was no exception. Texts like *Gui de Warewic*, *La Geste de Boun de Hamtone* and *La Queste del Saint Graal* left their mark on the literature of England, Ireland and Wales during the same period and seem to be part of the same pattern.[9]

Borrowing a romance from another language and culture poses more problems than purely linguistic ones. Even today, a modern translator may be obliged to provide footnotes to explain elements in the original text which, because of cultural differences between the two societies, will otherwise be incomprehensible to those reading the translation. The enormous differences between the cultures of France and of Wales can be appreciated visually by comparing, or rather contrasting, a fourteenth century Welsh manuscript with a French manuscript of the same period. The larger format of the latter, the better quality parchment, the more elegant *mise en page* and the rich, professional decoration, provide an eloquent commentary on the contrasting circumstances of literary production in the two societies. Those who first began to compose Welsh versions of French texts in the Middle Ages were only too aware of the problem posed by this

[8] The Corsini letters, private collections, auctioned at Christie's, London, 4 September 1984 and 11 June 1986, also Zürich, 30 October 1984.

[9] Ceridwen Lloyd-Morgan, 'A Study of *Y Seint Greal* in relation to *La Queste del Saint Graal* and *Perlesvaus*' (unpublished D. Phil. dissertation, University of Oxford, 1978), pp. 71–5. There is no full Welsh translation of *Gui de Warewic*, but references in the poetry of the period show that the story at least was familiar to the poets and their patrons.

décalage. Unfortunately the problem was further compounded by the time-lag: French texts composed in the early twelfth century, for example, might not be translated into Welsh until the late fourteenth.

The response of Welsh adapters of French material, naturally enough, was to follow the main narrative outline but to avoid close translation. The earliest examples we have of such a procedure are the three romantic tales of *Gereint*, *Owein* and *Peredur*, which correspond to the *Erec*, *Yvain* and *Perceval* of Chrétien de Troyes. Close comparison of the Welsh and French texts reveals that at times the Welsh redactors followed Chrétien's narrative very closely indeed, with passages of virtual word-for-word translation. Yet these three Welsh translations can scarcely be described as translations in the narrowest sense of the word. Rather they are re-tellings of the French narratives, and often very free re-tellings at that. In *Owein* and *Peredur* substantial chunks of narrative of purely native (Welsh) origin have been added, appended in the case of *Owein*,[10] but incorporated as an extra sequence of adventures in *Peredur*.[11] Moreover, in all three tales the narrative techniques, in fact the whole mode of telling the story, are essentially Welsh. Although the names of the main characters correspond to those of their counterparts in the French, in terms of behaviour and reactions they have far more in common with the older Welsh heroes, whose names they bear, than with the *chevaliers* who people Chrétien's fictional world. This process of adaptation may have taken place over a period of time; the earliest extant manuscript versions of the Welsh tales date from the late

[10] R.L. Thomson (ed), *Owein or Chwedyl Iarlles y Ffynnawn* (Dublin, 1968), lines 782–822 (the Du Traws episode).

[11] J. Gwenogvryn Evans (ed.), *Llyfr Gwyn Rhydderch* (second edition, Cardiff, 1973), columns 145–65.

thirteenth or early fourteenth century and we cannot now establish how many earlier written versions preceded them, nor how each successive scribe-redactor introduced further changes. Such a gradual editorial process may have also taken place in an oral context, for the tale of *Peredur* now exists in three main manuscript versions which seem to have evolved independently to some extent, and it may be that the narrative had circulated orally for a time before these separate versions were committed to writing.[12]

However many editorial stages lie behind these three tales as we know them today, there can be no doubt that those who first adapted *Yvain*, *Erec* and *Perceval* into Welsh were interested chiefly in the narrative aspects of the material. Wales already had its own stories about heroes who could be readily identified to a greater or lesser extent with the characters in the French romances, and so new tales could easily be incorporated into the corpus of material relating to those heroes, whether it were Arthur, Peredur, Owein or Cei, to name but a few. The extent to which the two stocks of stories could be linked is particularly well demonstrated in *Peredur*, where the so-called 'native sequence' of adventures was incorporated into what corresponds roughly to the middle of Chrétien's *Perceval* or *Conte del Graal*. If Perceval is

---

[12] The two complete versions are found in Llyfr Gwyn Rhydderch (the White Book of Rhydderch, MS Peniarth 4 in the National Library of Wales), c. 1300–50, and in Llyfr Coch Hergest (the Red Book of Hergest, MS Jesus College 111 in the Bodleian Library, Oxford), c. 1380–1410; these two versions agree fairly closely. Two fragments of the early part of the text are preserved in MSS Peniarth 7 and Peniarth 14, both tentatively dated c. 1275–1325 (see Ceridwen Lloyd-Morgan, 'Narrative structure in *Peredur*', *Zeitschrift für celtische Philologie* 38 (1981), 187–231 (pp. 193–95); and, for a general discussion, Brynley F. Roberts, 'Tales and Romances' in *A Guide to Welsh Literature*, volume 1, edited by A. O. H. Jarman and Gwilym Rees Hughes (Swansea, 1976), 203–43 (pp. 225–28).

perceived as the same character as Peredur then tales originally about Perceval can be linked to those about Peredur, and vice versa, and the same goes for other native characters. The use of the standard literary language of Middle Welsh and of native story-telling techniques helps to impose some stylistic unity on a text where material of disparate origins is brought together and treated as part of a single narrative. In other words, the entrance of Chrétien's romances into the Welsh literary context is a case of free adaptation rather than of slavish imitation or faithful translation. Nonetheless, the Welsh tales can be regarded as examples of translation in the broadest sense, as cases where a text has been carried over from one language and culture into another.

A century later, however, we begin to find in Welsh many examples of translation in the narrower sense. Curiously, we have no new native prose tales emerging in the fourteenth and fifteenth centuries, but instead a rapidly expanding corpus of literature in translation.[13] Texts in Latin and English as well as in French were translated into Welsh, and a wide variety of such material survives. This includes not only romances, *chansons de geste* and tales, but also non-fiction, such as religious and historical texts, and practical handbooks. The earliest surviving examples of such translations were made from Latin and include the *Brutiau* based on Geoffrey of Monmouth's *Historia Regum Britanniae*, and Welsh versions of the *Credo Athanasius* and *Turpini Historia*, all translated during the thirteenth century. *Bown de Hamtwn*,

---

[13] For general surveys and further references see Stephen J. Williams, 'Cyfieithwyr Cynnar', *Y Llenor* 8 (1929), 226–31, and 'Rhai Cyfieithiadau' in *Y Traddodiad Rhyddiaith yn yr Oesau Canol*, edited by Geraint Bowen (Llandysul, 1974), pp. 303–11; Ceridwen Lloyd-Morgan, 'A Study of *Y Seint Greal*', pp. 36–41, and 'Rhai Agweddau ar gyfieithu yn yr Oesoedd Canol', *Ysgrifau Beirniadol* 13, edited by J. E. Caerwyn Williams (Denbigh, 1985), pp. 134–45.

corresponding to the Anglo-Norman *Geste de Boun de Hamtone*, was perhaps translated in the mid thirteenth century, and the *Transitus Mariae* in the second half of the same century. New translations and re-copyings of the old ones then continued through the fourteenth and fifteenth centuries. Focussing on translations from French secular texts, we find three further tales from the Charlemagne and Roland cycle appearing in Welsh in the late thirteenth and the fourteenth centuries: *Cân Rolant*, based on the *Chanson de Roland*, *Pererindod Siarlymaen*, from the *Pèlerinage de Charlemagne*, and *Rhamant Otuel*, after the *Otinel*. Arthurian texts are also represented: the fourteenth century MS Llanstephan 2Ol in the National Library of Wales contains a fragment relating the birth of Arthur, which, although largely indebted to Geoffrey's history, includes a section derived from the French *Prose Merlin*, whilst the bulkiest translation of all, *Y Seint Greal*, was translated from two early thirteenth century French Grail romances, *La Queste del Saint Graal* and *Perlesvaus*, at the end of the fourteenth century.

If French was not the only language from which translations were made in the second half of the Middle Ages, there is nevertheless no doubt that such material was of especial interest to Welsh redactors and, presumably, to their patrons and audiences. Before looking more closely at their performance as translators the circumstances under which they worked should be considered.

These Welsh translators have left few names, but the scraps of scattered evidence that do survive show that some were churchmen, and that in many cases translations were commissioned by lay patrons from the *uchelwr* class.[14] Many

---

[14] The *uchelwyr* constituted a class of nobility below that of the native princes and emerged as the chief patrons of Welsh literature in the years after the conquest of 1282.

were working in south-east Wales where French and English made the earliest inroads in the years following the Norman conquest of Wales. In assessing the achievements of these translators the present-day concepts of translation can rarely be applied without major modifications. Unlike their modern counterparts, there is no evidence to suggest that the medieval Welsh translators had any special training. Of course, clerics sometimes translated secular material: their familiarity with the traditional mode of teaching Latin by translating and parsing each word in the sentence obviously provided an excellent training for a budding translator.[15] (And it is probably significant that translations from the Latin are generally more accurate and closer to their sources than are those made from medieval vernaculars.)

But the general run of translations from French into Welsh was a very different matter. Since some at least of the surviving translations from French have a south-eastern provenance, they were produced in an area where Norman French as well as English was a second language to Welsh. There it would be possible to pick up a little French, but normally the spoken rather than the written language, especially during the earlier period. By the fourteenth century, too, when translation into Welsh was at its height, Norman French was already disappearing as a living language in England and Wales. The last text in Norman French to be composed in either of those two countries, *Le Livre de Seyntz Medecine*, was written in 1354, and the author, Henri de Grosmont, Lord of Monmouth, felt it necessary to apologise

---

[15] Erik Jacobsen, *Translation. A Traditional Craft* (Copenhagen, 1948), pp. 44–99.

for the standard of his French.[16] As early as the late
thirteenth century French had ebbed to such an extent even
amongst the aristocracy in England that manuals began to
appear for teaching French to upper class children.[17] The low
standard of these manuals underlines the lack of help available
to the would-be translator, but there is no evidence that even
such poor tools as these English ones were available to Welsh
speakers anxious to acquire French. Dictionaries did not exist
either. The first full-scale Latin-English dictionary, the
Promptorium Parvulorum, was not prepared until 1440,[18] and
before that only short word-lists and vocabularies were
available, whilst the late adoption of alphabetical order meant
that convenience of reference was still unknown. If such
provision was minimal for Latin and English, it was non-
existent for French and Welsh. It could be argued that English
would be the first foreign language acquired by Welsh
translators, and that this would enable them to use such
English handbooks as existed, but to learn one foreign tongue
through the medium of another is not conducive to high
standards of accuracy in translation back to the mother tongue.

Welsh translators approaching French texts in the
thirteenth, fourteenth and fifteenth centuries were further
handicapped by difficulties of a non-linguistic nature. Many of
their productions reveal signs of haste, suggesting an impatient
patron anxious to have the finished work in his hands, or

[16] 'Si le franceis ne soit pas bon, jeo doie estre escusee, pur ceo qe jeo
sui engleis et n'ai pas moelt hauntee le franceis'. Henri de Grosmont, *Le
Livre de Seyntz Medecine*, edited by E. J. Arnould, Anglo-Norman Texts
Society, volume 2 (Oxford, 1940), p. 239.

[17] See for example W. Rothwell, 'The Teaching of French in Mediaeval
England', *Modern Language Review* 53 (1968), 37–46.

[18] See Nicholas Orme, *English Schools in the Middle Ages* (London,
1973), p. 250.

perhaps the need to return a rare and precious French manuscript to the owner from whom it had been borrowed.[19]

Comparison of the Welsh translations with the French tales on which they were based suggests that the redactors were also hampered by a lack of knowledge about France and French culture, including French literary tradition in general, which often led to mistranslation. Before examining their strengths and weaknesses, however, the avowed intentions of the translators should be considered. Unfortunately, compared with their counterparts in the Renaissance period, or indeed their contemporaries in other countries, medieval Welsh translators have left little in the way of theory or even simple declarations of intent. Nevertheless, the fragmentary evidence that has survived demonstrates that there was an awareness amongst them of the arguments for and against literal translation and the problems of retaining the feel and spirit of the original text as well as the surface meaning. Gruffudd Bola, one of the earliest translators, provides a rare insight into the attitude of the medieval Welshman faced with a text in another language, in this case the Latin *Credo Athanasius*:

Vn peth hagen a dylyy ti y wybod ar y dechreu, pan trosser ieith yn y llall, megys Lladin yg Kymraec, na ellir yn wastat symut y geir yn y gilyd, a chyt a hynny kynnal priodolder yr ieith a synnvyr yr ymadravd yn tec. Vrth hynny y troes i

---

[19] Books were certainly loaned by one Welsh nobleman to another, and even travelled some distance. In the fifteenth century, for example, the poet Guto'r Glyn composed a *cywydd* in which he asked Trahaearn ab Ieuan ap Meurig, of Penrhos Fwrdios near Caerleon, for the loan of a book, almost certainly a manuscript of *Y Seint Greal*, for Dafydd, abbot of the Cistercian house of Glyn Egwestl or Valle Crucis, near Llangollen. See *Gwaith Guto'r Glyn*, edited by J. Llywelyn Williams and Ifor Williams (Cardiff, 1939), pp. 303–04.

weitheu y geir yn y gilyd, a gveith ereill y dodeis synnvyr yn
lle y synnvyr heruyd mod a phriodolder yn ieith ni.[20]
[However, there is one thing you should know to start with,
when translating from one language to the other, as from
Latin into Welsh, it is not always possible to replace one
word with another whilst at the same time preserving fairly
the proper nature of the language and the sense of the diction.
For this reason I have sometimes translated word for word
and elsewhere followed the sense and meaning, according to
what was a natural and proper mode in our language].

Gruffudd Bola, however, was translating a devotional
work, and for him and his like fidelity to the original was of
prime importance, for mistranslation could even lead to
heresy. Whereas for such translators the word was the starting
point, the word often being synonymous with the word of
God, for those working on secular French texts the content
was the main interest. In the case of the translations of the
Charlemagne and Roland stories and the Grail romances, the
Welsh version is in most cases so close to the French source
that one can establish to which manuscript group or single
copy of the original it is most closely related. Close
comparison between the French and Welsh texts can then be
made, and reveals that the Welsh translators have made
significant changes, both deliberate and accidental.

Such textual comparison indicates that the Welsh
translators usually worked directly from the French, but still
translated quite freely at times. The commonest feature is
abridgement, which is found also in translation into other
European languages at this period. In the Welsh context,
however, there was a special justification. As a rule French
literary works translated into Welsh were considerably longer

[20] Henry Lewis (ed.), *Credo Athanasius, Bulletin of the Board of Celtic Studies* 5 (1930), 193–203 (p. 196).

than the native tales with which translator and patron — and potentially a wider audience — were familiar. In abridging, then, the translators may well have had in mind the need to adapt these long stories for a new audience and literary context. In their new, abbreviated, form they conformed more closely to what was the norm in native literary tradition, and presumably better adapted to reading aloud before an audience. In the case of *Cân Rolant* this has led to the loss of important passages such as Oliver's long speech criticising Roland's behaviour, and claiming that it is now too late to sound the horn. Moreover, the great battle between Charlemagne and Baligant, where the emperor of Christendom clashes with the king of the Pagans, has likewise disappeared, as has the Christians' revenge on the Saracens for killing Roland and his men. Similarly in *Y Seint Greal* a whole sequence of important adventures was abandoned towards the end of the second part, the translator rushing on to the conclusion and leaving ends untied.

Such abridgement inevitably led to, or went hand in hand with, the dismantling of what could be a very complex narrative structure in the source, a procedure already adopted at an earlier date by the redactors of the three romantic tales, *Gereint*, *Owein* and *Peredur*. By abridging or omitting paragraphs or entire episodes the translators broke down the intricate interlace of themes and adventures, imposing in its place a simpler pattern, a more paratactic structure with simpler episodes. In this way they imposed on the foreign material the kind of narrative structure which is more characteristic of the native Welsh tales such as *Culhwch ac Olwen*. By the same process the continental tales were divested of their more abstract elements and their psychological analysis. Thus in the translation of *La Queste del Saint Graal*, for instance, the spiritual and allegorical meaning of the adventures has virtually disappeared, as has the interest in the individual character and his or her emotional or psychological development. Instead, the emphasis is on action, on military exploits, on the bravery and valour of the heroes. It can be argued that the translators operated in this way because they were out of their depth, and failed to understand or fully appreciate the French texts, but on the other hand this did mean they reinterpreted the material before them so as to bring the narrative and the characters closer into line with what a Welsh audience would expect. It also seems likely that the impetus to change was often the translator's impatience or lack of interest in certain aspects of his source. Although the explanations of the theological significance of the adventures form a crucial part of the *Queste*, revealing the meaning and purpose of events, the Welsh translator soon begins to prune them away in a somewhat cavalier fashion, thereby causing havoc with the motivation of episodes and with the thematic structure as a whole.

Problems also arose from lack of familiarity with foreign fashions of thought and behaviour. The redactor of *Y Seint Greal* frequently has difficulty with the ideas and technical vocabulary of *fin'amors* and *courtoisie*, which leads him to misunderstand the behaviour and motivation of the main characters. Nonetheless, had such translators kept too closely to their original sources, their work would have remained largely incomprehensible to their audience.

Similarly, most Welsh translators of the later medieval period have chosen, no doubt consciously, to adopt a prose style as close as possible to that found in native Welsh prose. It is certain that the existence of a remarkably unified and standardised literary language also encouraged this response. Although the translator of *Y Seint Greal* uses a substantial number of French loanwords, some of which, admittedly, appear to have formed part of his own current vocabulary, rather than being lifted from his sources, the style is still surprisingly close to that found in earlier texts which were not translations. The translator frequently has recourse to the formulae and turns of phrase so characteristic of the earlier prose tales, and procedures such as the substitution of homely Welsh equivalents for French artefacts, and even the addition of references to earlier Welsh tales or traditions, all help to create an ambiance in which a Welsh audience would feel at home. And of course the audience, perforce without access to the French texts used by the translator, would be unaware of the examples of mistranslation that inevitably crept in.

From the mid fifteenth century onwards, the production of translations declines, though not so much from Latin, and the vogue for complete Welsh versions of important French texts seems to have waned. But this did not mean the end of Welsh interest in the French texts. During the fifteenth century and into the sixteenth, there began to emerge in addition a new breed of redactor, the antiquarian collector-scribe, who, magpie-like, would pick up tit-bits of narrative here and there. Sometimes these odds and ends of material, derived from manuscripts in Latin, English, French and Welsh, were worked up into complete narratives. A notable example is *Darogan yr Olew Bendigaid*, a fifteenth century text which combines Arthurian traditions, partly derived from the French Vulgate Cycle, with a Latin prophecy connected with Thomas Becket.[21] Sometimes such borrowings remained at the level of stray episodes, or even genealogies or name lists with minimal explanatory detail,[22] or they might be used to create

[21] See R. Wallis Evans, '*Darogan yr Olew Bendigaid* a *Hystdori yr Olew*', *Llên Cymru* 14 (1981–82), 86–91; Ceridwen Lloyd–Morgan, '*Darogan yr Olew Bendigaid*: Chwedl o'r bymthegfed ganrif', *Llên Cymru* 14 (1981–82), 64–85, and 'Prophecy and Welsh Nationhood in the Fifteenth Century', *Transactions of the Honourable Society of Cymmrodorion* (1985), pp. 9–26.

[22] P.C. Bartrum, 'Arthuriana from Genealogical Manuscripts', *National Library of Wales Journal* 14 (1965), 242–45; Ceridwen Lloyd-Morgan, 'Nodiadau Ychwanegol ar Achau Arthuraidd', *National Library of Wales*

triads modelled on the earlier ones of native origin.[23] It is noteworthy, however, that even at the end of the Middle Ages the interest in French written material remained keen, even if only amongst a restricted group of antiquarians and *conoscenti*. In their search for likely sources of interesting narrative material, these later redactors frequently had recourse to the very same French texts familiar to their predecessors.

Of the French Arthurian romances only the *Queste del Saint Graal*, *Perlesvaus* and part of the *Prose Merlin* had left substantial traces, but even in the full scale translations and in the triads there is evidence of familiarity with other such romances, notably the other romances of the Vulgate Cycle, the *Estoire del Saint Graal* and *Prose Lancelot* for example. Whether or not the same manuscript of the complete Vulgate Cycle, containing the *Estoire*, *Merlin*, *Queste*, *Lancelot* and *Mort Artu*, was still circulating in the fifteenth century or whether a few or even several copies were once available in Wales is difficult if not impossible to establish.[24] It seems unlikely, however, that any complete Welsh translation of a text such as the *Prose Lancelot* was ever undertaken, for if it had been, some evidence of this would surely have survived in the form of triads or more detailed references by the poets, even if all manuscripts of the translation itself vanished.

Interest in the French romances of the Vulgate Cycle did not peter out in the hands of the antiquarians, who simply quarried from them fragments of material to be noted down

---

Journal 21 (1980), 329–39.

[23] Examples include triads 86 and 91 in *Trioedd Ynys Prydein*, edited by Rachel Bromwich (Cardiff, 1961).

[24] For an account of a fragment of a *Prose Lancelot* manuscript with possible Welsh provenance, see John Scattergood, 'An Unrecorded Fragment of the Prose Lancelot in Trinity College Dublin MS 212', *Medium Aevum* 53 (1984), 301–06.

divorced from their proper narrative context. In the early sixteenth century a man who could be described, with hindsight, as the last of the medieval Welsh translators was busy at work in a house in Calais. Elis Gruffudd had come a long way from his native Flintshire, but had always maintained his Welsh literary interests, despite his employment in the retinue of the English king.[25] In his chronicle of the history of the world down to 1552 he included a section on the history of King Arthur, and, like his countrymen centuries before, he turned not only to Latin, Welsh and English sources, but also to the French romances.[26] An examination of his Arthurian sequence reveals his familiarity with the selfsame French romances as his predecessors, notably the Vulgate Cycle. But whereas the antiquarians of the fifteenth century had concentrated on picking out small morsels of material, and whilst translators of the thirteenth and fourteenth centuries struggled to produce Welsh versions of complete French texts, Elis Gruffudd's interest was in producing a comprehensive and coherent narrative of the career of Arthur, based on a multitude of source materials. Although, in consequence, he did not translate entire French tales or romances into Welsh, he often retold substantial portions. But in order to impose unity on his material, and perhaps also because he was not always working directly from his source

[25] For biographical details and a survey of Elis Gruffudd's military and literary careers, see Thomas Jones, 'A Welsh Chronicler in Tudor England', *Welsh History Review* 1 (1960), 1–18, and Prys Morgan, 'Elis Gruffudd of Gronant, Tudor Chronicler Extraordinary', *Publications of the Flintshire Historical Society* 25 (1971–72), 9–20.

[26] The chronicle, as yet mostly unpublished, is now NLW MSS 5276D and 3054D (formerly Mostyn 158), in the National Library of Wales. The Arthurian section occupies folios 321–40 of the former. A paper on the sources of this section was read at the International Congress of Celtic Studies, Swansea, July 1987.

manuscripts, Elis paraphrased and adapted to suit the needs and mood of his chronicle.

His avowed role was that of a translator, interpreting for his fellow countrymen the wealth of material in other languages to which they had no access.[27] In this respect he continued the tradition of large scale translation of the thirteenth and fourteenth centuries. But in his free adaptation of his sources and in his combination of this foreign material with narratives drawn from native Welsh tradition, he returns, in a sense, to the free re-telling of source material which is characteristic of the earlier adapters of French material, those responsible for providing Welsh versions of *Peredur*, *Owein* and *Gereint*. Having passed through a phase of full-scale, close translation of secular French texts, and of antiquarian patchwork, with Elis Grufudd we find the wheel has come full circle.

Changing circumstances, changing literary fashions and the aims, interests and capabilities of the individual redactor account for this development or evolution from the thirteenth to the sixteenth century, but ultimately all these translators and redactors have in common a desire to re-tell some of the finest medieval French narratives in a way acceptable to a new audience, whose own traditions and expectations were only too different from those of the French audiences who first received them. In this respect the task of the Welsh translators was no different from that of their counterparts in England and continental Europe. The same texts were being translated into the different vernaculars at the same period and, *mutatis mutandis*, gave rise to the same spectrum of responses. An examination of the translated literature in Middle Welsh demonstrates clearly that, far from being culturally introspective, during the second half of the Middle Ages

[27] NLW MS 3054D, f. 2.

Wales was looking east of its borders and was following new, European, literary trends.

The Monastery of Vadstena.
Investigating the Great Translation Workshop in Medieval Scandinavia

LARS WOLLIN

BY FAR the most important cultural institution in the Swedish
— and Scandinavian — later Middle Ages was the Monastery
of Vadstena. Much literary activity took place here,
particularly in the fifteenth century, mainly directed to the
translation into contemporary Swedish of internationally
current religious literature of all genres, almost exclusively
from the Latin. Through this industrious and continuous Latin
translating activity, the people of Vadstena clearly promoted
the development of written Swedish. Although it originated in
the oldest written forms of this language, developed earlier in
the Middle Ages, Vadstena Swedish was highly dependent on
continental, primarily Latin, style patterns.

1. St. Bridget and her Monastery

The Monastery of Vadstena was a creation of St. Bridget —
who was active, as we all know, in the fourteenth century, and
one of the central figures in medieval Scandinavia. Her
renown is chiefly based on her recapitulation of the 'Divine

Revelations', which she believed herself to have received through Christ's or the Holy Virgin's own mouth. Their contents are highly miscellaneous, and their style varies greatly; they were often charged with some kind of urgent request to central actors in contemporary Scandinavian and European politics.

St. Bridget herself laid down the general outlines for the Order for monks and nuns that she wanted to institute, with its centre located in Vadstena on the eastern shore of Lake Vättern in the province of Östergötland in southeastern Sweden. The idea was realized according to her instructions some years after her death, in connection with her canonization in Rome. The Monastery was inaugurated by the bishop of Linköping in 1384 and continued its work throughout the fifteenth century; after the Reformation in Sweden, in the early sixteenth century, activity there ceased in practice. The Monastery's contribution to history was, as mentioned, primarily one of literature and language. In printed editions, the works of translated literature from Vadstena extant today cover a few running metres of shelf space. 'Vadstena literature' and 'Vadstena language' have long been central concepts in research on the Middle Ages in Sweden and Scandinavia.

One of the very first tasks to be undertaken in the recently-established Monastery was presumably the presentation of the collected Revelations of the founder of the Order in stately Swedish language. St. Bridget herself had already received these celestial messages, and communicated them to those around her, in her maternal tongue, but only slight remains of the original Swedish version seem to have been preserved. All that certainly remains today are some trifling fragments.[1] The Revelations were translated immediately into Latin by St. Bridget's confessors and dispersed throughout the world in this language. The fact that Sweden's first, and for a long time sole, contribution to the literature of the world was thus delivered in Latin is nothing to be wondered at, in an essentially Latin-writing medieval Europe. But the nuns of the Monastery did not understand Latin. For them — and reasonably also as an expression of sorts of a national Swedish consciousness — a retranslation of the entire collection of Revelations into Swedish was begun. The result of this undertaking is the extant Old Swedish version of the text — much of it revised shortly afterwards, in varying stylistic expressions. At least, this is the conception of the course of events that generally prevails among scholars today.[2]

As a pioneering achievement in the new Monastery, the task of the translator — or the translators — was apparently a heavy one, at least in a strictly quantitative sense. In modern print, it is a matter of roughly 1,500 pages of text, and today philologists think that most of this text was completed in good Vadstena Swedish as early as the 1380s.[3]

[1] B. Högman (ed.), *Heliga Birgittas originaltexter*, SSFS [= Samlingar utgivna av Svenska Fornskriftsällskapet] 58 (Uppsala, 1951).

[2] Surveys are given by C-G. Undhagen (ed.), *Sancta Birgitta. Revelaciones. Book I*, SSFS, ser. 2, vol. VII:1 (Uppsala, 1978), p. 7 with note 10, and Sten Eklund, 'A Re-assessment of the Old Swedish Bridgettine Text Corpus', in *Kungl. Humanistiska Vetenskaps-Samfundet i Uppsala. Årsbok 1983–1984* (Uppsala), pp. 5–24 (pp. 6–9) — both with further references.

[3] This view was first held by K. B. Westman, *Birgitta-studier* (Uppsala, 1911) and S. Kraft, *Textstudier till Birgittas revelationer*, Kyrkohistorisk Årsskrift 29 (Uppsala, 1929), and has been further strengthened by e.g. B. Bergh (ed.), *Sancta Birgitta. Revelaciones. Book V*, SSFS, ser. 2, vol. VII:5 (Uppsala, 1971), pp. 16–33.

The several subsequent translation undertakings in the Monastery present, to the extent to which they have been preserved, a linguistic form and a relationship to their originals in line with the first great translation of the Revelations themselves. This continuity is of course hardly surprising, since the given conditions and the external framework of the activities in the Monastery basically remained the same throughout the Middle Ages.

The Vadstena translators worked with great fidelity to the Latin texts — often giving the impression of close stylistic imitation — but also, undeniably, with considerable independence and skill. It still happens that linguistic and literary historians speak condescendingly of the 'slavish' translation technique of these monks, and of their 'mechanical aping' of the 'ungenuine' form of the Latin originals. To a certain extent, these conceptions can be traced back to a common idealization of Swedish literature of the earlier Middle Ages, particularly the provincial laws. This kind of literature has been considered, partly in a romantic spirit, more 'genuine' or 'popular' than later literary achievements, thus suggesting an erroneous contrast with the later, continentally influenced, Latinized language of Vadstena.

In fact, the Latin translators of the Monastery developed a professionalism that seems to have stabilized rapidly, within the given limitations. In Vadstena they not only learned to write Swedish in a routine fashion never previously experienced, characterized by speed, quantity, and steadiness of hand, all within a richly varied, sometimes very abstract field. They also acquired, more or less consciously, a certain ideal of style, something of a very loose norm, to which a relatively large number of writers over a relatively long period of time subordinated themselves and adapted their language, with a fair degree of consistency. In medieval Scandinavia this was something new. It may be asserted that the monks of

Vadstena, translating from the Latin, took the very first steps towards standardizing the Swedish language.

2. Investigating medieval translation

Despite its importance for the development and stabilization of a standard written language in Sweden, the Latin translation at Vadstena has scarcely attracted the interest of philologists and historical linguists — at least not as *translation*, with the accent on the process. For several years I have been working to fill this lacuna, at the same time trying to work out a model for the closer — and more general — analysis of some central aspects of the process proper.[4] I shall now present a general outline of these attempts.

My methodological point of departure was the vigorous research on modern spoken language, carried out in Sweden and elsewhere in the 1960s and early 1970s. Generally, this work had socio-linguistic aims, inspired primarily by Basil Bernstein's theories; its main object was to determine and measure social differences of language use in modern Sweden. Theoretically based on a structuralist view of language, this research was highly orientated to syntax: one defined and classified sentences and clauses, which were broken up into constituents for further systematic classification and description on a large scale and in quantitative terms. The concentration on spoken language required new principles for the segmentation of these syntactic units — prosody replacing

---

[4] L. Wollin, *Svensk latinöversättning I. Processen*, SSFS 74:1 (Lund, 1981) and *Svensk latinöversättning II. Förlagan och produkten*, SSFS 74:2 (Lund, 1983). (Also published in Lundastudier i nordisk språkvetenskap, A 34, 35).

punctuation as a main marker of the speaker's own segmentation.

It is obvious that this model for syntactic analysis, based on living spoken language, has particular significance to the philologist working with medieval texts. Such texts often lack consistent punctuation; in printed editions, punctuation is normally the work of the editor, and as such dependent on his private, often unconscious, and essentially irrelevant syntactic analysis. The principles used for the segmentation and classification of syntactic units in modern spoken Swedish, then, could be easily applied to written texts in Old Swedish and medieval Latin. These principles start from an autonomous judgement of syntactic relations on different levels: between and within units such as sentences, clauses, and clause constituents.

Given the general questions, the theory and the method, the Vadstena literature offered an abundance of material for a systematic investigation of late medieval Swedish translation. The five Latin original texts I chose are the following:[5]

1. St. Bridget: *Revelationum Liber VII*
2. St. Bridget: *Revelationes Extravagantes*
3. Mechthild of Hackeborn: *Liber Specialis Gratiae*
4. ps.-Bonaventura: *Meditationes Vitae Christi*

[5] Editions of the Latin texts: 1. *Den heliga Birgittas Revelaciones. Bok VII*, edited by B. Bergh, SSFS, ser. 2, vol. VII:7 (Uppsala, 1967). 2. *Den heliga Birgittas Reuelaciones extrauagantes*, edited by L. Hollman, SSFS, ser. 2, vol. V (Uppsala 1956). 3. *Revelationes Gertrudianae ac Mechtildianae II. Sanctae Mechtildis Liber specialis gratiae*. Ed. Solesmensium O.S.B. Monachorum cura et opera. Pictavii & Parisiis 1877. 4. *Sancti Bonaventurae ... operum tomus sextus*, Mogvntiae, 1609. 5. S. Bernardi, *Clarae-Vallensis abbatis primi, opera omnia*, edited by J. P. Migne, Patrologiae cursus completus. Bibliotheca patrum latinorum, vol. 184 (Paris, 1879), coll. 1199–1306.

5.   Thomas de Froidmont: *Liber de Modo Bene Vivendi ad Sororem*

These five texts represent, with some simplification, two separate genres in medieval European religious literature: the Brigittine and Mechthild texts relate divine revelations, whereas the two others reflect ordinary Christian edification. All these Latin texts were translated at Vadstena.[6] The Swedish is oldest in No. 1, which is part of the main Brigittine text mentioned above; No. 4 was probably translated around 1400, No. 3 in 1469, Nos. 2 and 5 some time in the latter half of the fifteenth century.

3. Translating strategies

In the initial stage of the investigation, the five translations together with their Latin originals were systematically analysed with regard to their syntactic qualities, especially sentence structure. The text of each version was segmented into major syntactic units such as sentences and primary constituents. These units are, to express it again in a slightly simplified manner, the same as those resulting from a traditional grammatical analysis, although segmented somewhat more systematically. In the example below, the constituents of the Latin and the Old Swedish sentence are

---

[6] Editions of the Old Swedish texts: 1. *Heliga Birgittas uppenbarelser*, edited by G. E. Klemming, SSFS 14:3 (Stockholm, 1861), pp. 233–95. 2. *Heliga Birgittas uppenbarelser*, edited by G. E. Klemming, SSFS 14:4 (Stockholm, 1862), pp. 49–120. 3. *Hel. Mechtilds uppenbarelser*, edited by R. Geete, SSFS 32 (Stockholm, 1899). 4. *Bonaventuras betraktelser öfver Christi lefverne*, edited by G. E. Klemming, SSFS 15 (Stockholm, 1860), pp. 1–256. 5. *Helige Bernhards skrifter*, edited by H. Wieselgren, SSFS 16 (Stockholm, 1866), pp. 1–195.

separated by slanting lines (/).

> et / ab illo tempore / ego et dyabolus / discordamus et
>   certamus
> oc / af them timanon / missämiom / wi / oc stridhom
> and of that time disagree we and fight

Exactly 300 ordinary affirmative sentences and varying numbers of non-affirmative ones were thus segmented in each Old Swedish TL (Target Language) text, corresponding to roughly the same number in the Latin SL (Source Language) text. This makes a total of about 1800 sentences in each version, comprising about 27 000 words in the SL and about 33 000 words in the TL version.

At the second and more significant stage, the *relations* between the corresponding units of each version were systematically analysed and classified — an undertaking not directed by any previous model. My intention was to make a quantitative survey that thoroughly described the translating process, as it appears in a large body of authentic text.

The relations accounted for are those described on the basis of the diagram below (Figure 1). Here six dimensions of the translating process are arranged hierarchically. The terms refer directly to the principal descriptive unit of the investigation, i.e. the primary constituent (as segmented in the initial stage). They are written in rectangles: content, lexicon, syntactic structure, number, extension and level. Under each dimension the translator is faced with the binary choice of either *identity* or *transformation*. Choosing the latter, he has the same two alternatives in the following lower dimension, and so forth.

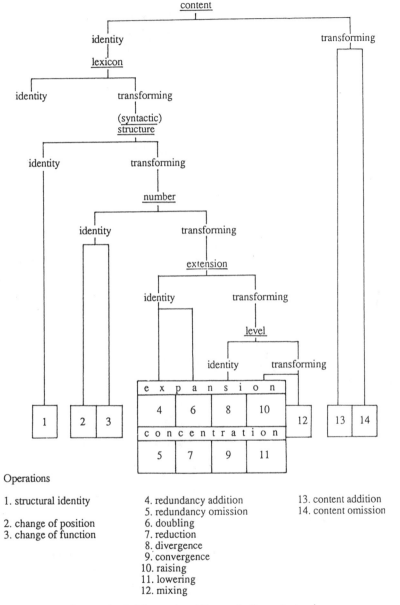

Operations

1. structural identity

2. change of position
3. change of function

4. redundancy addition
5. redundancy omission
6. doubling
7. reduction
8. divergence
9. convergence
10. raising
11. lowering
12. mixing

13. content addition
14. content omission

Figure 1. A hierarchy of translating strategies

The 'translating strategies' — which I refer to as *operations*, i.e. the translator's actual measures which realize these dimensions — are listed at the bottom of the diagram (Nos. 1–14). One example of each main type of operation is given below.

   1.   Structural identity
     Text No.1
     Adhuc / deficit / ei / corona (13:67)
     Än / bristir / hanom / kronan (p. 268, 28)
     Still lacks him the crown

   2.   Change of position
     Text No. 4
     Regnum celorum / *pauperum* / est (p. 366 A)
     himerikis rike / är / *fatika manna* (p. 130.1)
     Heaven-realm's realm is poor men's

   3.   Change of function
     Text No. 2
     Mater Dei / loquitur / *sponse Christi* (6:1)
     Gudz modher / talar / *til christi brudh* (p. 55, 21)
     God's mother speaks to Christ's bride

   4.   Redundancy addition
     Text No. 4
     Numquid / Domina / reservavit / sibi? (p. 341 B)
     Hwat / munde / ey / varfrw / läggia / *thät* / nidhir (p. 3, 5)
     Might Our Lady hide it away?

   5.   Redundancy omission
     Text No. 3
     sed / *hoc* / scias, / quod tunc multo vicinius tibi cor meum
         sociatur (p. 177)
     wtan / thu / skalt / wita / at tha är mit hiärta tik mykit
         nämmare (p. 222, 2)
    but thou shalt know that then is my heart thee much nearer

6.   Doubling

Text No. 2

Quid / *confert* / audienti? (1:2)

huat / *gagna* / thät / *ällir froma* / them thät höra (p. 49, 20)

what avails that or benefits those it hear?

7.   Reduction

Text No. 5

nullo modo / dubites, / *nullo modo* / de misericordia Dei /
    desperes (col. 1248)

jäfwa / *ey* / älla wanhopa / af gudhz miskund (p. 92, 13)

doubt not or despair of God's mercy!

8.   Divergence

Text No. 1

et / ab illo tempore / ego et dyabolus / *discordamus et*
    certamus (11:3)

oc / af them timanom / *missämiom* / wi / *oc stridhom* (p.
    254, 27)

and from that time disagree we and fight

9.   Convergence

Text No. 2

et / *ibi* / sedes mea / est, / *ubi voluntas mea perficitur*
    (24:4)

oc / *hwar som min wili fulkompnas ther* / är / mit säte (p.
    76, 9)

and where my will is done, there is my seat

10.   Raising

Text No. 4

et / cum grandescente / grandescas, / *semper tamen*
    humilitate conservata (p. 344 A)

oc / swa / skalt / thu / waxa / til / lika vp mädh honom.
ödhmiuktena / *skalt* / *thu* / *tho* / *altidh* / *göma* (p. 16, 9)

And so shalt thou grow to like up with him. The humility
    shalt thou yet always preserve.

11. Lowering

Text No. 3

Oculi Domini / sunt / nobis / specula divinae veritatis: *ibi / agnoscere / valemus / tenebras nostrae infidelitatis.*[7]

Hans hälghasta öghon, the / äro / oss / späghil gudhligz sanhethz, *j huilkom wi skulum skodha wars otrolighetz mörker* (p. 258, 21)

His holiest eyes, they are us a mirror of divine truth, in which we shall behold our disbelief's darkness.

12. Mixing

Text No. 5

Fides / nequaquam / vi / *extorquetur* (col. 1205)

tron / *kan* / aldrigh / *nödhdraghas* / *wt* (p. 2, 26)

The faith can never be need-pulled out

13. Content addition

Text No. 4

Ego / sensi / virtutem / ex me exijsse (p. 355 A)

Jak / kände / *väl* / at dygdhen gik af mik (p. 72, 23)

I felt well that the virtue went off me

14. Content omission

Text No. 4

Et / per ista / *maxime* / peruenire / possumus / ad cordis puritatem (p. 350 B)

ok / mädh thässom fyrom / maghom / vi / koma / til hiärtans renlek (p. 45, 1)

and by these four may we come to the heart's purity

The total number of operations in the material is close to 7,400. As to the characteristics of these translation activities, it is sufficient to establish the following: first, that the lowest numbered operations (Nos. 1–3, implying either structural

---

[7] Missing in printed edition; for manuscript reading, see Wollin 1981, p. 262.

identity, or structural transformation followed by number identity) are the least complex ones; secondly, that the more complex operations, those implying number transformation (Nos. 4–11), occur in two parallel series, referred to as *expansional* and *concentrational* restructuring — the No. 12 'mixing' operation forming a third class.

4. Linguistic implications

The frequencies of these different operations in each particular translation reflect fundamental individual properties of the translator's technical strategies. Different translations can be distinctly contrasted and compared in significant details.

Three relationships are important in this context: that of identity to transformation; that of expansion to concentration; the levels of awareness and free choice operating behind the measures taken by the translator. Some hints of this are given in the proportions in the tables below.

Table 1.   Structural identity and transformation
Operations: percentage distribution

Text No.	1	2	3	4	5	Total
Identity	54	63	53	39	45	50
Transformation	46	37	47	61	55	50

The even distribution in the total material between structural identity and transformation   (Table 1; operation No. 1 compared to the rest) is not reflected in the individual translations: identity dominates in texts Nos. 1–3, whereas the opposite is the case in the purely didactic texts, Nos. 4 and 5. This difference may possibly be, but is not necessarily, connected with the differences between the two literary genres. (I will return to these basic relationships below.)

78 **Lars Wollin**

Table 2.   Expansion and concentration
A. Operations: percentage distribution

Text No.	1	2	3	4	5	Total
Expansion	14	16	20	23	14	17
Concentration	12	5	9	16	18	13

B. Number of words in SL, TL; percentage increase

Text No.	1	2	3	4	5	Total
SL text	6480	4829	5761	4549	5153	26772
TL text	7107	6158	7986	5983	5670	32904
Increase %	10	28	39	32	10	23

In four of the five translations, expansional operations are predominant over concentrational ones (Table 2A). At the same time we can see (Table 2B) that the TL version in each pair of texts is longer, in terms of word number, than the SL version. The translator has, in all these cases, expanded the text.

The figures might give some hints of the increase in redundancy that is often said to be essential to most translating activity. According to some frequent theoretical conceptions[8], this is due to the need to make explicit in translation what is implicit in the original. Apparently this is accomplished by various means of expansion — syntactic and lexical — when restructuring the message in the TL.

The Swedish translator's purely mechanical analysis of Latin structure, resulting in the transferring of finite forms into finite and non-finite forms and into pronouns functioning as grammatical subjects, in the adding of particles of different kinds and so on, accounts for a considerable portion of these expansional operations. The quantitative enlargement, then, as

[8] E.g.: E.A. Nida, C. R. Taber, *The Theory and Practice of Translation*, (Leiden, 1974), pp. 163–65.

described in table 2, is brought about in a rather automatic manner. Accordingly, one has to take into account the essential difference difference between *intentional* and *non-intentional* adjustment of the structure.

Another important distinction is made between such measures of the translator as may be regarded as *obligatory* — i.e. required by the 'un-Swedish' structure of the original, unconditionally demanding some kind of transforming — and those *voluntary* ones not performed under that kind of pressure.

A typical example of these structural obligations may be seen in No. 2 above: the Latin clause has a predicative (*pauperum*) in the position between the subject and the finite verb, a complement which splits the nexus of relationship between subject and predicate, which Swedish (even Old Swedish) syntax is forced to keep unsplit in affirmative main clauses — in conformity with German word order rules, but principally unlike English.The translator solves the dilemma — which he probably did not conceive as a dilemma — by transposing the predicative (*fatika manna*) and the finite verb (*är*), so that the latter lands in its grammatically regular position as the second element of the clause.

The non-intentional and the structurally obligatory operations make up about the half of all the transforming operations in my texts. If we leave them out of account, thus isolating those operations made *intentionally* and *voluntarily* by the translator, we can neutralize the balance between expansional and concentrational operations: the percentage relationship of 17:13 according to Table 2A changes into 9:8 in Table 3 below.

Table 3. Expansion and concentration.
Intentional, non-obligatory operations: percentage
distribution

Text No.	1	2	3	4	5	Total
Expansional	5	6	11	13	8	9
Concentrational	6	3	4	10	16	8

In four of the five translations — the rather insignificant exception being No. 3 — the tendency toward concentration has now strengthened its position in proportion to expansion. This means that the textual expansion in the translation is, to a varying but not negligible extent, a question of either unconscious manipulations, performed in more or less mechanical connection with the SL grammatical structure, or compulsory arrangements, enforced by an SL structure that does not lend itself to immediate imitation. In those cases, however, where the translator is acting deliberately, and in the position to allow himself the free choice between structural imitation and restructuring, he is still slightly more inclined to use expansions, but the proportions become evener. The idea of Nida, and others, that some kind of textual expansion is intrinsic to all translating activity is essentially modified by these observations. When the Swedish TL texts in this material use more words than the Latin SL texts, this is, to a considerable extent, due to differences in the grammatical structures of Latin and Swedish, requiring numerous translating manipulations with an expanding, text-extending effect, but unrelated to deliberate considerations or to the possible stylistic endeavours of the translator. — Incidentally, this can be confirmed by observations in translation from present-day English into Swedish: the TL version normally becomes slightly shorter, because of the somewhat more synthetic character of Swedish language structure as compared to English.

a. All (i.e. intentional and non-intentional) operations
b. Intentional (i.e. voluntary and non-voluntary) operations
c. Voluntary operations

+ = more than average
− = less than average

Text No.	a					b					c				
	1	2	3	4	5	1	2	3	4	5	1	2	3	4	5
2 change of pos.	+	−	−	−	+	+	−	−	−	+	−	−	−	+	+
3 change of funct.	−	−	−	+	+	−	−	−	+	+	−	−	−	+	+
4 redundancy add.	−	−	+	+	−	−	−	+	+	−	−	−	+	+	−
5 redundancy om.	+	−	+	+	−	+	−	+	+	−	+	−	+	−	+
6 doubling	−	−	+	+	+	−	−	+	+	+	−	−	+	+	+
7 reduction	−	−	−	−	+	−	−	−	−	+	−	−	−	−	+
8a divergence a	−	−	−	+	+	−	−	−	+	+	−	−	−	+	+
9a convergence a	−	−	−	+	+	−	−	−	+	+	−	−	−	+	+
8b divergence b	+	+	−	+	−										
9b convergence b	+	−	+	−	−										
10a raising a	−	−	+	+	+	−	−	+	+	+	−	−	+	+	+
11a lowering a	+	−	−	+	−	+	−	−	+	−	+	−	−	+	−
10b raising b	−	−	+	+	−	−	−	+	+	+	−	−	+	+	+
11b lowering b	−	−	−	+	+	−	−	−	+	+	−	−	−	+	+
12 mixing	−	−	−	+	+	−	−	−	+	+	−	−	−	+	+
13 content add.	−	−	−	+	+	−	−	−	+	+	−	−	−	+	+
14 content om.	+	−	−	+	+	+	−	−	+	+	−	−	−	+	+
expansional	−	−	+	+	−	−	−	+	+	+	−	−	+	+	+
concentrational	−	−	−	+	+	−	−	−	+	+	−	−	−	+	+
numb. transform.	−	−	−	+	+	−	−	−	+	+	−	−	−	+	+
str. transform.	−	−	−	+	+	−	−	−	+	+	−	−	−	+	+

(NB: The operation types Nos. 8–11 are further classified in subtypes not accounted for in this paper.)

Table 4. Operation types. Frequency: relation
to average occurrence

Distinguishing the intentional, non-obligatory operations
in a text also helps us to sharpen the image of the two
'schools' that can actually be discerned within the translation
tradition at Vadstena: one more 'slavishly' imitative,
stylistically Latinizing school, and one 'freer'. To the former
school belong the two Brigittine texts, to the latter both the
edificatory texts — the Mechthild revelations occupying an
intermediate position. This fundamental pattern was intimated
in table 1; in table 4 above it appears with closer
representation of details. Here is marked, for each single
operation type, in each single pair of texts, higher (+) and
lower (-) frequency than the average for each type. Moreover,
the pattern is being gradually clarified by the successive
rejection, first, of non-intentional, and then of obligatory,
operations.

It is column c that most sharply contrasts the genres. The
difference between them, thus defined in some detail, cannot
be traced back to differences between Latin and Swedish
languages; it is due more or less exclusively to the translators'
free choices, conditioned by their individual variations in
competence and stylistic ambition. This variation is not
insignificant — whether it is dependent on the diversity of the
two literary genres or strictly individual, is a different
question.

5. Philological implications

Though applied to a rather specific and confined text corpus,
these observations concerning the translation process, its
course and effects, may be reasonably assumed to have some
implications for our general conceptions of the nature of this
process itself. Furthermore, the relations detected in
investigating the process give rise to some philological
considerations; the principal reference is to the textual history

of the works of St. Bridget, represented here by the texts Nos.
1 and 2, so central to the literature of late medieval Sweden.
The current conception of the relationship between Latin and
Old Swedish version was noted above (p. 66 ff.) and can be
summarized by viewing a Latin SL and an Old Swedish TL
version. Text No. 1 is part of the great pioneering translation
work of the 1380s, whereas text No. 2, the TL version of
which is dated a hundred years later, comprises a small part
of St. Bridget's literary remains — mainly a commentary on
the 'Regula Salvatoris', formulating St. Bridget's own statutes
for her Order. For several reasons, this section of the text was
left outside the corpus and was not translated until a later date.

It appears from the investigation that the earlier translator
worked in slightly different ways from the later. Although
both are characterized to a fair degree by fidelity to the
syntactic structures of their originals — what we might call
the 'more closely stucture-copying school' — the patterns are
not entirely identical: translator No. 2 is a bit more 'slavish'
than his pioneering colleague. More importantly, they diverge
in 'effect' as regards the textual expansions in the TL version
(see Table 2B). There is considerably more expansion in text
No. 2 — 28% — as compared to 10% in text No. 1. The
average for all five text pairs is 23%. (Text No. 5 shows as
low an expansion rate as text No. 1, but that is another story.)

Examining text No. 1 more closely, we find several
explanations for the modesty of its expansions. In 28% of the
SL and 23% of the TL text (counted in numbers of words)
either the SL and the TL structures are equally long, or the SL
structures are longer. In the latter case, the translator has
abbreviated or concentrated the text, instead of expanding it in
accordance with the common pattern. In these parts the text
volume is decreased by 9%; in the rest of the text it is
increased by 17%, which is close to the average total. In text
No. 2, on the other hand, expansion is more constant
throughout.

A tangible example of this kind of text shrinkage, brought about by a translator, is given in example No. 15:

15.   *Text No. 1*

    et / ex hoc / tanta *caritate* / cepit / deum *diligere*, quod ... (13:21)

    ther / fik / han / aff / swa storan *kärlek* til gudz at ... (p. 263, 30)

    there got he of so great love to God that ...

The translator has reduced the double concept of *caritate ... diligere* into a single word *kärlek* ('love'); the operation applied is, in my terms, reduction (No. 7). In this case, it exclusively hits the redundancy of the assertion, which is diminished as an effect of the translator's selections, without loss of relevant information.

Reduction of content, however, is obvious in example No. 16:

16.   *Text No. 1*

    Cum sponsa Christi esset in Roma continue residens, et quodam die orando staret *in elevatione mentali*, tunc Christus apparuit ei sic dicens: ... (6:1)

    Nar christi brudh var daghlica sitiande j rom oc stodh een dagh a bönom syntis christus hänne sighiande swa: ... (p. 246, 26)

    When Christ's bride was daily sitting in Rome and stood one day on prayers, was seen Christ to her saying so: ...

The phrase *in elevatione mentali* has been omitted in translation, which has undeniably reduced the message of the SL text.

6. A test case: the Old Swedish Revelations

It is tempting to link these observations to the longstanding debate of Brigittine philologists about the relationship between the Latin and the Old Swedish versions of the Revelations. Attempts have been made to modify, or even to revise, the common view of a Swedish retranslation in the 1380s — generally by adducing passages in the Old Swedish text which suggest non-Latin priority — or in some isolated cases even positively proving Swedish priority. An instructive example is No. 17:

> 17.   *Text No. 1*
> Nam non solum ablatus est michi saccus, verum etiam
>   peccata, quibus erat repletus (13:41)
> här är borto baadhe säkkir ok saka (p. 266, 6)
> here are away both sack and guilts

The Old Swedish version is laconic and pithy, it is rhythmic and doubly alliterated (borto baadhe säkkir ok saka); the character of good, genuine Swedish is unmistakable. It is easy to see how the Latin translator, insensitive or indifferent to the stylistic qualities of the Swedish, fills the structure with phrases only loosely equivalent, thus producing a lengthier, more garrulous version, quite lacking the vigorous density of the original. It is at least arguable that the version preserved in the Old Swedish translation provides a more authoritative witness to the Saint's original Swedish.

Examples like Nos. 15 and 16, however, are never referred to in the discussion about the relationship. The stylistic differences between the versions are not so evident in these cases, and it has been impossible to claim seriously that reducing and cancelling operations as such would be less likely to be used by a translator than the doubling and adding ones, which would follow from our assumption of Swedish priority. Nevertheless, quantitative relations like those

accounted for above, applicable to large parts of the text, may
provide a basis for argument in that direction. Cases like No.
4 can then serve as undisputable evidence: they prove that
certain elements of the Saint's Swedish original undeniably
exist in the extant Old Swedish text. The question is how
many and how coherent these elements are, if they do not
actually comprise the entire text, and how to trace and identify
these brief passages — or more extended sequences. Of
course, a plausible explanation of this complex relationship
between Latin and Old Swedish version would be welcome.

One reasonable hypothesis emerges immediately. It
implies that the extant Old Swedish text is neither
unambiguously a translation from the Latin, nor throughout
identical with the original of the same Latin version. Instead,
the Swedish text is the result of a compilation, carried out at
Vadstena in the 1380s by an editor, who began his work
collecting both what he had to hand, and what he could hunt
up, of Swedish manuscripts still extant from St. Bridget's own
days, possibly by her own hand. He would have used this
original material in its existing condition, provided it agreed
adequately with the official Latin text, which had just been,
or was just going to be, sanctioned by the Holy See; the
discrepancies between the original Swedish text and the Latin
translation, which may have been numerous and profound,
were then corrected in translation against the Latin. For large,
possibly very large, parts of the text the translator had no
access to any original Swedish material; in these cases he had
no other choice than to make a new translation of his own
from the Latin. The result of this very pragmatic, and certainly
very rational, procedure would of course have been an Old
Swedish text that as a whole presents several strata of different
relationship to the Latin: pure original, (more or less) revised
and corrected original, translation mixed with remaining
original elements, pure translation. Everything is deposited in

layers, in an elusive pattern, which may be concealed from us for ever.

To the contemporary scholar the matter is further complicated by the fact that a double text tradition began almost immediately in the Monastery. The Old Swedish text has undergone more or less radical revisions, the relations of which to the Latin are uncertain, and we probably also have to take account of interference occurring between the Latin and Old Swedish versions during the next century and a half. In addition, recent observations have been reported by Brigittine latinists, stating that even in the Latin text tradition — which has developed in diverging branches of a vast stemma — there are in some cases several layers, apparently distinguished by different degrees of stylistic elaboration.[9] — Despite more than a hundred years of research, we still lack a comprehensive investigation of this classic complex in Swedish medieval philology.

The idea that such a relationship exists between the Latin and Old Swedish versions of St. Bridget's Revelations is in itself far from new. It has been occasionally mentioned in the debate, in general terms, often in connection with the study of some individual chapter or passage, for which Swedish priority has been suggested or argued. As early as the beginning of this century, one scholar[10] maintained that the Latin version was stylistically inferior and so less likely to be the original. Since he based his argument on intuition rather than on fact, it was easy for later critics to build up the picture prevailing today of a more or less unambiguous Latin SL and Old Swedish TL relation. The arguments of these critics were presented in the thorough study of individual passages,

[9] S. Eklund, *op. cit.*

[10] R. Steffen, cf. Eklund *op. cit.*

deliberately selected from those large parts of the text where the relationship they have asserted is undisputable.

The hypothesis presented above might be tested in the light of the quantitative data accounted for here. It is tempting to undertake an inventory of the entire Revelations text — or, at first, maybe just of particularly significant sections such as book 7 (the basis of text No. 1) — in a detailed analysis, directed not at scattered phenomena, chosen more or less by impression, which has hitherto been a common procedure, but proceeding systematically from one operation to the other. The sorting of the operations according to proportional increase and decrease in the number of words involved would be combined with the study of the presence, or absence, of accompanying manipulations in grammatical structure, in connection with stylistic observations of the same kind as those applied to example No. 4 above. The pattern resulting might give some hints as to the priority in each single case. However, this task is so extensive that the present paper can do no more than point the way and suggest the outcome.

Julius Caesar, Philip Augustus, and the Anonymous Translator of *Li Fet des Romains*

JEANETTE BEER

JULIUS Caesar was not among the early heroes of vernacular French literature, and it was not until the thirteenth century that his potential as a heroic model was realized through the activities of an anonymous cleric, who saw analogies between his own monarch and the Roman conqueror of Gaul. That translator's project to translate into French all known material about Caesar reached fruition just before the king (Philip II of France) confronted that most crucial military enterprise: the Battle of Bouvines.

Li Fet des Romains[1] represents medieval translation at its most ambitious. The sources for Julius Caesar's life were extensive: the seven books of Caesar's own *Commentarii de bello gallico* plus an appended eighth book by Hirtius, Suetonius's *Vitae Caesarum* I, Sallust's *Catilina*, Lucan's *De bello civili*, and multiple lesser sources such as Isidore of Seville's *Etymologiae*, Flavius Josephus's *Bellum Judaicum*,

---

[1] L.-F. Flutre and K. Sneyders de Vogel (eds), *Li Fet des Romains*, 3 vols (Paris and Groningen, 1938) (emphasis mine in all quotations).

Petrus Comestor's *Historia*, St. Augustine, and the Bible. Moreover, it was the plan of the translator to provide a similar biography for all the twelve emperors: of whom, as he mistakenly believed, Julius Caesar was the first. 'Et comencerons nostre conte principalment a Juille Cesar, et le terminerons a Domicien, qui fu li douziemes empereres, si que nos i metrons meinte persone qui orent diverses dignetez a Rome au tens des .xij. empereeurs, dont Juilles fu li premiers'.[2] [And we shall begin our narration with Julius Caesar first and foremost, and we shall end it with Domitian, who was Rome's twelfth emperor; and it is our plan to include in it many diverse Roman dignitaries from the period of the twelve emperors, of whom Julius was the first.]

The particular usefulness of the subject to an ambitious French monarchy of the early thirteenth century was obvious. As a military manual it presented — and sometimes solved — such diverse tactical problems as the naval superiority of an enemy fleet (from Armorica), mass immigration (of the Helvetians), two (German) invasions, unusual war formations, unbesiegeable cities, midwinter snows, impassable rivers, and the revolt of all Gaul. If, therefore, the translator had done nothing but render the *Commentarii* into the vernacular (which for pages at a time he often does!), his translation would have been both justified and welcome. The activities of the Romans contained both negative and positive military lessons for the present.

The translator has broader intentions, however. He echoes Isidore of Seville's view of the utility of pagan history when he asserts that in the deeds of the Romans 'puet en trover

---

[2] Julius Caesar was, in fact, extremely careful to avoid all titles that might suggest possible tyranny to the Roman people. By a historical accident, however, that non-imperial status made his situation even more analogous to Philip's than the translator realized.

assez connoissance de bien fere et de mal eschiver' (p. 2) [one may come to a real knowledge of doing good and avoiding evil]. This statement must not be too narrowly interpreted. The accomplishment of good and the avoidance of evil was obviously not restricted to a military context, even in times of war. Indeed, such restriction would be alien to the holistic aims of medieval translation. The translator's assumptions about his function are therefore crucial, and an understanding of them will prevent the circularity of argumentation that is so frequent in analyses of medieval translation (for example, 'adaptation is not translation — medieval translation is adaptation — therefore medieval translation is not translation').

The sources for our information are necessarily the text itself, but it may be significant that the translator did not think to reveal his identity. Might he have been one of the many 'clerici regis', a situation that would have allowed him time for a major project in the king's service? Certainly he speaks complicitously to his public, and to his king, of Paris and of the king's appearance as an adolescent. Yet his prologue contains no mention of official patronage, suggesting that he himself had realized the analogies, immediate and potential, between Caesarean and Capetian ambitions.

Anonymous or not, he is unusually explicit about the importance of his role. His prologue attributes as much merit to the 'litteratus' who records significant prowess as to the military hero who performs it: 'cil ... qui font les proesces *ou qui les recordent et metent en escrit*, cil font a loer' (p. 2) [Those who perform acts of heroism or those who record them in writing, *they* are praiseworthy]. Even more explicit is the passage where he consoles Philip for his illiteracy since literacy was potentially dangerous in a ruler. Letters had only incited Julius Caesar to evil, whereas King Philip was without malice — 'et encontre ce que J(uilles) fu letrez, est li rois sanz malice, car la letreüre aguisa Juilles a meint malice' (pp. 18–19) [Whereas Julius Caesar was literate, our King is devoid of malice, for Caesar was spurred to sundry acts of malice by literacy]. The compliment is, I believe, a reminder of Anselm's quip 'non militia sed malitia'.[3] Its implications are clear. The thirteenth-century monarch will be superior to Caesar by his virtue, not by his literacy. In any new Augustan age, therefore, the acquisition of military glory would be tempered by the Christian qualities that a cleric would encourage in his privileged role as 'litteratus'.

This role is assumed early in the work, where the translator's attitude toward his monarch combines respect, affection, and didacticism. He makes a comparison between Julius Caesar and Philip, leaving little doubt of the intended relevance of his translation: 'Quant ge lis de Juilles Cesar que Luces Silla l'apeloit le valet mau ceint, si me membre de monseignor Phelipe le roi de France ...' (p. 18) [When I read of Julius Caesar that Lucius Sulla used to call him the ill-girt boy, I am reminded of my lord Philip, King of France]. At the same time, there is none of the fulsome adulation that characterizes the language of the king's official admirers. The translator skilfully conveys an instructional message about the appropriate dress for monarchs by the subtlest of psychological means. Suetonius had alluded to the unsuitability of Julius's dress, including Lucius Sulla's warning to the Senate 'ut male praecinctum puerum caverent'[4] [to beware the ill-girt boy]. Caesar wore a senator's striped tunic which had, however, long fringed sleeves, a sign of effeminate exoticism. With it he wore a girdle which was loosely tied ('fluxiore cinctura'), a further indication of his homosexual inclinations. The source description is well rendered by the translator's 'le valet mau ceint', but his shift to specificity ('que l'en pooit bien apeler le valet *mau*

---

[3] Cf. *Epistola de incarnatione verbi*, I.

[4] *Vitae*, I, 45.

pingnié') [who could justly be called the *uncombed* boy] and his careful delimitation 'quant il estoit joenes' [when he was young] convert the comparison into a complicitous congratulation that those messy days of youth are now over.

The king is then complimented on his 'sens' and experience, both of which are equal to Caesar's except in the area of literacy (see above). No specific mention is made here or in the source of sexual conduct. There is no doubt, however, that the translator was aware of the sexual aspects of Julius Caesar's 'malice'. Toward the end of *Li Fet des Romains* the translator comments perceptively that public jesting about Caesar's 'youthful misdeeds' could only have occurred before Caesar's acquisition of real power and his subjugation of 'France': 'Mes il n'estoit pas lors dou pooir dont il fu puis, car encor n'avoit il pas France conquise ne Pompee sormonté; por ce li osoient plus reprover les meffez de sa jovente' (p. 72O) [But at that time he was not possessed of the power he had afterwards, for he had not yet subjugated France or subdued Pompey; therefore they reproached him more daringly for his youthful misdeeds]. He then renders into perfect — and perfectly vulgar — French an army rhyme about Caesar's sodomy with Nicomedes.[5] The translation is impeccable and, once again, the didactic responsibilities assumed by the translator have been fulfilled with such delicacy that no offence to the reigning monarch can possibly have resulted.

[5] 'Gallias Caesar subegit, Nicomedes Caesarem:/ Ecce Ceasar nunc triumphat qui subegit Gallias,/ Nicomedes non triumphat qui subegit Caesarem' (*Vitae*, I, 49) [The Gauls came under Caesar. Caesar came under Nicomedes. Look now at Caesar triumphant — the Gauls came under Caesar! Nicomedes is not triumphant — Caesar came under Nicomedes] becomes 'Cesar a mise France soz soi, Nichomedes Cesar soz lui. Cesar a ore triumphe, qui a France sozmise; Nichomedes n'en a point, qui a Cesar sozmis' (p. 72l).

The translator's purposes are not always achieved as delicately, especially when they concern the king's political enemies. He expands[6] Lucan's meagre facts about Marius into a passionately propagandist declaration of loyalties, illustrating the degree to which medieval translation was a vital literary activity, reflecting contemporary events, ideas, aspirations, and even — as here — military jingoism. *Li Fet des Romains* has added to the source's 'mox vincula ferri/ exedere senem longusque in carcere paedor' (*De bello civili* II, 72–73) [Subsequently iron bonds and prolonged filth in prison destroyed the aged Marius] the inherited legend of a Gallic or Cimbrian soldier (now labelled 'Tyois' i.e. German) who was ordered into Marius's cell to kill him. The inability of this pseudo-German to assassinate a defenceless man is then used to excoriate the cowardice of all Germans, and the foolishness of the English and the Normans to ally themselves with such a race: 'Totes eures que il me membre de ceste chose, je tieng por fox et Anglois et Normanz, qui ont fole esperance et quident que Octes li escomeniez, que Diex et seinte Eglise ont degité, doie France envaïr par itel gent. Ne sont pas de grant hardement, quant uns d'els n'osa pas ferir de s'espee celui (qui) estoit enchaennez en une chartre et qui sa gent avoit essilliee' (p. 365) [Whenever I remember this, I consider both English and Normans to be crazy. Fondly they hope and believe that the excommunicated Otto, cast out by God and by our Holy Church, is destined to invade France with such a people. Germans have no great courage when one of them dared not even lift his sword against a shackled prisoner exiled by his countrymen!].

---

[6] The particular translating techniques that the translator chose in order to incorporate Lucan's florid rhetorical verse into his prose history are discussed in Jeanette Beer, *A Medieval Caesar* (Geneva, 1976).

The mention of Philip's political rival, Otto of Brunswick, Emperor, as 'li escomeniez' resembles an epic tag. The translator has conveniently forgotten the papal interdict that was once incurred by his own monarch, and an interdict was not anyway equivalent to an excommunication! Meanwhile, in a context of political upheaval it was clearly useful to vilify excommunicates, especially when they were the unworthy heirs to the Roman 'imperium'.[7]

From military bravura to the quality of mercy was not an impossible transition for the translator during his narration of Roman *exempla* for an ideal medieval monarch. Moreover, the theme of clemency was a 'given' in his sources. He had only to translate them word by word. Paradoxically, it is by this meticulous adherence to the source that the translator most radically departs from it — just one more illustration of the futility of a 'translation'-versus-'adaptation' approach to medieval texts. 'Clemency' for Caesar was a political buzz-word. It was useful for him in the *Commentarii* to remind the Roman public frequently of his 'clementia' toward the 'barbari' (ignoring, obviously, his own barbarous harassment of the barbarians even in peacetime!). Caesarean generosity at home and abroad was stressed so frequently that perhaps even its promoter came to believe in it. This political ploy becomes, almost necessarily, bland in translation. Irony is not a word-by-word translatable, since it depends both upon shared knowledge of a context but also on shared attitudes *within* that context. Admittedly the translator was handicapped by his century's ignorance that the real author of the *Commentarii* was the perpetrator of the Gallic Wars, Caesar himself.[8] But

---

[7] See John Baldwin, *The Government of Philip Augustus* (Berkeley, Los Angeles, and London, 1986), p. 387.

[8] The translator calls him Julius Celsus, and tries to supply him with convincing credentials. See *A Medieval Caesar*, pp. 29, 30, 31, 34, 35, 144.

even had he known that fact, a literal translation of these passages could not have been different. Moreover, it is Caesar's continuator, Hirtius, who produces the most blatant example of Caesar's 'generosity' to which, as usual, the translator remains faithful for his own reasons.

Hirtius reports that Caesar was aware that his leniency ('suam lenitatem') was well-known to all (VIII, 40). Thus he ordered the right hand of every man who had borne arms to be cut off, but granted each his life. It is difficult — and irrelevant — to guess whether or not the translator was sincere when he here rendered Caesar as a model of humane virtues. 'Cesar, qui bien savoit que sa (de)bonairetez estoit asses conneüe partot et mesure voloit tenir en jostise, que li autre ne s'amorsissent a fere autretel, il fist les poinz destres coper a toz cels qui armes pooient porter. Ne les vost pas ocirre, que l'en nel tenist a cruel *contre sa nature, qui estoit douce et piteuse*' (p. 33l) [Fully cognizant that his generosity was universally known and wishing to maintain moderation along with justice, Caesar, as a cautionary measure lest the others attempt similar action, ordered that the right fists of all men capable of bearing arms be lopped off. He did not want to kill them lest he be considered cruel, contrary to his nature which was kind and merciful]. Such constant reminders of the conqueror's clemency were useful as a reinforcement of accepted chivalric values. And so 'as princes des citez il parloit cortoisement et lor donoit riches dons; as citeains il ne voloit rien enjoindre qui lor grevast, ne tailles ne treüs; et por ce qu'il le troverent douz et debonaire et sanz grevement au derrien, il les tint assez plus legierement en pes' (p. 335) [To princes of cities he spoke courteously and gave them rich gifts; on citizens he would not impose anything that might harm them, neither taxes nor tributes; and because they found him gentle and liberal and no tyrant in the end, he kept them more easily in peace]. Caesar's calculated mildness in the last stages of his subjugation of Gaul added one more *exemplum* for the benefit of future rulers, Philip Augustus not the least among them, and the Caesarean image promoted by *Li Fet des Romains* became an accepted part of all European literatures.

It is interesting to speculate whether that image would have been as effective in the Middle Ages if the full degree of its cynicism and calculated cruelty had been visible in translation. And its appeal continued in French literature, tempting no less a personage than the Emperor Napoleon III to attempt its revival with his own analysis of Caesarean strategies. Possibly the twentieth-century image of Julius Caesar has at last been stripped of old irrelevancies — only to acquire new ones! Translation in the twentieth century remains a dangerously vital process.

The Translator and his Reader: Jean de Meun and the Abelard-Heloise Correspondence

LESLIE C. BROOK

FOLLOWING his completion of the *Roman de la Rose* (*c.* 1275), Jean de Meun embarked upon the translation of several works from Latin into French prose. He himself provided a list of them in the preface to his translation of Boethius's *De Consolatione Philosophiae*:

> A ta royal majesté, tres noble prince, par la grace de Dieu roy des François, Phelippe le Quart, je Jehan de Meun qui jadis ou Rommant de la Rose, puis que Jalousie ot mis en prison Bel Acueil, enseignai la maniere du chastel prendre et de la rose cueillir et translatay de latin en françois le livre Vegece de Chevalerie et le livre des Merveilles de Hyrlande et la Vie et les Epistres Pierres Abaelart et Heloys sa fame et le livre Aered de Esperituelle Amitié, envoie ore Boece de Consolacion que j'ai translaté de latin en françois.[1]

---

[1] V. L. Dedeck-Héry, 'Boethius' *De Consolatione* by Jean de Meun', *Mediaeval Studies*, 14 (1952), p. 168 ('To your royal highness, Philip IV, most noble prince, by the grace of God king of the French, I, Jean de Meun, who formerly in the *Roman de la Rose*, from the point at which Jealousy imprisoned Fair Welcome, showed how to capture the castle and pluck the

The five works which he thus claimed to have translated are: *De re militari* by Vegetius, *De Mirabilibus Hiberniae* by Giraldus Cambrensis, the Correspondence of Abelard and Heloise, *De Spirituali Amicitia* by Aelred of Rievaulx, and the *De Consolatione Philosophiae* of Boethius. We have no reason to doubt that this list is arranged chronologically and is complete, the translation of Boethius being his last. Of the five texts only the translations of Vegetius, the Correspondence of Abelard and Heloise, and Boethius survive.

For whom were these works translated? Several MSS of the Vegetius translation have an explicit attached which informs us that the work was carried out for the young Jean de Brienne, otherwise known as Jean 1er, comte d'Eu, in the year 1284.[2] The Boethius translation, as we have seen, was dedicated to Philippe IV (Philippe le Bel) sometime before 1305, the date of Jean de Meun's death. There is no indication of any patron in the unique MS of the translation of the Correspondence of Abelard and Heloise, B.N. fr. 920.

The preface to the Boethius translation is important also for the remarks which Jean de Meun made concerning his concept of the translator's role. He presents them as a kind of defence against possible attack for his method, and partly shelters behind his patron:

---

rose, and translated from Latin into French Vegetius's work on military affairs, the book on the wonders of Ireland, the life and letters of Peter Abelard and Heloise his wife, and Aelred's work on spiritual friendship, now send you Boethius's *Consolation of Philosophy*, which I have translated from Latin into French').

   [2] See *Li Abregemenz noble honme Vegesce Flave René des Establissemenz apartenanz a Chevalerie*, traduction par Jean de Meun de Flavii Vegeti Renati ..., éditée par Leena Löfstedt, Suomalainen Tiedeakatemia, Sarja B, 200 (Helsinki, 1977), p. 10.

Ja soit ce que tu entendes bien le latin, mais toutevois est de moult plus legiers a entendre le françois que le latin. Et por ce que tu me deis — lequel dit je tieng pour commandement — que je preisse plainement la sentence de l'aucteur sens trop ensuivre les paroles du latin, je l'ai fait a mon petit pooir si comme ta debonnaireté le me commanda. Or pri touz ceulz qui cest livre verront, s'il leur semble en aucuns lieus que je me soie trop eslongniés des paroles de l'aucteur ou que je aie mis aucunes fois plus de paroles que li aucteur n'i met ou aucune fois mains, que il le me pardoingnent. Car se je eusse espons mot a mot le latin par le françois, li livres en fust trop occurs aus gens lais et li clers, neis moiennement letré, ne peussent pas legierement entendre le latin par le françois.[3]

For this translation, then, Jean de Meun envisaged a wide readership: firstly his patron, whom he tactfully compliments on his Latin while adding that French is far easier to follow; secondly a wider public, with no Latin; and thirdly clerks, for whom Boethius would be an important work to be studied, but who might find the Latin on its own too difficult.

It is perhaps less likely that Jean de Meun would expect as many readers for the translation of the Abelard-Heloise Correspondence, and it may even be that it was intended for the unknown patron only. Given the official condemnation of Abelard, their letters could hardly be seen as *textes d'étude*

---

[3] Dedeck-Héry, p. 168 ('Although you understand Latin well, it is nevertheless easier to understand a French text than a Latin one. And since you asked me — and I interpret this as an instruction — to take the author's meaning as a whole, without following the Latin words too slavishly, I have done my humble best to conform to your grace's instructions. And now I beseech all who read this book to forgive me if it seems to them that in places I have strayed too for from the author's words, or that sometimes I have used more words than he, and sometimes fewer; for had I used the French to expound the Latin word for word, the book would have been too obscure for lay folk, and even clerks with a reasonable understanding of Latin could not easily have followed the Latin from the French').

alongside, say, Boethius. On the other hand, how far should we assume that the translation of the Correspondence was intended as a substitute for the original? All that can be said for certain, in the light of the remarks made in the preface to the Boethius translation, is that it could have functioned as a substitute for some, and depending on the ability of the patron who commissioned it, perhaps for all.

On this basis it seems permissible to consider the French text from the standpoint of a medieval reader with no Latin, and to try to assess his comprehension and appreciation of it; and while the modern critic may look for accuracy or inaccuracy, or a stylish rendering, the medieval reader is more likely to have to take fidelity to the original on trust and ask only that the French text make sense, and read in such a way that it holds the attention and interest. The advantage of the prose medium for translation is that it can be subtly persuasive in terms of accuracy. A prose translator can present himself as the servant and interpreter of the original, whereas a verse translator proclaims his intention to recreate within a chosen structure.

Any attempt, though, to put oneself in the position of the reader of the translation of the Abelard-Heloise Correspondence is undoubtedly hampered by the fact that we possess only one MS (late fourteenth or early fifteenth century). Allowance must therefore be made for distortions, and indeed MS 920 has proved notoriously difficult overall to edit successfully.[4] Nor is it always easy to pin down the Latin

---

[4] The first letter only (*Historia Calamitatum*) was edited by François Génin, *Bulletin du Comité historique des monuments écrits de l'Histoire de France: Histoire, Sciences, Lettres*, vol. 2 (Paris, 1850), pp. 175–191, and 265–292, and by Charlotte Charrier, *Jean de Meun, traduction de la première épître de Pierre Abélard (Historia Calamitatum)* (Paris, 1934). Charrier (p. 7) intended to publish an edition of the complete text, but did not do so. The full text was eventually edited by Fabrizio Beggiato, *Le*

version from which Jean de Meun must have worked, as his translation does not correspond in every detail with any of the ten complete or partial Latin MSS which are extant, several of which date roughly from the time of Jean de Meun. Nevertheless it has been possible to apply in retrospect to the translation of the Correspondence the precepts lying behind Jean de Meun's remarks in the preface to Boethius, and to show that in general he is a meticulous but flexible translator.[5] Charrier in fact described him as 'le meilleur interprète français des Lettres d'Abélard et d'Héloise'.[6]

While it is generally true that in the process of translation Jean de Meun is scrupulous to the extent that no Latin word is left aside, and each finds its equivalent somewhere in the French, the reader is more likely to feel confidence from the natural flow of the French prose, and moreover, be held by its energy and expressiveness. The naturalness is achieved by a simple rearrangement of the order of clauses or phrases, and where appropriate of the word order within the clause or phrase, as the following two examples from Heloise's first letter will show:

'Je te rens graces de ce que tu me escrips souvent, car au moins te monstres tu a moy en telle maniere comme tu pues'

lettere di Abelardo ed Eloisa nella traduzione di Jean de Meun, 2 vols (Modena, 1977), but see the review by E. Hicks in Romania, 103 (1982), pp. 384–397.

[5] See Charrier, pp. 35–56; Beggiato, vol. 2, pp. 18–30.

[6] Charrier, p. 56.

(61.2)[7] (Quod frequenter mihi scribis gratias ago. Nam uno modo potes te mihi ostendis).[8]

Tu dreças ce tabernacle divin et dedias propre temple du Saint Esperit es couches des bestes sauvaiges et es repostailles des larrons, la ou Dieu ne seut pas estre nommez (62.10)[9] (In ipsis cubilibus ferarum, in ipsis latibulis latronum ubi nec nominari Deus solet, divinum erexisti tabernaculum et Spiritus Sancti proprium dedicasti templum).

In the first example the order of the clauses in each of the Latin sentences, a, b, a, b, is replaced in the French by the pattern b, a, b, a; in the second example the pattern of phrase or clause a, b, c, d, is replaced by c, d, a, b. Latin participial constructions are replaced by subordinate clauses, with finite verbs: '*Quo completo*, reversus sum in Franciam ...' becomes '*Et quant ce fut fait*, je m'en reving en France ...' (6.4),[10] and '*Missam ad amicum pro consolatione* epistolam, dilectissime, vestram ad me forte quidam nuper attulit', 'Tres chiers amis, voz homs m'a nouvellement monstré vostre espitre *que vous*

---

[7] 'I thank you for writing to me often, for at least you are in my presence in the only way you can be'. All the French quotations are taken from my own unpublished edition of the text, and the numbers in brackets after each quotation indicate the page and line of the MS.

[8] All quotations from the Latin text of the Letters are taken from the critical edition by J. T. Muckle in the following volumes of *Mediaeval Studies*: 12 (1950), *Historia Calamitatum*, pp. 163–213; 15 (1953), Letters 1–4, pp. 68–94; 17 (1955), Letters 5–6, pp. 241–281. I append an English translation of Latin quotations corresponding to a piece of quoted French text only in those rare instances in which there are significant differences between the two versions. For a modern English translation of the Latin Correspondence, apart from Letter 6, see *The Letters of Abelard and Heloise*, translated by Betty Radice, Penguin Books (Harmondsworth, 1974).

[9] 'You built this sanctuary to God, and dedicated a special shrine to the Holy Ghost, in the lairs of wild beasts and in the hiding-places of brigands, where the name of God is never uttered'.

[10] 'And when this was done, I returned to France'.

envoyastes a nostre ami pour confort' (58.26);[11] or again
'Divisis itaque sic nobis adinvicem ...' is turned into the
adverbial clause *'Puis doncquez que nous feusmes ainsi
departiz l'un de l'autre ...'* (84.2).[12]

As for the vigour, that is perhaps most apparent in the
rhetorical passages, in which the translator makes the French
every bit as eloquent as the Latin. A clear example of this is
to be found when Heloise deplores her loss, in her first letter
to her former lover:

> Car li quelz des roys ou des philosophes pooient aconsuivre
> ta renommee? Quelle re(li)gion, quelle cité, quelle ville ne te
> desireroit, ci que quant tu venoies au commun, ne se hastast
> de toy regarder et ne t'ensuivoit a col estendu et aus yex
> esdreciez quant tu destendroies? Qui estoit la mariee, qui
> estoit la pucelle, qui ne te couvoitoit la ou tu n'estoies pas,
> et qui n'ardoit pour toy ou tu estoies presens? Quelle royne,
> ou quelle dame puissant, n'avoit envie de mes joies ou de
> mes chambres? Deulx choses, bien le r[e]cognois, estoient
> especialment en toy par quoy tu pooie(e)s tantost atraire le
> couraige de toutes femes, c'est assavoir grace de dicter et de
> chanter. Ces .ij. choses n'avons nous pas trouvees que cil
> autre philosophe aient aconceues, par quoy tu, en recreant si
> come par un geu, et en reconfortant le travail de l'estude de
> philosophie, lessas pluseurs chançons et ditez amoureux, fais
> par vers ou par rimes, qui, par la grant douceur et du dit et
> du chant, souvent hanté, faisoient sans cesser toutes manierez
> de gens parler de toy, si que neis a ceulx qui n'estoient pas

[11] 'Dearest love, your servant recently showed me your letter which you
sent to our friend in order to console him'. This differs from the Latin,
which means: 'Dearest love, someone recently brought me by chance your
letter which you sent to a friend in order to console him'.

[12] 'When we had in this way separated from one another'.

lettrez la douceur de la melodie ne te lessoit oblier; et de ce
soupiroient mesmement femmes en l'amour de toy (66.22).[13]

Equally effective is the way that Abelard, in his final letter,
expounds the story of Christ and the woman of Samaria at the
well:

> Qui est neis cil qui n'esmerveille celui parlement si privé, si
> familier, et si lonc par quoy il seul daingna diligenment
> enseigner cele seule feme paienne et Samaritainne, dont li
> apostres mesmes se esbahirent moult forment? De ceste
> famme mescreant et reprinse de la multitude de ses hommes
> volt il requerre a boivre, ne nous n'avons pas cogneu qu'il
> eust oncquez puis de nul autre requis quelque chose de
> norrissement. La le servoient li apostre et lui offroient les
> viandes qu'il avoient achetees, et lui disoient: 'Maistre,
> menjue'. Ne nous ne veons pas qu'il eust receus les viandes,
> ainsoys les mist au devant ces parolles, aussi comme en
> excusacion: 'Je ay a menger viandes que vous ne [savez
> pas]'. I requiert bevraige de la feme, et elle s'escusoit de cest
> benefice, et li dist: 'Et tu, comme tu soies Juifs, comment
> requier[s] tu a boire de moy, qui [sui] femme Samaritainne,
> car les Juis n'ont pas communicacion avec les Samaritains?'

---

[13] 'For what king or philosopher could match your fame? What region,
city, or township did not long for you, so that whenever you moved
amongst the people, they hurried to catch a glimpse of you and follow you
with craned necks and straining eyes as you went on your way? What wife,
what damsel, did not desire you in your absence, and lust after you in your
presence? What queen, what great lady, did not envy me my joys and my
bed-chamber? I admit that you had two special gifts, with which you could
immediately win the heart of any woman: your skill with verse and in
singing. We know of no other philosopher with such attainments, through
which you, as a recreation and diversion, and to alleviate the labour of
philosophical study, left many songs and amorous ditties in verse or meters.
By the sheer charm of their words and tune, which were constantly heard,
they caused all manner of people to speak of you, and the sweetness of the
melody ensured that even the unlettered could not forget you, and in
particular women sighed for love of you'.

Et de rechief: 'Tu n'as pas en quoy tu puisses; le puis est
parfont'. Il, donques, qui n'a(s) cure des viandes des quelles
li apostres lui offrent, requiert beuvraige de la femme
mescreant, et qui le lui dennie (l94.11).[14]

Jean de Meun proves himself well able to match the
longer Latin sentences with French ones of equal complexity,
while at the same time making the exposition clear and easily
readable. In his first letter, Abelard, relating his early troubles,
gives an account of his theological studies under Anselm of
Laon, for whom he felt little respect, and from whose lectures
he began absenting himself. While still his pupil he had been
challenged by fellow-pupils to lecture on the text of the
prophet Ezekiel. These lectures were something of a *succès de
scandale*, until two jealous colleagues of Abelard, Alberic of
Rheims and Lotulph of Lombardy, alerted the old man and
Abelard was forced to stop. The French text reads as follows:

Lors estoient es escolles a ce viellart dui escolier qui
sembloient estre li plus vaillans de touz les autres, c'est
assavoir Auberi de Rains et Lotulphes li Lombars; que de
tant comme il avoient greigneur presumpcion de eulx

[14] 'Who indeed does not wonder at that conversation, so private, so
intimate, and so lengthy, in which He deigned to instruct carefully only the
pagan woman of Samaria? Even the Apostles were greatly astonished. Of
this woman, an unbeliever and rebuked by her own menfolk, He asked a
drink. We know of no further occasion on which He sought refreshment
from anyone. The Apostles served Him, offering Him meat that they had
bought, saying: "Master, eat"; but we do not witness Him accepting the
meat, rather He addressed these words to them as though by way of excuse:
"I have meat to eat that ye know not of". He seeks drink from this woman,
and she declined the favour, saying: "How is it that thou, being a Jew,
askest drink of me, which am a woman of Samaria? for the Jews have no
dealings with the Samaritans". And again: "Thou hast nothing to draw with,
and the well is deep". He, therefore, who has no care for the meat offered
Him by the Apostles, asks drink of the unbelieving woman, who refuses it
Him'.

mesmes, de tant estoient il plus embrasez contre moy. Icil
viellart, troublez par l'amonestement de ces .ij., si comme fu
puis aperceu, n'ot pas honte de moy deffendre a gloser ou
lieu de sa mestrise sur ce que je avoye commancié, et metoit
avant ceste reson, car il se doubtoit, ce disoit il, se je comme
rude en ceste science escripsisse par aventure aucune chose
par erreur en ceste euvre, que ce ne li fust mis sus. Et quant
ceste chose vint aus oreilles de mes escolliers, il furent
esmeus par trop grant desdaing sur la chalenge de si aperte
envie, qui n'estoit onques avenue a autres, si comme ilz
disoient; et de tant comme elle fu plus apperte, de tant me fut
elle plus honorable et me fist plus glorieus par sa persecucion
(8.l0).[15]

[15] 'At that time there were in the old man's school two pupils who stood
out from the rest, Alberic of Rheims and Lotulf of Lombardy, and because
of the high esteem in which they held themselves, they were the more
incensed against me. The old man, urged on by the promptings of these two,
as it later became clear, was not ashamed to forbid me to expound the text
that I had begun in the place where he taught, on the grounds, so he feared,
that should I, being untrained in the art, peradventure write something in the
work in error, that it might then be attributed to him. And when this reached
the ears of my students, they felt nothing but great indignation at the
hostility of such manifest spite, which had never happened to anyone else,
as they pointed out; and the more open it was, the more it brought me fame
and renown through his persecution'. Compare Latin: 'Erant autem tunc in
scholis huius senis duo, qui ceteris praeminere videbantur, Albericus scilicet
Remensis et Lotulphus Lombardus, qui quanto de se maiora praesumebant,
amplius adversum me accendebantur. Horum itaque maxime suggestionibus,
sicut postmodum deprehensum est, senex ille perturbatus impudenter mihi
interdixit inceptum glossandi opus in loco magisterii sui amplius exercere,
hanc videlicet causam praetendens ne si forte in illo opere aliquid per
errorem scriberem, utpote rudis adhuc in hoc studio, ei deputaretur. Quod
cum ad aures scholarium pervenisset, maxima commoti sunt indignatione
super tam manifesta livoris calumnia quae nemini unquam ulterius acciderat.
Quae, quanto manifestior, tanto mihi honorabilior exstitit et persequendo
gloriosiorem effecit'.

In this excerpt Jean de Meun puts light into the text, and so aids the reader's ready comprehension, by the addition of the parenthetic 'ce disoit il', and 'si comme ilz disoient'.

In the earlier letters only, and especially in the translation of Abelard's first letter, he enlivens his translation by the occasional aside such as: 'et ce s'acorde a ceste parolle: qui premier est coulx en la ville, derrenier le scet' (13.6), 'mauvaise haste n'est preus' (23.2), or 'n'est pas merveilles se les dames les heent!' (22.6), in reference to eunuchs.[16] The effect of such interventions, which do not go beyond page 98 of the MS, out of a total of 213 pages of text, is to establish a rapport between translator and reader, by showing an interest in and reaction to the text that is being translated. He does not, however, add a comment to Heloise's statement in her first letter to Abelard that she would rather be his whore than empress of Rome, a statement which he had already designated in the *Roman de la Rose* as 'une merveilleuse

---

[16] The complete list of these asides is as follows: 'et ce s'acorde a ceste parolle: qui premier est coulx en la ville, derrenier le scet (13.6) ('and this accords with the saying: he who is cuckolded, is the last in the town to know of it'), 'et ce faisoit la belle pour son honnour garder' (20.9) ('and the fair Heloise did this to protect her (his?) honour'), 'n'est pas merveilles se les dames les heent!' (22.6) ('it is not surprising that women hate them!'), 'mauvaise haste n'est preus' (23.2) ('indecent haste is unwise'), 'Certes, nuls ne doit dire ce' (41.24) ('Indeed, no man should claim this'), 'C'estoient li moyne au deable!' (55.18) ('They were monks from the devil!'), 'or valu pis' (56.1) ('now things were worse'), 'Nota le confort qui vient a Abaielart des lettres a s'amie, etc. etc.' (61.4) ('Note the comfort that Abelard derives from his loved one's letters'), 'Nota, oncquez femme ne parla plus saigement' (90.18) ('Note, never did a woman speak more wisely'), 'et pour ce sont les cotes mautaillees en religion'(98.5) ('and for this reason tunics worn in religious life are ill-cut').

parole' (v. 8781)[17] before paraphrasing her words. Jean de Meun may also be responsible for the division of the text into sections under headings, most of which occur within the *Historia Calamitatum*, Abelard's first letter; for example, 'Or conclut son propoz la saige Heloys en eschivant le mariaige' (l9.l).[18] These certainly help the reader to find key passages which might interest him, though the final letter of sixty-five pages proceeds with no such headings beyond the introductory one (p. 148), which is in any case and exceptionally a translation of a Latin introduction.

One notable way in which the translator gives good value to his reader is by using two terms to translate one Latin one: for example, 'mon famillier et mon privé' (35.21) for 'mihi familiaris', or 'chançons et ditez' (67.6) for 'carmina'. There are in all over 200 examples of this phenomenon spread throughout the text, and they provide a variety of effects, from rhetorical emphasis to the imparting of complementary meanings of the Latin, or a greater clarification of it. On the whole these synonymic pairs do not display the predetermined fixity of the cliché, but an element of spontaneity, and overall they serve to enrich the prose of Jean de Meun.[19]

For the reader's benefit two classical names are explained at the beginning of the text: 'Mars, qui est diex de batailles' (1.21), and 'Minerve, qui est diuesse de science' (1.22).[20]

[17] Guillaume de Lorris et Jean de Meun, *Le Roman de la Rose*, publié par Félix Lecoy, CFMA, 3 vols (Paris, 1965–70). All references to the *Roman de la Rose* are to this edition.

[18] 'Wise Heloise concludes her arguments against marriage'.

[19] For a full analysis of this feature, see L. C. Brook, 'Synonymic and near-synonymic pairs in Jean de Meun's translation of the Letters of Abelard and Heloise', *Neuphilologische Mitteilungen*, 87 (1986), pp. 16–33.

[20] 'Mars, who is the god of war'; 'Minerva, who is the goddess of science'.

Elsewhere classical imagery may appear to have been tamely
rendered: 'assorbiz par cest peril' (19.5) ('haec Charybdis
absorbeat'), 'de com grant demourement de peril'(107.2) ('a
quantae Charibdis voragine'), 'saillir en un feu' (69.11) ('ad
Vulcania loca ... properantem'), and 'neis en feus me vaudrois
tu asuivre' (104.6) ('etiam ad Vulcania profiteris te sequi
velle).[21] Yet such renderings at least convey the essence of
the images to a reader with no classical background. In any
case in the medieval *Lexiques* published by Roques, every MS
which lists 'caribdis' has 'peril de mer' or 'un peril de mer'
as its equivalent, and for 'vulcanus', 'feu ou dieu de feu'.[22]

This brings us to the question of the difficulty which
some Latin words inevitably posed for a translator, though in
the Correspondence the difficulty is never such as to cause
Jean de Meun frankly to admit defeat, as he at one point had
to in the Vegetius translation, when faced with explaining or
translating the names of various winds.[23] Whenever he is

[21] 'Swallowed up by this peril' ('this Charybdis should swallow you
up'), 'from such a mighty abyss of peril' ('from the abyss of such a mighty
Charybdis'), 'leap into the flames' ('leaping into the Vulcanian regions'),
'you would be willing to follow me even into the flames' ('you declare that
you would be willing to follow me even into the regions of Vulcan').

[22] M. Roques, *Recueil général des Lexiques français du moyen âge*, 2
vols (Paris, 1936–8).

[23] 'Mais pour ce que cist aucteur Aristotes et li poete neis et diverses
nations avoec nomment et ordennent diversement ces vens, et pour ce neis
que ie ne les sai mie proprement nomer en françois, ie, Iehans de Meun,
translatierres de cest livre, ne voeil du tout ensuivre ne les uns ne les autres,
mais ie vous nomerai et ordenerai des .IIII. venz principaus et de touz lor
compaingnons proprement les nons en latin si comme li Latin les noment
ore communement et en ont fait vers que vous orroiz ci emprés', Löfstedt,
ed. cit. p. 188 ('But since Aristotle and the poets and other peoples too
name and classify differently these winds, and since I do not know how to
give them their appropriate names in French, I, Jean de Meun, the translator
of this book, do not wish to follow one or the other, but will give you the

forced by the context or merely chooses to use a word which he knows to be a Latinism, he normally adds some explanation of its meaning. At one point he could hardly avoid using the literal term, before adding an explanation, since the Latin text explains how the word 'sanctimoniales', meaning 'holy women', was derived. The French text, with some editing, reads as follows: 'car la seule religion neis de cestes est seule ennobl[i]e du nom de sainteté, [come] de [*sanctimonia*, c'est a dire sainteté, elles sont dites] sanctimoniables, c'est a dire saintes nonnains' (183.19).[24] On another occasion he is not forced but chooses to use a learned term, but again he adds an explanation: '"Je ne diray pas", dist il, "ravir, mes se aucun ose les saintes vierges neis atempter tant seulement par cause de mariaige, ferus soit de paine capital", c'est a dire que l'en lui coupe la teste' (206.7).[25] He checks himself, too, when he writes 'a la plenitude' as a translation of 'ad...plenitudinem', adding 'c'est a la planté', the normal Old French word (161.14). There are in all fifteen examples of explanations introduced by 'c'est' or 'c'est a dire', not necessarily following a Latinism, but always

names and classification concerning the four principal winds together with related ones in Latin, as Latin writers now normally refer to them, and write verses about them, as you shall later hear').

[24] 'For only the devotion of these women is honoured with the name of holiness, for from "sanctimonia", that is, holiness, they are called "sanctimoniales", that is, holy women' ('Quarum quoque religio sola ex nomine sanctitatis est insignita cum ipsae a sanctimonia, id est, sanctitate, sanctimoniales sint dictae').

[25] 'It is not a question of ravishing, but if any man dares even to tempt one of these holy virgins with marriage, he shall be smitten with capital punishment, that is to say his head will be cut off' ('Si quis, inquit, non dicam rapere, sed attemptare tantum causa iungendi matrimonium sacras virgines ausus fuerit, capitali poena feriatur').

showing a concern for the reader's comprehension.[26] In one
case he does not even attempt to find an equivalent word in
French, but renders 'eius qui catechumenus sit defunctus
salutem' ('the salvation of one who had died as a
catechumen') by a perfect definition: 'le salu de celui qui
estoit mort sans baptesme, mes oi avoit les parolles de la foy'
(212.9).[27]

Towards the end of the final letter, which is on the
history of holy women, there occurs some rather unusual
ecclesiastical vocabulary in a passage which compares the
Christian with the primitive pagan church, and shows the debt
of the Church to its forebear. Jean de Meun seems to have
made an honest and effective attempt at conveying the passage
in French. Unfortunately the scribe of MS 920 has failed him,
for the transcription is far from accurate, with some key words
missing, so that the original translation can in.places only be
surmised. The passage in question, with emendation and
suggested restoration, reads as follow:

> Car qui est cil qui ne saiche que l'Eglise a pris [de] la
> signagogue toutes les ordres des clers, de l'uiscier jusques a
> l'evesque, et l'usaige mesmes de la tonsure ecclesiaste, par
> quoy il sont fait clerc es jeunes des quatre temps, et les
> sacrefices de Pasques, et les aournemens neis des vestemens
> aus prestres, et neis pluseurs sacremens ou dediement ou des
> autres? Qui est, neis, qui ne saiche que elle a retenu par tres
> pourfitable dispensacion non mie seulement les degrez des
> dignetés seculiers es rois et [es] autres princes, et pluseurs
> decrez de lois, ou pluseurs enseignemens de la discipline et
> de philosophie es paiens convers, ainçois neis reçut elle de
> eulx aucuns degrez de dignetés ecclesiastres, ou la forme de

[26] For a complete list, see Brook, 'Synonymic and near-synonymic pairs
...', p. 33.

[27] 'the salvation of one who had died without baptism, but had heard the
words of the faith'.

continence, et la religion de corporel netteté? Car certaine
chose est que li evesque et li arcevesque sont ore en l'estat
ou lors estoient [li flamines et li arceflamines. Et] li temples,
qui lors estoient establis au[s] deables, furent aprés consacrez
en nostre Seigneur ou ennoblis des memoires des sains. Et
savons que l'onnesteté et la hautesce de virginité resplendi
avant mesmement es paiens, come la maleiçon de la loy
contrainsist les Juis aus noces, et que ceste vertu ou ceste
netteté de char fut tant aggreable aus paiens [que grans
couvens de femmes] se vo[o]ient en ceste vie en leur
temples. Dont Jheriaume, en l'*Epistre aus Galachiens*, ou
tiers livre, qui dist: 'Que avient il que vous faciez, en la
condempnacion des quiex (des quiex) Juno a ses nonnains
veuves d'un mari, et Veste ses nonnains vierges, et li autres
ydole leur continens?' [Et il dist 'nonnains veuves d'un mari'
et 'nonnains vierges', si comme les moynesses qui ont
cogneu les hommes] et les moynesses [vierges]. Et vient cist
mos de moynes, qui sonne autant en grec comme en latin, et
d'ilec est dist cist mos moynes, ce est a dire solitaires
(201.6).[28]

[28] 'For who who does not know that the Church has adopted from the
synagogue all its clerical orders, from ostiary to bishop, as well as the
practice of ecclesiastical tonsure, by which clerics are ordained on ember
days, the Easter sacrifice, even the adornments of priestly vestments and the
sacraments, be they dedicatory or other? And who does not know that she
has retained, through her most fruitful dispensation, not only the degrees of
secular dignities in respect of kings and princes, a number of laws, and from
pagan converts the many teachings of philosophy, but also certain degrees
of ecclesiastical dignities, the pattern of self-denial, and the scrupulous
observance of bodily cleanliness? For it is clear that bishops and
archbishops now preside as once did *flamines* and *archiflamines*; while
temples formerly honouring demons were subsequently consecrated in the
name of Our Lord, or dedicated to the memory of saints. We know that the
honour and dignity of virginity flourished firstly among the pagans, at a
time when the cursed law forced the Jews into wedlock, and that this virtue
or bodily purity was so prized by the pagans that large assemblies of women
consecrated themselves to this way of life in their temples. Thus Jerome, in

The first point of interest is the translation 'les sacrefices de Pasques' for 'azymorum sacrificium' ('the Feast of Unleavened Bread'). The use of the word 'Pasques' instead of the technically correct 'azymes', which already existed in the thirteenth century, makes the reference more immediately understandable. As for the conjectured 'flamines' and

his commentary on the Epistle to the Galatians, book III, wrote: "What does it behove you to do, when you stand rebuked by the fact that Juno has her nuns who are widows of one husband, Vesta has her virgin nuns, and other idols their celibate devotees?" And he says "nuns who are widows of one husband" and "virgin nuns", like "moynesses" (female monks) who have known men and virgin "moynesses". This word derives from "moynes" (monk), which is the same in Greek as in Latin (viz. "monachos" and "monachus"), whence (i.e. from the Greek) "moynes", meaning "solitary" ('Quis enim nesciat universos clericorum ordines ab ostiario usque ad Episcopum, ipsumque tonsurae usum ecclesiasticae, qua clerici fiunt, et ieiunia quattuor Temporum, et azymorum sacrificium, nec non ipsa sacerdotalium indumentorum ornamenta, et nonnulla dedicationis vel alia sacramenta a synogoga ecclesiam assumpsisse? Quis etiam ignoret ipsam, utillissima dispensatione, non solum saecularium dignitatum gradus in regibus, ceterisque principibus, et nonnulla legum decreta vel philosophicae disciplinae documenta in conversis gentibus retinuisse, verum etiam quosdam ecclesiasticarum dignitatum gradus, vel continentiae formam et corporalis munditiae religionem ab eis accepisse. Constat quippe nunc episcopos vel archiepiscopos praesidere ubi tunc flamines vel archiflamines habebantur, et quae tunc templa daemonibus sunt instituta, postea Domino fuisse consecrata et sanctorum memoriis insignita. Scimus et in gentibus praecipue praerogativam virginitatis enituisse, cum maledictum legis ad nuptias Iudaeos coerceret, et in tantum gentibus hanc virtutem seu munditiam carnis acceptam extitisse, ut in templis earum magni feminarum conventus caelibi se vitae dicarent. Unde Hieronymus, in Epistolam ad Galatas, libro tertio: "Quid nos, inquit, oportet facere, in quorum condemnationem habet Iuno univiras, et Vesta univirgines, et alia idola continentes?" Univiras autem et univirgines dicit quasi monachas quae viros noverant, et monachas virgines. Monos enim, unde monachus, id est, solitarius dicitur, unum sonat'. In this extract 'univirgines', the reading of most Latin MSS, replaces Muckle's 'virgines').

'arceflamines', it is clear from the context that Jean wrote something for the corresponding Latin words, and even if he did use the forms suggested and they were Latinisms, their sense would have been clear enough from the context. In the quotation from Jerome the unusual words 'univiras' and 'univirgines' are clearly and correctly explained by the translator ('nonnains veuves d'un mari' and 'nonnains vierges' respectively). The final sentence of the passage cited is, however, problematical, and is probably based on a slightly different reading from that of the extant Latin text.[29]

In return for conveying the meaning of the text as clearly as he could, Jean de Meun would not expect his reader to be squeamish. In the *Roman de la Rose* he had repeatedly used the coarse terms 'coilles' or 'coillon' and 'viz' to designate the male sexual organs, and defended the blunt use of such words in a long discourse by Raison (vv. 6913–7154). Likewise in the translation of Abelard's first letter, in a passage referring to his mutilation and the exclusion from heaven of eunuchs, Jean de Meun does not flinch from using similar terms, with repeated use of 'coillons' and 'escouillez', and once of 'vit'. Was his intended reader male? If his sensibilities were not offended, those of a later reader of MS 920 certainly were, since each of these words on pages 21 and 22 of the MS have been scratched out, though a modern reader can still decipher them with confidence.

---

[29] Abelard's explanation of the sense of 'univiras' is in fact incorrect, its true meaning being 'women who have known one husband'. His comment on the Jerome quotation means: 'He says "univiras" and "univirgines", just like "monachas" who have known men and "monachas" who are virgins; for "monos", whence "monachus", which means "solitary", corresponds to "unum"'. Jean de Meun appears to have read the Greek 'monachos' for 'monos' in his translation 'qui sonne autant en grec comme en latin' ('monachos ... unum sonat'); see my translation of the final sentence in his version in note 28 above.

Although in general Jean de Meun is very helpful to his reader, there are some occasions when he expects him to cope with a certain literalness of rendering which imparts a learned flavour to the translation: for instance, 'Et se nous desvelopons toute l'ordenance du Viez Testament...' (186.22) ('Si totam Veteris Testamenti seriem revolvamus ...'), or 'Par le jugement desquelz la feste est de tant eue plus celebrable ...' (99.3) ('Quorum quidem iudicio tanto festivitas habetur celebrior ...').[30] Sometimes, too, under the influence of the Latin sentence, the French one seems unnecessarily complex, as in the following example;

> Comme tuit cil, a qui par renommee fut portee ceste chose faite si cruelment et sans regart, la repreissent et blamassent trop forment, tuit cil qui present y avoient esté ostoient le blasme et la coupe sur eulx et la metoient sur les autres, en tele maniere que nostre envieus meismes desnioent que ceste chose eust esté faite par leur conseil, et li legaz mesmes sur ce fait blasmoit et maudisoit l'envie des François (33.l5).[31]

[30] 'If we turn through the whole sequence of the Old Testament', and 'By whose judgment the festival is held to be the more worthy of celebration'. For further examples of a literalness that does not seem quite natural in French, see L. C. Brook, 'Comment évaluer une traduction du treizième siècle? Quelques considérations sur la traduction des Lettres d'Abélard et d'Héloïse faite par Jean de Meun', in *The Spirit of the Court*, edited by Glyn S. Burgess and Robert A. Taylor (Woodbridge, 1985), pp. 62–68 (p. 67).

[31] 'As everyone to whom the news spread of this act committed so cruelly and wantonly censured and condemned it outright, all those who had been present shifted the blame and the censure from themselves onto others, so much so that even my rivals denied that it had been done on their advice, while the legate himself blamed and denounced the jealousy of the French in this matter' ('Cum autem hoc tam crudeliter et inconsiderate factum omnes, ad quos fame delatum est, vehementer arguerent, singuli qui interfuerant a se culpam repellentes in alios transfundebant, adeo ut ipsi quoque aemuli nostri id consilio suo factum esse denegarent, et legatus

Jean de Meun can also pose problems at the lexical level, when he uses a word the sense of which is far from clear, although it corresponds closely to the equivalent Latin word. A case in point occurs at the very beginning of the first letter:

> Essamples attaignent ou appaissent souvent les talens des hommes plus que ne font parolles. Et pour ce, aprés aucun confort de parole dire entre nous en ta presence, ai ge proposé a escripre a toy, qui es ores lontains, une confortable espitre des propres esperimens de mes meschances, pour ce que tu cognoisses que tes temptacions sunt ou nules ou petites au regart de[s] moyes, et que tu les portes plus legierement (1.1).[32]

Here the word 'temptacions' translates the Latin 'tentationes'. Its sense in medieval Latin, apart from 'temptation', was 'trial, torment, affliction',[33] and this is the meaning intended by Abelard. Such a meaning is is not, however, attested in either the Godefroy or Tobler-Lommatzsch dictionaries for the French 'temptacions', yet unless the meaning 'trial' is understood in Jean de Meun's translation, the sentence could be a little misleading. Again, what precisely is the sense of the word 'provablement' in the following sentence, which refers to the dedication of a shrine to the Holy Ghost: 'a qui neis ce semble que temples doit estre donnez es escrips plus provablement que a nulle des autres personnes, se nous

---

coram omnibus invidiam Francorum super hoc maxime detestaretur').

[32] 'Often examples either incite or calm human passions more so than words; and so, following the few words of comfort spoken in your presence, I propose addressing to you, now that you are far away, a consoling letter concerning my own experience of misfortune, so that you may appreciate that your temptations (? trials) are as nothing in comparison with mine, and so that you may bear them more easily'.

[33] See J. F. Niermeyer, *Mediae Latinitatis Lexicon Minus* (Leiden, 1976).

entendons plus diligenment l'auctorité de l'Apostre et l'evre
du Saint Esperit mesme' (42.8)?[34] The corresponding Latin
term 'probabilius' means either 'more probably' or 'more
fittingly', and it is in this second sense that Abelard used the
word. For 'provablement' Godefroy gives the meaning
'probablement', and Tobler-Lommatzsch 'wahrscheinlich': but
could the French word also carry the sense of 'fittingly',
'reasonably'? It would be interesting to know how the
medieval reader understood these problematic terms.

In a few relatively minor ways Jean de Meun can
inadvertently mislead his reader, particularly over one or two
Biblical allusions. In the story of Judith and Holofernes he
treats the Latinized Greek word 'abra' as a proper name, and
so translates as follows: 'Et Judith desarmee, avec Abra sa
chamberiere ['cum abra sua'], envai l'ost espoentables et
coupa la teste a Holoferne de son propre glaive mesmes ...'
(185.18).[35] He refers to the prophetess Deborah, who judged
Israel according to Judges 4. 4, as 'vainquerresse du pueple
nostre Seigneur' (185.15),[36] because he evidently read in his
Latin MS 'vindex' in place of 'iudex' in the description of
her: 'Dominici iudex populi'. Through insufficient familiarity
with the story of Zacharias in Luke 1.20 he misrepresents the
situation: 'Elizabeth tenoit encore mu par la deffiance de sa
mescreantise Zacharie son mari, grant prestre de nostre

---

[34] 'to whom it would seem that a shrine should be dedicated more
fittingly (?) than to any of the other Persons (i.e. of the Trinity), if we heed
more closely the authority of the Apostles and the work of the Holy Ghost
Himself'.

[35] 'And Judith unarmed, with Abra her handmaiden, penetrated the
fearsome host and cut off Holofernes's head with his own sword'.

[36] 'conqueror of the people of Our Lord'.

Seigneur ...' (190.2l).[37] In the corresponding Latin sentence
Jean de Meun has taken 'Elizabeth' and 'diffidentia' to be
respectively nominative and ablative, instead of genitive and
nominative. The sentence should mean: 'The husband of
Elizabeth, Zacharias, a great priest of the Lord, the diffidence
of unbelief still kept dumb ...'. Elsewhere through a literal
rendering of 'per visum' as 'par le regart' Jean de Meun
diminishes the effect in Matthew 27.19 of the warning given
to Pontius Pilate by his wife concerning her dream of Jesus:
'"Tu et cist droituriers homs n'avez que fere ensemble. Et si
ay huy maintes choses souffertes pour lui par le regart"'
(198.l4).[38] Apart from these Biblical inaccuracies he refers to
'le psiaume Atanaise' (32.17) for 'Symbolum Atanasii',[39]
although he translates the word 'symbolum' further on in a
different context by 'symbole'.[40] Also, by misunderstanding
the sense of 'tertio', he makes an inaccurate statement
concerning the Benedictine Rule. Taking 'tertio' as an
adjective agreeing with 'anno', instead of as an adverb
meaning 'for the third time', or 'three times', he translates as
follows: 'Ou en quel lieu esprouva il en ung an l'esprouvance,
c'est l'estableté du couraige des femes qui sont a recevoir, et
au tiers an les enformacions (et) enseigna, quant la regle leur

---

[37] 'Elizabeth still kept dumb, because of the diffidence of his unbelief,
Zacharias her husband, a great priest of Our Lord'. Compare Latin: 'Virum
Elizabeth Zachariam magnum Domini sacerdotem incredulitatis diffidentia
mutum adhuc tenebat'.

[38] 'Nihil tibi et iusto illi; multa enim passa sum hodie per visum propter
eum'; 'par le regart' means no more than 'through what I saw'.

[39] 'the Athanasian psalm' for 'the Athanasian Creed'.

[40] 'En ung autre lieu apelle elle(s) le(s) Filz Dieu *symbole*, c'est
conseille(l)eur ou conseil' (191.24) ('Alio loco Filium Dei symbolum
appellat, id est consiliarium vel consilium').

eust esté leue, si comme il est commandé?' (124.10).[41] It is
in fact clear from the Rule (chapter 58) that it was read to the
novices three times, after the second, eighth, and twelfth
months.

It would nevertheless be unfair to Jean de Meun to lay
too much stress on such misrepresentations, especially as on
a couple of occasions he gives his reader the benefit of
alternative readings of the Latin. Thus, unsure whether the
Latin should be 'vinis' or 'venis', he translates both words: 'es
vins et es vainnes' (123.2);[42] and unable to decide between
'quid profiteretur' and 'quid proficeretur' he translates: 'quelz
homs il estoit et de quelle cité' (18.19).[43]

The modern reader of MS 920 will not be reading the
translation precisely as Jean de Meun intended it, and there
seems likely to have been at least one intermediary lost MS
between the original and this MS.[44] Even so it is possible to
see that the intended reader of the translation would have been
able to appreciate both the pathos and the rhetoric of this
Correspondence, in a version which would have been both

---

[41] 'And wherever was tested in one year the strength or constancy of the
heart of those women who are to be received, and in the third year the
instructions taught them, when the Rule was read to them, as it is laid
down?' Compare Latin: 'aut suscipiendarum feminarum constantiam uno
anno probaverit, easque tertio perlecta Regula, sicut in ipso iubetur,
instruxerit?'

[42] 'in the wines and in the veins'.

[43] There is nevertheless an obscurity here in respect of the Latin. Both
Du Cange and Baxter and Johnson (*Medieval Latin Word-List* ...) list
'proficere' as an alternative to 'proficisci'; 'proficeretur' is the reading of
three Latin MSS, but 'quid proficeretur' should normally mean 'what had
been attained (achieved)'. For it to have Jean de Meun's interpretation we
would expect 'quo proficeret' (for 'quo proficisceretur'), which no extant
Latin MS has.

[44] See Brook, 'Comment évaluer ...', p. 65.

sophisticated and clear. Jean de Meun was no amateur, and though at times he may not have been strictly accurate by the standards that we expect today of translators, his translation is an honest attempt at conveying the original, unlike the later travesty of Bussy Rabutin. From the perspective of the medieval reader both inaccuracies and inspired moments of translation alike are less important than general clarity and overall coherence; and MS 920, despite its sorry state, allows us to be confident that Jean de Meun would have served his reader well.

Translation and Response:
Troilus and the *Filostrato*

N. S. THOMPSON

TRANSLATION, as most will agree, is not simply a case of substituting one word for another. If it is a *translatio*, it is from one set of signs to another and both those sets of signs depend upon a cultural context for their legibility. Thus in considering Chaucer's *Troilus and Criseyde*[1] as a translation — or even as a poem resulting from a translation — we must be prepared not only to investigate Chaucer's interest in the culture and letters of fourteenth-century Italy, but also to see him altering the teleology of his source poem, Boccaccio's *Il Filostrato*,[2] to fit new strategic demands. It is part of the thesis of this paper that these come from deepening certain implications inherent in the Italian poem, so that although Chaucer's version may be radically different, its genesis lies in the source work. Chaucer takes aspects which in Boccaccio refer solely to the world of the *dolce stil nuovo* and applies

---

[1] *Troilus and Criseyde* in *The Riverside Chaucer*, 3rd edition, General Editor, L. D. Benson (Boston, Houghton Mifflin Company, 1987).

[2] *Il Filostrato, Tutte le opere di Giovanni Boccaccio*, vol. 11, ed. V. Branca (Milan, 1964–).

them to a broader context; one, however, for which his Italian reading prepared him.

Several works and articles in recent years have helped to expand our knowledge of Chaucer's Italian background: the studies by Barry Windeatt and his dual-text edition of *Troilus and Criseyde*;[3] the studies by Piero Boitani and his anthology *Chaucer and the Italian Trecento*;[4] and recently David Wallace's detailed study *Chaucer and the Early Writings of Boccaccio*,[5] which gives an excellent exposition of the cultural and literary background to the *Filostrato*, presenting a clear case for Chaucer's intimate knowledge both of Italian and of Boccaccio's text.

As we know, Chaucer's work is a *rifacimento* of the *Filostrato*, with radical changes to Boccaccio's original characters.[6] Often his language is more subdued, often it is more colloquial; he omits scenes and events and adds his own, which gives him opportunity to create brilliant exchanges of dialogue, especially between Pandarus and Criseyde; nevertheless, as Wallace shows, for a good part of the

[3] B. Windeatt, 'The "Paynted Process": Italian to English in Chaucer's Troilus' *English Miscellany*, 26–27 (1977–8), pp. 79–103; idem, 'Chaucer and the Filostrato' in Boitani, *Trecento*, pp. 163–83 (full reference, n. 4 below); idem (ed.), *Troilus and Criseyde. A New Edition of 'The Book of Troilus'* (London, 1984).

[4] P. Boitani, *Chaucer and Boccaccio*, Medium Aevum Monographs, NS, VIII (Oxford, 1977); idem (ed.), *Chaucer and the Italian Trecento* (Cambridge, 1983).

[5] D. Wallace, *Chaucer and the Early Writings of Boccaccio* (Woodbridge, 1985).

[6] For a full bibliography of the relations between the two poems, see Windeatt's edition, 1984. R. A. Pratt discusses the case for the French prose translation in 'Chaucer and Le Roman de Troyle et de Criseida', *Studies in Philology*, 53 (1956). The case is examined by Wallace, pp. 106–7.

narration and dialogue, he is following Boccaccio stanza for stanza, if not line for line, and even building on those stanzas where he directly wishes to embellish.[7] What is more, he is preserving the self-conscious quality which pervades the *Filostrato*'s narration. The narrator's voice and his reasons for narration are paramount; so too his relationship both with an inscribed audience of courtly lovers and ultimately, of course, with the actual reader, all of whom can expect to share his interest in his own narrative. In Boccaccio, the narrator has an interested, particular relationship with his narrative: it will enable him to gain sympathy for his plight, as well as furnishing a moral for courtly lovers. This persona dramatizes his situation as unsuccessful lover and (successful) narrator (which role is not without its difficulties). In Chaucer, the narrator is at first more distantly placed, then gradually becomes involved in the narrative — especially in Book III — before moving out of the lovers' world in the Palinode. The moral he wishes to draw is not simply for a narrow circle of courtly lovers, but for Christians in general. This new context for reception of the text comes, as I hope to show, from a deepening of Boccaccio's text, a deepening of the aesthetic of reception as much as of the characters and their narrative.

Dr Wallace cites Geoffrey of Vinsauf's analogy between laying foundations for a house and writing a poem, then says:

> It is quite clear that Chaucer pondered for years on the theme and design of Troilus before setting his hand to the task of composing; the *Filostrato*, by contrast, is a youthful piece written in haste.

And he continues:

_____

[7] See Wallace, chapter 6, pp. 106–140.

Chaucer's obeisance to the *Poetria Nova* at this point...
functions as a private critique of the *Filostrato* and as
something of a personal manifesto.[8]

We cannot be sure about the time scales here. Is it a
'youthful piece', and did Boccaccio really write 'in haste'?[9]
Did Chaucer own a copy of the text for years before he began
composition? It is possible he came to it relatively late, but
having meditated upon the *matière* and *sens* in other contexts.
Perhaps he even began a faithful translation at one stage, as he
appears to have done with the *Teseida*. What is certain is that
at some point before he created *Troilus and Criseyde* he had
a firm grasp of the overall design he wanted, one that
involved a greater participation on the part of the reader. I
would suggest that his version is not so much a 'private
critique' as a public debate about the issues involved: the
narrative is a 'hypothesis',[10] in the technical, rhetorical sense
of the word, for soliciting audience reaction in the arena of a
debate. We can see this design in embryo in the *Filostrato* and
it is this, just as much as the individual word, line or stanza
which Chaucer 'translates'. Thus I would like to make a case
for *Troilus and Criseyde* as a *public critique* of the *Filostrato*.
It offers a dialectical investigation of the lovers' narrative,
inviting a response from its audience (real and inscribed) as if
it were a *demande d'amour* in a fictional love debate, a
quaestio in the Schools or a *quodlibet* debate.

---

[8] Ibid. p. 104.

[9] See A. Balduino, *Boccaccio, Petrarca e altri poeti del Trecento*
(Florence, 1984): 'Reminiscenze petrarchesche nel "Filostrato" e sua
datazione', pp. 231–247, where he puts the case for a later dating, *c.* 1339,
as opposed to the usual 1335.

[10] See Wesley Trimpi, 'The Ancient Hypothesis of Fiction: An Essay on
the Origins of Literary Theory', *Traditio* XXVII (1971), pp. 1–78. Cf. his
later article in *Traditio* XXX (1974).

In view of this, one wonders if, beyond his 'design', Chaucer had any theoretical orientation when meditating upon his *rifacimento*. I now want to consider this point before looking at the effects of the design in both poems and the responses they engender.

*   *   *

A time-honoured theory of translation exists, one which Chaucer was able to apply indiscriminately to suit his purposes, sometimes translating 'word for word' and sometimes 'sense for sense'. However, a theory of imitation did exist, which Petrarch talks about in his letter to Boccaccio, *Familiarum Rerum Libri*, XXIII, 19.[11] He is talking about his amanuensis, Giovanni Malpaghini, whose love of Virgil led him to insert lines or passages from the latter into his own compositions, a practice which elicited a kindly and fatherly reproof from Petrarch:

> ...curandum imitatori ut quod scribit simile non idem sit, eamque similitudinem talem esse oportere, non qualis est imaginis ad eum cuius imago est, que quo similior eo maior laus artificis, sed qualis filii ad patrem. In quibus cum magna sepe diversitas sit membrorum, umbra quedam et quem pictores nostri aerem vocant, qui in vultu inque oculis maxime cernitur, similitudinem illam facit, que statim viso filio, patris in memoriam nos reducat, cum tamen si res ad mensuram redeat, omnia sint diversa; sed est ibi nescio quid occultum quod hanc habeat vim. Sic et nobis providendum ut cum simile aliquid sit, multa sint dissimilia, et id ipsum simile lateat ne deprehendi possit nisi tacita mentis indagine, ut intelligi simile queat potiusquam dici. Utendum igitur ingenio alieno utendumque coloribus, abstinendum verbis; illa

---

[11] F. Petrarca, *Familiarum Rerum Libri* in *Prose*, eds. Martellotti, Ricci, Carrara, Bianchi (Milan, 1955); cf. *Fam.* I, 8; XXII, 2, 10, etc.

enim similitudo latet, hec eminet; illa poetas facit, hec simias.
Standum denique Senece consilio, quod ante Senecam Flacci
erat, ut scribamus scilicet sicut apes mellificant, non servatis
floribus sed in favos versis, ut ex multis et variis unum fiat,
idque aliud et melius.[12]

... the imitator must seek to be similar, not equal, and the
similarity must not be that which exists between a copy and
its original, where the closer the more praiseworthy it is, but
like that which exists between a son and his father. Between
these two, in fact, although different in appearance, is
something indefinable which painters call an 'air' and which
is revealed above all in the face and eyes, producing a
similarity that, when one looks at the son, straightaway
recalls the father, even if, when one begins a detailed
examination, everything appears different. In the same way,
when imitating, we should work in such a way that, if there
is a similarity, there is also much that is, on the other hand,
dissimilar, and that which is dissimilar should be so hidden
that it can only be discovered by a quiet inquiry of the mind
and which it befalls us above all to intuit rather than
demonstrate. One can make use of another's imagination and
colours [rhetorical expressions] but not his words; the
imitation of the former remains hidden, and is what poets do,
while the latter is apparent and is what apes do. In the end it
is necessary to follow the advice of Seneca, which was first
given by Horace, that one writes in the way bees make
honey, not by gathering the flowers but by transforming them
into honey, fusing various elements into a single unity, which
is different and better.

Thus Petrarch offers two similes for the reworking of poetic
models; the new work should be as son to father, and the
creative process is likened to that of bees creating honey: out
of a variety of elements they create something which is

---

[12] ibid. pp. 1018–1020. My translations throughout except where stated.

different and better. Thus the inference is that, whilst admiring
and even using old models, the poet should actively seek to do
better and differently. This is not what we generally
understand by the idea of 'imitation',[13] but Petrarch, as he
says, is taking his ideas from Seneca (Epistle LXXXIV) and
Horace (Carm. IV 2, 27–32). Writing to Lucillius about the
relationship of reading and writing, the former says:

> ... nos quoque has apes debemus imitari et quaecumque ex
> diversa lectione congessimus, separare, melius enim distincta
> servantur, deinde adhibita ingenii nostri cura et facultate in
> unum saporem varia illa libamenta confundere, ut etiam si
> apparuerit, unde sumptum sit, aliud tamen esse quam unde
> sumptum est, appareat.

> We also, I say, ought to copy these bees, and sift whatever
> we have gathered from a varied course of reading, for such
> things are better preserved if they are kept separate; then, by
> applying the supervising care with which our nature has
> endowed us, — in other words, our natural gifts, — we
> should so blend those several flavours into one delicious
> compound that, even though it betrays its origin, yet it
> nevertheless is clearly a different thing from whence it
> came.[14]

As writing is the fruit of study, it should be a product, as that
of son to father:

> Etiam si cuius in te comparebit similitudo, quem admiratio
> tibi altius fixerit, similem esse te volo quomodo filium, non
> quomodo imaginem; imago res mortua est.

---

[13] For a Renaissance view see Sidney's *A Defense of Poetry*. For a
general bibliography on imitation in the Renaissance, see Thomas M.
Greene, *The Light in Troy: Imitation and Discovery in Renaissance Poetry*
(New Haven and London, 1982), p. 312, n. 34.

[14] Seneca, *Ad Lucilium Epistulae Morales*, vol. II, ed. & tran. R. M.
Gummere. Loeb Classical Library (London, 1925), p. 278.

> Even if there shall appear in you a likeness to him who, by
> reason of your admiration, has left a deep impress upon you,
> I would have you resemble him as a child resembles his
> father, and not as a picture resembles its original; for a
> picture is a lifeless thing.[15]

Seneca emphasizes the process of uniting separate elements
into one new substance, e.g.:

> ... haec enim omnibus, quae ex quo velut exemplari traxit,
> formam suam inpressit, ut in unitatem illa conpetant.

> ... for a true copy stamps its own form upon all the features
> which it has drawn from what we may call the original, in
> such a way that they are combined into a unity.[16]

Thus imitation is not a process of slavishly copying an
exemplar, but, one might say, taking the best from a variety
of exemplars to create something new. This is the meaning
Petrarch uses in his letter to Boccaccio and, judging from his
practice, it appears to be the process that Chaucer follows:
from the various sources which nourished the work he creates
something which is *aliud et melius*.

One way of looking at this is to see the different
weighting that Chaucer gives to the themes of tragic (or high)
poetry that Dante outlines in *De Vulgari Eloquentia*:

> ...et iste quem tragicum appellamus summus videtur esse
> stilorum, illa que summe canenda distinximus isto solo sunt
> stilo canenda: videlicet salus, amor et virtus... (II, iv, 8)[17]

---

[15] Ibid. p. 280.

[16] Ibid. p. 280.

[17] D. Alighieri, *De Vulgari Eloquentia*, ed. Pier Vincenzo Mengaldo,
Opere Minori, Tomo II (Milan-Naples, 1979), p. 166.

... and so that which we have called the tragic shows itself to be the highest of styles, and those themes we have delineated as the highest style should only be sung in it, that is to say, health, love and virtue...

which themes he earlier defined (II, ii) as the worthiest themes of vernacular poetry, based on the Aristotelian division of man's three souls and the ends they seek:

Ad quorum evidentiam sciendum est quod sicut homo tripliciter spirituatus est, videlicet vegetabili, animali et rationali, triplex iter perambulat. Nam secundum quod vegetabile quid est, utile querit, in quo cum plantis comunicat; secundum quod animale, delectabile, in quo cum brutis; secundum quod rationale, honestum querit, in quo solus est, vel angelice sociatur <nature>. Propter hec tria quicquid agimus agere videmur... (II, ii, 6)[18]

In order to know them [i.e. the themes], one must know that, as man has three souls, the vegetative, the animal and the rational, so he follows three ways. Following the vegetative, he looks for the useful, and this he has in common with plants; following the animal, he looks for pleasure, and this he has in common with the beasts; following the rational soul he looks for honesty, and in this he is alone or is like the nature of angels. Whatever we do it is clear we do it because of these three ends.

Thus the vegetative soul seeks the useful, the animal soul seeks pleasure and the rational soul seeks honesty. But each of these ends, says Dante, has aspects among its major components which are of supreme importance:

Et primo in eo quod est utile: in quo, si callide consideremus intentum omnium querentium utilitatem, nil aliud quam salutem inveniemus. Secundo in eo quod est delectabile: in

[18] Ibid. p. 150.

quo dicimus illud esse maxime delectabile quod per
pretiosissimum obiectum appetitus delectat: hoc autem venus
est. Tertio in eo quod est honestum: in quo nemo dubitat esse
virtutem. Quare hec tria, salus videlicet, venus et virtus,
apparent esse illa magnalia que sint maxime pertractanda, hoc
est ea que maxime sunt ad ista, ut armorum probitas, amoris
accensio, et directio voluntatis. (II, ii, 7)[19]

In the first place, in the useful: if we look closely at the
intention of all those who seek the useful, we find nothing
other than the preservation of life. In the second place, in
pleasure: in this let us say that the greatest pleasure is
enjoyed for the most longed for object of the senses, amorous
enjoyment. In the third place, in honesty, there is no doubt
that it is virtue that is sought. These three ends, the
preservation of life, amorous enjoyment and virtue appear as
the great and marvellous things that must be treated in the
greatest of ways, that is, in those things that most pertain to
them — prowess in arms, the fire of love, and the probity of
the will.

In other words, the most important part of the useful is
the preservation of life, or health; the most important aspect
of pleasure is sexual pleasure, and that of honesty is virtue.
We can see how Boccaccio alludes to these three great themes
in the *Filostrato* at I, 44 where the narrator is speaking of
Troiolo:

> Ciascun altro pensier s'era fuggito
> della gran guerra e della sua salute,
> e sol nel petto suo era sentito
> quel che parlasse dell'alta virtute
> della sua donna; e, così impedito,
> sol di curar l'amorose ferute
> sollicito era, e quivi ogni intelletto

---

[19] Ibid. pp. 150–152.

avea posto, e l'affanno e'l <u>diletto</u>.
(my emphasis)

> All thought of the <u>great war</u> and of his own <u>well-being</u> had
> fled from him, and in his breast he only listened to that
> which spoke of his lady's <u>high virtue</u>, and, thus blocked, he
> was eager only to heal the <u>amorous wounds</u> and to that end
> he had given all his intellect, his effort and <u>delight</u>.

In saying that health or life (*salus*) is preserved by arms
(*armorum probitas*), Dante is stretching a point in order to
introduce the martial themes of chivalry into his argument.
But in the *Filostrato* they are intimately linked. Troiolo has to
preserve his life both against the dangers of war and against
the wounds of love (*amorose ferute*). He is successful in the
short run in the latter case, but not, in the long run, in the
former. While the *alta virtute* of his lady turns out to be false,
we see Troiolo as the true repository of virtue and if he is
something of a martyr to his cause, unlike Chaucer's Troilus
in the eighth sphere, he learns nothing from the experience,
and receives no reward for his suffering.

All this acquires a much greater moral significance in
Troilus and Criseyde. We have the background of war (and
the increased perspective of death); we have the virtue caused
by love, which is contrasted with that stemming from
Christian love. But Chaucer also introduces the idea of
survival through procreation (whereby mankind overcomes
death), set against the survival of the soul, which is brought
about by virtue. In contrast to Troilus' virtue — his eternal
love, which ultimately leads him to his death — Criseyde (like
her father) survives in this life only by betrayal.

It will be instructive to look at Chaucer's translation of
the above passage because *in nuce* it represents a good
example of all of Chaucer's heightening techniques.

Alle other dredes weren
   from him fledde,
Both of th'assege and his
   savacioun;
N'yn him desir noon
   other fownes bredde,
But argumentes to his
   conclusioun:
That she of him wolde
   han compassioun,
And he to ben hire man,
   while he may dure.
Lo, here his lif, and from
   the deth his cure!
(I, 463–9)

Ciascun altro pensier s'era
   fuggito
della gran guerra e della
   sua salute,
e sol nel petto suo era
   sentito
quel che parlasse dell'alta
   virtute
della sua donna; e, così
   impedito
sol di curar l'amorose
   ferute,
sollicito era, e quivi ogni
   intelletto
avea posto, e l'affanno e'l
   diletto.

In the Italian, Troiolo only wants to cure his *amorose ferute*, to which end he applies his *intelletto*, *affanno* and *diletto*, with a simple opposition operating between his personal effort and Criseida's *alta virtute* (reference to which Chaucer notably omits). Chaucer's stanza is much less direct about the relation between the two protagonists, but it exhibits a more sophisticated use of language and register. Boccaccio speaks conventionally of the 'amorous wounds' which Troiolo wishes to 'cure' by using his intellectual and physical faculties, mentioned at the stanza's close. Chaucer begins his stanza with a direct translation of the first two lines of the Italian, correctly interpreting *pensier(o)* in this context as 'worry' or 'care' (cf. Petrarch's canzone 129, *Di pensier in pensier*) — rather than simply as 'thought' — with his 'dredes', and using 'assege' for the 'great war' and 'savacioun' for 'well-being'. He then introduces an unusual metaphor, where Troilus's desire breeds 'fownes' (fawns), that is 'fledgling desires' which — rather surprisingly — are not 'tender thoughts' but 'argumentes' to a 'conclusioun'. Thus he moves quickly from metaphorical elaboration to the language of scholarly debate. This 'conclusioun' is not a logically demonstrated point (and therefore a metaphorical use of the word) but yet another protestation in indirect speech of Troilus's hope and love, with the perspective of death as always much in evidence, viz. 'while he may dure' and 'from the death his cure'. If we take this last phrase as belonging to the relative clause beginning 'That she of him wolde han ...', then Criseyde (as Pandarus often states) is nothing less than a cure for Troilus's 'deth', i.e. his fatal love-sickness. The expressions of Criseyde's 'compassioun' and Troilus's being 'hire man' are more formal and certainly less erotic than the directly Ovidian curing of love's wounds, which Boccaccio has. Significant, too, is the change from Troiolo's effort to gain his end to Troilus's desire to establish the relationship along courtly lines, which is again less erotic in the Ovidian sense.

On the other hand, Chaucer leaves out the mention of Criseida's *alta virtute*, that most courtly of qualities which in Boccaccio's version is seen as an impediment or obstacle to Troiolo's 'cure'. Similarly, he omits to translate stanza II, 23, where Pandaro explicitly states that the only problem to Troiolo's attaining Criseida is that 'above all other women' (*più che altra donna*) she is *onesta*. Chaucer inverts this and makes it more complex. Pandarus says that Troilus will win Criseyde because her virtue is a sure index of her having some compassion for him (I, 897–900), thus introducing the formula from the *dolce stil nuovo* where *gentilezza=virtute* and, as Chaucer translated loosely from Guinizzelli, 'Pitee renneth soone in gentil herte'. At the same time he puts the argument of *carpe diem* to Criseyde: she is gradually getting older and must enjoy love to the full while her beauty still allows it. Elsewhere, Pandarus suggests their possible fruitful union because of their common humanity (I, 976–980), to whose laws they are bound; he also asks Troilus to think of 'Kynde' making Criseyde feel pity for his plight (II, 1375–9).

This over-determinism gives a multiple choice of motivation, and overlies the internal debate of the characters, which, in turn, provokes a debate with the reader. I will now turn to how the design of both poems affects this reaction.

                              *   *   *

What, firstly, is the *Filostrato*'s design? We know the narrative details and that it is a dramatization of a performance — or recitation — echoing the influence of the *cantare*, or popular Italian romance.[20] A narrator guides the reader through the poem, but he is much closer to the material, identifying himself far more with his lovesick hero than the Chaucerian narrator.

Il *Filostrato* opens with a prose *proemio* which explains the fictional genesis of the poem (at one time considered to be autobiographical); in it the narrator also explains the poem's twofold design on its audience. Both *proemio* and poem are addressed to a noble lady by a narrator who presents himself in the role of unrequited lover, one — even if he is not of noble origin — used to debating *questioni d'amore* in the Courts of Love. He says he has been a servant of the God of Love since almost his early youth:

> quasi dalla mia puerizia infino a questo tempo ne' servigi d'Amore sono stato
>
> > (Proemio, 1)

Among the 'noble men' and 'beautiful ladies' of Love's court, he has heard the following question disputed:

[20] See Vittore Branca, *Il cantare trecentesco e il Boccaccio del Filostrato e del Teseida* (Florence, 1936).

a young man fervently loves a woman, but nothing is
conceded to him by Fortune except sometimes being able to
see her, or other times being able to talk about her to
someone, or being able to think sweetly about her by himself.
Which of these things therefore gives him the most pleasure?
(Proemio, 2–3)[21]

The narrator's theoretical position was to defend the last
option, 'being able to think sweetly about her by himself'.
Then we find that his *experience* (however fictional this is)
has come to tell him something different. We learn that the
nobilissima donna whom he loves has left Naples and moved
to Sannio, and that Fortune has thus corrected his error:

Now I know, *me miserum*, now I feel, now I most openly
discern how much more good, how much more pleasure, how
much more sweetness there is in the true light of your eyes,
and to see them with my own, than there was in the false
flattery of my thoughts. (Proemio, 20)[22]

Rather than privileging presence and reality here, it is the
proper emphasis on the true grace to be found in the sight of
the lady's eyes stressed repeatedly by Cavalcanti[23] or Dante
in the *Vita Nuova*.[24] Here the narrator is showing he knows

[21] ... uno giovane ferventemente ama una donna, della quale niun'altra
cosa gli è conceduta della fortuna se non il poterla alcuna volta vedere, o
talvolta di lei ragionare con alcuno, o seco stesso di lei dolcemente pensare.
Quale gli è adunque di queste tre cose di più diletto? (Proemio, 2–3).

[22] Ora, misero me, il conosco, ora il sento, ora apertissimamente il
discerno, quanto di bene, quanto di piacere, quanto di soavità, più nella luce
vera degli occhi vostri, veggendole co' miei, che nella falsa lusinga del mio
pensiero dimorasse. (Proemio, 20).

[23] Guido Cavalcanti, *Rime*, ed. Giulio Cattaneo (Turin, 1967), XXIV,
XXV, XXVI, XXVIII, XXX, XXXI.

[24] Dante Alighieri, *Vita Nuova*, ed. Domenico De Robertis, Opere
Minori, Tomo I, Parte I. XXI.

the trappings of 'new style' doctrine and also, like a true
scholastic, that he can recognize fine distinctions in his own
cognitive perception.

His lady's absence causes the narrator to suffer until, if
it had continued much longer, he would certainly have died,
he says. Fortunately, he is able to find a remedy, that of
narrating his sufferings in a lyric manner: *cantando narrare li
miei martiri*, which points to an interesting generic mix that
Chaucer preserves. Once he has found a suitable story in that
of Troiolo, composition not only restores his ailing health, but
should so move his lady, he hopes, when she reads of
Troiolo's sufferings, that she will restore to him the sight of
her *angelico viso* (for he cannot ever hope that his catharsis
will extend to the physical delights of Part III). In its fiction,
then, the poem is a means of persuasion.

But, at its outset, it is also addressed to an audience of
courtly lovers, whom the narrator similarly seeks to move to
compassion:

> E voi, amanti, priego ch'ascoltiate
> ciò che dirà 'l mio verso lagrimoso
> e se nel core avvien che voi sentiate
> destarsi alcuno spirito pietoso,
> per me vi priego che Amor preghiate,
> per cui, sì come Troiolo, doglioso
> vivo, lontan dal più dolce piacere
> ch'a creatura mai fosse in calere.
>
> (Part I, 6, 1–8)

And you lovers, I beg you to listen to what my tearful verse
has to say, and if it happens that you feel in your heart any
spirit of pity awaken in you, I beg you to pray for me to the
God of Love, through whom, like Troiolo, I live a sorrowful
life, far from the sweetest pleasure that any creature could
hold dear.

Like the address to the noble lady, the poem is an appeal for an affective response through the fine feelings of courtly love, Italian style: courtly lovers will be awakened to pity in the same way, the narrator hopes, as his lady.

Chaucer adopts both the narrator's persona and the role of unrequited lover, appealing for his audience of courtly lovers to be moved:

> For I, that God of Loves servantz serve,
> Ne dar to Love, for myn unliklynesse,
> Preyen for speed, al sholde I therfore sterve,
> So fer am I from his help in derknesse ...
>
> (I, 15–18)

> But ye loveres, that bathen in gladnesse,
> If any drope of pyte in yow be,
> Remembreth yow on passed hevynesse
> That ye han felt, and on the adversite
> Of othere folk, and thynketh how that ye
> Han felt that Love dorste yow displese,
> Or ye han wonne hym with to gret an ese.
>
> (I, 21–28)

The narrator's description of himself as a 'servant of the God of Love'[25] is more subtle and humorous than Boccaccio's narrator, but in so doing he sets himself apart from courtly lovers, which is something that the latter narrator appears not to do. In relating his education in the courts of Love, the *Filostrato* narrator seems to be saying that he was on a par with the nobles there, but more by the fact of his presence than by his sharing their noble blood:

> ritrovandomi nella corte intra i gentili uomini e le vaghe donne dimoranti in quella parimente con meco
>
> (*Proemio*, 1–2)

---

[25] See note to Book I, line 15, p. 1025, *Riverside Chaucer*.

finding myself in (Love's) court among the noble men and beautiful women dwelling there as equally as myself.

The expression itself suggests some distance: he does not say 'with other young noblemen like myself', which, in any case, given that Boccaccio came from the merchant class, the conventions of authorial personae of the time would not permit him.

Chaucer's narrator is also inviting his inscribed audience of courtly lovers to remember what they have felt in love, and to weigh their own experience against that of the tale, and — should they be moved to feel any pity — he requests them to pray for the various categories of unfortunate and fortunate lovers that he lists in the bidding prayer (I, 29–56).

The bidding prayer is usually taken to be a Chaucerian addition, but if we look at the last stanza (33) of Part VIII of *Il Filostrato*, we find that the narrator also asks for the prayers of his inscribed audience:

> Dunque siate avveduti, e compassione
> di Troiolo e di voi insiememente
> abbiate, e fia ben fatto; ed orazione
> per lui fate ad Amor pietosamente,
> che'l posi in pace in quella regione
> dov'el dimora, ed a voi dolcemente
> conceda grazia sì d'amare accorti,
> che per re donna al fin non siate morti.

> Therefore be cautious, and have compassion both for Troiolo and for yourselves, and things will be well; and pray to the God of Love for him with pity, so that he will rest in peace in the place where he remains, and also so that Love may sweetly concede you grace to love sensibly, so that in the end you do not die for a wicked woman.

This striking transposition of material is by no means unique. We have, for example, the inspired switch of Troiolo's hymn to Venus, after the consummation in Part III (74–79), to the voice of the narrator in the Prologue to Book III, which is almost too well known to require comment. Perhaps more extreme is the use of Arcita's otherworldly vision (*Teseida*, 11, 1–3) for the Troilus story. Even individual lines of Boccaccio are treated similarly. The description of Troilus fainting in the bedroom scene (III, 1112–5), for example, as Dr. Wallace shows, ironically echoes that of Troiolo's fainting when he hears that Criseida is to be exchanged for Antenore (IV, 19, 5–8).[26] Consequently, we may surely conclude that Chaucer's bidding prayer is derived from the Boccaccian stanza at the end of Part VIII. Once more, that is, we see Chaucer amplifying the interaction between narrator and inscribed audience.

But Boccaccio's poem assumes a homogenous audience; the fiction of a recitation for an audience of lovers is maintained throughout. The poem's 'moral' is aimed at them and both involves and sustains the canons of *stilnovismo* love. In the stanza quoted above, therefore, the narrator warns his audience against the type of *rea donna* represented by Criseida. Although she has the right status and sensibility, she is not constant, therefore she is not virtuous, therefore she is no courtly lover. Consequently, the last words of the narrative make plain and unambiguous her new status: *Criseida villana* (VIII, 28, 8).

A rather curious rubric introduces the warning to young lovers which follows on the above, where the 'author' says that 'it is better to place one's love in mature women than in young ones',[27] and stanzas 31 and 32 of Part VIII continue the polemic against fickle young women who think themselves capable of being courtly lovers simply because they are nobly

[26] Wallace p. 125.

[27] Parla l'autore a' giovani amadori assai brievemente, mostrando più nelle mature che nelle giovinette donne porre amore.

born:

> And even more because they are descended from a high lineage and know how to count off their ancestors, they think they must have some preference over others in love, and they consider good manners an offence: they turn up their noses and go about with a scornful air. Shun these ladies and consider them common [i.e. low-born], because they are not noble women but beasts.

> The perfect [noble] woman has a firm desire to be loved, and delights in love. She discerns and sees what is to be avoided: she chooses and she leaves alone, she looks ahead and she maintains her promises. These are the ladies to be followed. But even then, one should not choose in a hurry, as they are not all sound, just because they seem older, and these are the less worthy. (VIII, 31–32)[28]

Although this 'new style' moral employs the right kind of opposition between *gentile* and *vile*, it perhaps also smacks of a bourgeois writer snubbed by a haughty young *gentil donna*.

---

[28]   E molte ancor perché d'alto lignaggio
discese sono, e sanno annoverare
gli avoli lor, si credon che vantaggio
deggiono aver dall'altre nell'amare,
e pensan che costume sia oltraggio,
torcere il naso, e dispettose andare;
queste schifate ed abbiatele a vili,
ché bestie son, non son donne gentili.

     Perfetta donna ha più fermo disire
d'essere amata, e d'amar si diletta;
discerne e vede ciò ch'è da fuggire,
lascia ed elegge provvida, ed aspetta
le promission; queste son da seguire,
ma non si vuol però scegliere in fretta,
ché non son tutte sagge perché sieno
più attempate, e quelle vaglion meno.

At the same time, however, it does make an appeal for inner virtue — one that was extended to rulers in the previous Part:

re è colui il quale per virtù vale
non per potenza
(VII, 99, 6–7)

a king is worthy because of his virtue, not because of his power.

On the whole, such moralizing sits uneasily with the poem's lighter stylistic features, and with its almost hedonistic portrayal of the love affair. But it is precisely this lack of unified sensibility which the well-read Chaucer might well have noted and thought that he could make new. It is his knowledge of the *dolce stil nuovo* that enabled him to make much more of the ethics in *Il Filostrato*, and broaden its argument to virtue in general.

Chaucer was evidently taken with Guido Guinizzelli's line *Al cor gentil rempaira sempre amore*,[29] which opens the Bolognese poet's famous canzone, and which Chaucer probably knew from its citation by Dante in the last tractate of the *Convivio* (IV, xx), or even possibly from Dante's version in *Inferno* V, 100: *Amor, ch' al cor gentil ratto s'apprende*. The *Convivio* enlarges on the theme of Love's swifter entry into the gentle (or noble) heart by bringing in Aristotle's claims about true nobility in the *Nicomachean Ethics*: it arises from virtue.

In the *Filostrato*, Boccaccio even quotes a line directly from the third canzone of the *Convivio*, which opens the Fourth Tractate:

[29] Guido Guinizzelli, *Poesie*, a cura di E. Sanguineti (Milan, 1986), IV, pp. 22–24. See Kn T, 1761; Sq T, 479; Mer T, 1986; LGW Pro F, 503, cf. MLT, 660, and *T & C*, III, 4–5.

E gentilezza dovunque è virtute
(VII, 94,1)

Only virtue can give true nobility, just as virtuous love is the only true courtly love — and virtue, of course, demands constancy.

The *Ballade of Gentillesse* shows Chaucer at least influenced by the *Convivio*'s arguments about virtue and its power to endow judgment, if he is not directly translating:

> The firste stok, fader of gentilesse —
> What man that desireth gentil for to be
> Must folowe his trace, and alle his wittes dresse
> Vertu to love, and vyces for to flee.
> For unto vertu longeth dignitee,
> And noght the revers ...
>
> (Gentilesse, 1–6)

The argument is repeated in the Loathly Lady's speech in the *Wife of Bath's Tale* (*CT* III, 1109–1147), where Dante is openly acknowledged.

In *Troilus and Criseyde*, Chaucer leaves the idea of virtue merely implicit in the references to loving:

> Plesance of love, O goodly debonaire,
> In gentil hertes ay redy to repaire!
>
> (III, 4–5)

> ... for every wyght, I gesse,
> That loveth wel, meneth but gentilesse.
>
> (III, 1147–8)

Troilus's constant references to 'trouthe' remind us of the fact, but the argument is also about Criseyde's virtue — or lack of it — and ultimately the reader's own, in the face of worldly temptation and necessity.

Chaucer was equally well acquainted with questions of love and love debates, just as his language demonstrates a knowledge of the terms of scholastic debate: one only has to think of the *Prologue to the Legend of Good Women* and the parody of the *Parliament of Fowls*. In the latter debate, one of the most outraged, if genteel, voices is that of the turtle dove, who says:

> 'Nay, God forbede a lovere shulde chaunge!'
>
> (*PF*, 582)

> 'Though that his lady everemore be straunge,
> Yit lat hym serve hire ever, til he be ded.'
>
> (*PF*, 584–5)

The Goose has just voiced the opinion that:

> 'But she wol love hym, lat hym love another!'
>
> (*PF*, 567)

which the Duck seconds:

> 'That men shulde loven alwey causeles!
> Who can a resoun fynde or wit in that?'
>
> (*PF*, 590–1)

Chaucer is creating an opposition between Courtly Love and Nature here. If the two young tercels who are not chosen remain chastely faithful, then, to quote the Monk in the *General Prologue*, 'How shal the world be served?'.

In the *Filostrato* Boccaccio is measuring Criseida's behaviour ostensibly against the *dolce stil nuovo*'s canon of love, while at the same time asking the audience to test the experiences of Troiolo against their own. What the Chaucerian narrator does is to invite the audience of lovers to compare and assess the 'hypothesis' of the narrative against their own experience: the question about the lovers' respective attitudes ultimately rebounds on the actual reader in a Christian context, as we shall see.

It is significant that Chaucer included Criseyde in the *Explicit*, because the poem is as much about her plight as it is about that of Troilus. In a fairly impossible situation, what is she to do? She may be 'slydynge of corage' (V, 85), but she knows how to cope with change and, most of all, she survives.[30] One might again consider the words of the duck:

> 'That men shulde loven alwey causeles!
> Who can a resoun fynde or wit in that?'

In the same way, the actual reader may be alerted to reading the narrative in the light of experience (or reason!) and debate the issues in his or her mind.

We have seen how the appeal to experience enters Chaucer's poem at the very beginning, in the bidding prayer. Similarly, the narrator appeals to his own experience:

> O blisful nyght, of hem so longe isought,
> How blithe unto hem bothe two thow weere!
> Why nad I swich oon with my soule ybought,
> Ye, or the leeste joie that was theere?
>
> (III, 1317–20)

which is, of course, a very double-edged compliment: on the one side, terrestrial bliss crooks a beckoning finger, on the other lies the cost of eternal damnation. Not many lines later in this climactic point in the tale, the audience is specifically invited to consider both narrative and presentation in the light of their own 'felyng":

> For myne wordes, heere and every part,
> I speke hem alle under correccioun
> Of yow that felyng han in loves art,
> And putte it all in youre discrecioun
> To encresse or maken dymynucioun
> Of my langage, and that I yow biseche.
>
> (III, 1331–36)

---

[30] This may possibily have been Henryson's chief dissatisfaction with the poem; see his *The Testament of Cresseid.*

Further addresses to the audience can be noted in the same book, for example the very last stanza.

In a more subtle fashion, we have the assertions and concealments of the narrator. His separation from the common judgment of Criseyde, and especially his partisan position with regard to her must surely give the actual reader cause for thought:

> Men seyne — I not — that she yaf hym hire herte.
>
> (V, 1050)

> And if I myghte excuse hire any wise,
> For she so sory was for hire untrouthe,
> Iwis, I wolde excuse hire yet for routhe.
>
> (V, 1097–9)

One feels that if the actual audience has a true feeling for experience and its hard knocks then it, too, should follow suit.

But the 'question' of Criseyde does not stop at the confines of courtly love. In the same way that the inscribed audience of lovers addressed at the beginning of the poem fragments in the bidding prayer into the various and opposed experiences of the lovers — their own and others' — so the inscribed audience of courtly lovers fragments at the end of the poem into a further set of hypothetical and actual readers, all with contrasting expectations.

It is here that Chaucer engenders the final atmosphere of debate. He foregrounds six different expectations around the Trojan narrative and in the process forces the reader to question his or her own assumptions and preferences in the act of reading. In so doing, he moves the reader out of the anachronistic world of Trojan Courtly Love and into the Christian universe.

The narrator begins by excusing himself to the male (or perhaps general) reader for not having written a romance of martial exploits:

And if I hadde ytaken for to write
The armes of this ilke worthi man,
Than wolde ich of his batailles endite;
But for that I to writen first bigan
Of his love, I have seyd as I kan, —
His worthi dedes, whoso list hem heere,
Rede Dares, he kan telle hem alle ifeere —

(V, 1765–71)

and then, addressing 'every lady bright of hewe', excuses himself for not having written an edifying legend of a good woman, like Penelope or Alcestis (V, 1772–78). In the envoi (V, 1786–92) he turns to the expectations of the scholarly reader, when he tells his 'litel bok' to be subject 'to alle poesie', with the implication to compare it with the great works of Classical antiquity; and, with the Christian moral that they should put their faith in the eternal love of God, rather than in the 'feyned loves' of the transitory, sublunar world, he addresses his group of potential lovers (the 'yonge fresshe folkes') directly, before inviting criticism from two professionals, literary and philosophical, namely Gower and Strode, who might be expected to pronounce on the literary performance and philosophical content and thus measure the poem's serious intent. But the final horizon is universal, addressing the Christian soul, where God forms the final frame of reference, circumscribing everything and constituting the ultimate (or absolute) — and non-literary — horizon of expectation.

Thus we are moved through a variety of perspectives on narrative, starting with that of the simple chivalric romance of 'batailles' and 'worthi dedes', appealing to a predominantly male audience, and that of an equally simple moral tale for women, through levels of increasing literary specification (scholarly, courtly love, named poet and philosopher) only to be led to the totally general in the end in the all-encompassing perspective of the Christian universe, against which not only literature, but all life, must be read. Just as fiction has to be weighed against experience, so experience has to be weighed against the expectations of Christianity. And, although he does not condemn his protagonists in the face of it, despite the stricture about 'payens corsed rites' (V, 1849), it is these expectations that Chaucer subsitutes for those of the *dolce stil nuovo* found in the *Filostrato*.

In her article 'Dante, Chaucer and the Ending of *Troilus and Criseyde*', Bonnie Wheeler states that:

> In denying us final judgment of his characters and their situation, Chaucer is suggesting that such questions are appropriately left unsolved. Ethics and philosophy reflect on the intractable, problematic nature of human experience. The poet does not join the narrator in attempting to freeze over our manifold responses to the poem in a single, indelible statement. The audience is left with moral and philosophical cleavage between the body of the poem and its ending; the fulfilment of that most ordinary desire for reconciliation would entail the very judgement and certainties which the poet through his narrator has here been denying as the appropriate end of poetry. Such decisions are best left to the moral Gower and the philosophical Strode; the process is itself open-ended.[31]

But as I hope I have shown, the process, while it is indeed 'open-ended' is not one of mere apostasy on the part of the poet: Chaucer is provoking response, and it really is for the reader to decide. As Dr. Wheeler admits, there is 'genuine resolution' in the last ten lines of the poem, but this is not poetic closure. The finite human world is seen from the perspective of the infinite (anticipated by Troilus' view from the 'eighthe spere' [V, 1807–27]), both of which lie beyond

---

[31] B. Wheeler, in *Philological Quarterly*, 61 (1982), pp. 105–123, p. 117.

the realm of fiction, but it is only against this perspective (human experience) that the actual reader can form an adequate response to the poem. What that may be Chaucer does not force upon his reader, but his narrator's compassion indicates that it might lie within the realm of *caritas*.

Boccaccio examines the behaviour of a courtly lover: Criseida has the right attributes and intentions, but fails to act well; he ends the work with the injunction on the prospective lover to discriminate and choose well. The narrative is both an exemplum and a 'hypothetical' cautionary tale. The narrator's simple message is 'Don't be caught out like Troiolo!'.

In a similar way, Chaucer's tale is cautionary. The narrator tells the prospective lovers not to confuse the transient love to be found in this world with the eternal love of God. But we must remember the arguments on courtly love to be found in the *Parliament of Fowls*: if the Christian swears love only to God, in chastity, how shall Nature, God's creation, be served? Like the good medieval scholar, he or she must make distinctions.

In this brief exposition, I have tried to show how Chaucer has remained faithful to the design of Boccaccio's poem, presenting a hypothetical narrative to a fictional (and, of course, a real) audience in the hope of eliciting its passions and compassion, and of alerting it to its own powers of judgment. Nevertheless, a huge cultural translation has taken place. Whereas the *Filostrato* remains within the narrow confines of courtly debate, its rather superficial references to the profounder ethical issues of the *dolce stil nuovo* provide a springboard for Chaucer to open out a full ethical debate about human aspirations and failings, set against a wide variety of perspectives, from literature to theology.

Middle English Translations of the
Tractatus de Purgatorio Sancti Patricii

ROBERT EASTING

THE STORY of the journey through purgatory and the Earthly
Paradise of the Irish knight Owein was one of the most
popular and enduring of the Middle Ages. It was first told in
the *Tractatus de Purgatorio Sancti Patricii* (hereafter *T*), a
Cistercian Latin prose text of the early 1180s, compiled by
H[enry] of Sawtry (Saltrey), Huntingdonshire. This text was
widely copied and translated throughout Europe. It exists in
two main redactions,[1] known as α and β, printed in parallel
by Karl Warnke.[2] It was also imitated by many subsequent
visitors to the pilgrimage site on Station Island, Lough Derg,
who left both Latin and vernacular accounts of their
experiences in the 'cave' of the Purgatory. Despite intermittent

---

[1] See the fundamental discussion of the Latin, Anglo-Norman and
Middle English manuscripts in the British Library by H.L.D. Ward,
*Catalogue of Romances in the Department of Manuscripts in the British
Museum*, ii (London, 1893), 435–84, especially pp. 444–54.

[2] *Das Buch vom Espurgatoire S. Patrice der Marie de France und seine
Quelle* (Bibliotheca Normannica, 9, Halle/Saale, 1938).

suppression, St Patrick's Purgatory has survived to this day as the foremost pilgrimage of Ireland.[3]

The popularity of Owein's story in medieval England is indicated by the large number of translations: five Anglo-Norman and three Middle English versions survive. It is these last that I shall examine here, for they provide an interesting example of the 'Englishing' of the same tale over some one hundred and fifty years.

The three Middle English versions are all in verse and are independent of each other.[4] The earliest version (hereafter *pa*)[5] is found under 'St Patrick' in the South English Legendary (SEL, late thirteenth-century);[6] the second, known as *Owayne Miles*[7] (*OM*1), survives in a unique acephalous copy in the Auchinleck manuscript[8] (A, 1330–40); the last, also known as *Owayne Miles* (*OM*2), probably early fifteenth-century, is the couplet version found in two

[3] For the most recent and substantial account of the pilgrimage's early development, see *The Medieval Pilgrimage to St Patrick's Purgatory: Lough Derg and the European Tradition*, edited by Michael Haren and Yolande de Pontfarcy (Dublin, 1988). For the *Tractatus*, see also the discussion and recent English translation in *Saint Patrick's Purgatory: a twelfth century tale of a journey to the other world*, translated by Jean-Michel Picard, with an introduction by Yolande de Pontfarcy (Dublin, 1985).

[4] This was recognised by E. Kölbing in the only previously published survey of the relationships between the Middle English, French and Latin versions: 'Zwei mittelenglische Bearbeitungen der Sage von St Patrik's Purgatorium', *Englische Studien*, 1 (1877), 57–121, at 57–98.

[5] This designation follows Manfred Görlach, *The Textual Tradition of the South English Legendary* (Leeds, 1974), pp. 149–51.

[6] See *A Manual of the Writings in Middle English 1100–1500* [hereafter *Manual*], edited by J. Burke Severs, vol. 2 (New Haven, 1970), V [321] a.

[7] So listed in Carleton Brown and R.H. Robbins, *The Index of Middle English Verse* (New York, 1943), no. *11.

[8] *Manual*, 2, V [321] b.

incomplete copies, British Library, MS Cotton Caligula A ii (C, mid-fifteenth century) and Yale University Library, MS 365, the 'Book of Brome', a commonplace book from Brome near the Norfolk/Suffolk border (Y, last quarter of the fifteenth century). Though there is much variation between these last two manuscripts, it is evident that C and Y are divergent copies of the same version, not two different versions as listed by Foster.[9] Foster lists as two further versions the 'Harley' and 'Hearne' fragments.[10] These are not, however, further separate translations: 'Harley' is a stanzaic reworking of *pa*, and 'Hearne' is a transcription of an extract from 'Harley'.[11] The fifteenth-century prose *Vision of William of Stranton*[12] is not a translation of *T* but an independent work. In this paper I discuss the three Middle English translations, *pa*, *OM*1 and *OM*2.[13]

Before dealing with these texts separately, a word about what they have in common: all three show common omissions of material found in the long texts of *T*; these may well be due to the omission of such passages from the *T* texts used by the original Middle English translators, for the Latin manuscripts, both α and β, often reduce their material

[9] *Manual*, 2, V [321] c, d.

[10] *Manual*, 2, V [321], e and f respectively.

[11] See Easting, 'The Middle English "Hearne" fragment of St Patrick's Purgatory', *Notes and Queries*, New Series, 35:4 (1988), 436–37.

[12] *Manual*, 2, V [321] h.

[13] I have dealt more fully with *pa* in Easting, 'The South English Legendary "St Patrick" as Translation', *Leeds Studies in English*, New Series XXI (1990), 119–40. For fuller discussion and texts of *OM*1, *OM*2, *Stranton*, and *T*, see Easting, 'An Edition of *Owayne Miles* and other Middle English texts concerning St Patrick's Purgatory', unpublished D.Phil. thesis, University of Oxford, 1976. A revision of this work is scheduled for publication by the Early English Text Society in 1991.

similarly, though the Middle English omissions may well indicate particular choices.

Whereas *T* is a Cistercian text directed specifically to a monastic audience, the Middle English versions are clearly designed for the laity. As such the translations all omit the two homilies found more or less complete in *β* and *α* manuscripts of *T* respectively, but also frequently omitted from both groups. These meditations occur at major breaks in the narrative, the first when Owein leaves purgatory, the second when he leaves the Earthly Paradise. Likewise the translations omit Henry of Sawtry's Dedication, Prologue and Epilogue, all the exemplary tales which Henry recounts to substantiate his main narrative, and the historical account of how he came to learn of the story of Owein from Gilbert of Basingwerk.[14] In other words, the Middle English translations preserve only the story of St Patrick founding the Purgatory entrance, and Owein's visit. These poems therefore have an 'historical' and dramatic force undiluted by narrative digression or by the theological and meditative emphases of the monastic Latin redactions.

I. South English Legendary version — *pa*

I turn now to the earliest Middle English version, the account given under 'St Patrick' in the SEL. This is the most faithful of the three translations, and its fidelity readily shows us that it derives from an *α* text of *T*. For example, one of the readiest indicators of the *α* and *β* texts is the way they

---

[14] The following sections in Warnke's edition (hereafter W) are all omitted by all the Middle English texts: I. Dedicatio; II. Prologus; III. Narratio I.2, II. 1–4; Homilia I; Homilia II; XXI.2–XXVI; Epilogus. W does not print the homilies complete.

describe the broadening of the narrow bridge above the river of hell.

α   Et ecce post paululum latitudo pontis exciperet carrum onustum, et post modicum uia erat ita larga ut sibi obuiarent in ea duo carra.   (W98:55–62)

pa   ...so longe forth he eode,
Þat it was so brod þat þere miȝte : a carte gon for neode,
And so longe, þat tuei cartes miȝte : meten heom wel i-nouȝ.   (437–39)[15]

β   Et ecce post paululum tantum creuit pontis latitudo ut etiam duo carra exciperet sibi obuiantia.

As might be supposed from this brief passage, *pa* for the most part closely follows the line-by-line order of the narrative details of *T*. In some places, however, the translator appears to have worked differently. As the following longer example shows, the translation process occasionally seems to have involved the reading and absorption of an extended section from which details are culled and reshaped into a new sequence with a good deal of new material added (as there is throughout the translation). Here Owein is taken to the hill in purgatory whence a wind blows the souls, himself, and the fiends into an icy river. (New material in *pa* is in italics; the Latin passages translated are numbered according to the lineation in Warnke, pp. 88–90; where *pa* translates more loosely or adapts, the Latin is in parentheses.)

325   heo nomen him *in grete wrathþe : and harleden him ferrere more,*

[15] I cite *pa* from Bodleian Library, MS Laud Misc. 108 (Ld), edited by Carl Horstmann, *The Early South-English Legendary*, EETS 87 (1887), 199–220.

protrahentes eum (1–2)

326 *And brouȝten him* opon a *swyþe gret* hul : *ful of sorewe and sore.*
(perrexerunt) contra montem unum (2–3)

327 *he stod and bi-heold a-boute : þo he cam þare-op an heiȝ;*

328 him wondrede of þe manie *gostes : þat he þare i-seiȝ.*
miraretur miles quid hec multitudo (13–14)

329 Alle *þe pinene* þat he hadde er i-seiȝe : *þare-aȝen nouȝt nere:*
(pauci) uiderentur ei omnes quos ante uiderat (7–9)

330 I-cluiȝte heo seten ope heore ton : and quakeden *revliche for fere.*
super digitos pedum curuatam (5–6)   cum tremore (10)

331 *In the south-half of þe hul : a deop water þare was and louȝ,*

332 Þat foule stonk, and caldore was : *þane ani ys oþur snovȝ.*
fetido et frigidissimo (27)

333 A norþerne wind *faste blevȝ : þat him þouȝte is flesch to-rende;*
ab aquilone uentus (23)

334 *Euere þare* seten *gostes : and a-ȝein þe winde heom wende,*
sedere (multitudinem) (7–8)   (ad aquilonem) erant uersi (11–12)

335   heo quakeden and *chyuereden faste : in grete pine*
      and stronge,
      cum tremore (10 cf. Ld330b)

336   Ase *ho-so seith* a-bidet *þare heore time : heore* deth
      for-to a-fonge.
      quasi mortem ... exspectantes (10–11)

337   "*lo*," seide on of þe feondes : "þov nost nouȝt ȝwat *is*
      tis;
      unus demonum dixit (15) (miraris ... quid ... populus
      hic exspectat (16–18))

338   bote þov torne þi þouȝt sone : þou schalt i-wite,
      i-wis."
      nisi ... consentiens reuerti uolueris, scies hoc
      certissime (18–20)

The Latin line numbers here show readily how *pa* moves
about within this section until the last couplet picks up the
direct order of *T* again. Unsurprisingly, given that the
translator is rendering prose as verse, the rhyming clauses are
usually new: here the only rhyme words to depend directly on
the Latin are *wende* (334b) after *uersi*, and *i-wis* (338b) after
certissime; the rhyming word or clause of the first line of
every couplet is new. 329 shows that the whole concept of the
line has been slightly shifted: whereas *T* compares the
numbers of souls previously seen, *pa* compares the number of
torments. In 331 the 'south' side is inferred from *T*'s northern
wind (23 cf. 11–12) which blows the souls into the water; this
is not reached until line 27 in *T*. 330b and 335 repeat
quakeden, based on the single occurrence of *cum tremore*, and
335a reinforces this with *chyuereden faste*; both processes of
duplication (repetition and reinforcement) are found elsewhere
in *pa*.

The italicised additions and expansions here are typical of the tendency of the translator to enhance the dramatic forcefulness of the narrative, often by emphasising the physical and spiritual pain of Owein and the souls in purgatory. This is very similar to the 'heightened depiction of the sufferings and joys of the protagonists' in the scenes of martyrdom elsewhere in the South English Legendary, discussed by Jankofsky.[16]

Elsewhere Jankofsky has identified four major principles whereby SEL texts translated from the *Legenda Aurea* seek to instruct, edify and entertain: these principles he summarizes as simplification, expansion, concretization or dramatization, and acculturation or 'Englishing' in the sense of 'adaptation of essentially Latin sources to an English audience'.[17] Although only the opening 54 lines of the "A" redaction of *pa* are translated from the *Legenda Aurea*, these principles do duty also for the translation here from *T*.[18]

Simplification of theological-dogmatic material is obviously most evident in the outright omission of all the

[16] Klaus P. Jankofsky, 'Entertainment, Edification, and Popular Education in the *South English Legendary*', *Journal of Popular Culture*, 11 (1977), 706–17 (quotation from p. 711).

[17] Jankofsky, '*Legenda Aurea* Materials in *The South English Legendary*: Translation, Transformation, Acculturation', in *Legenda Aurea. Sept siècles de diffusion. Actes du colloque international sur la Legenda Aurea: texte latin et branches vernaculaires à l'Université du Quebec à Montréal 11–12 mai 1983* (Montreal and Paris, 1986), pp. 317–29, esp. p. 320. This formulation is a development of points made in his earlier paper, cited in the previous note (p. 709).

[18] For the term "A" redaction, see Görlach, *Textual Tradition*. For the text, see Cambridge, Corpus Christi College, MS 145 (Co), edited by Charlotte d'Evelyn and Anna J. Mills, *The South English Legendary*, EETS 235 (1956), pp. 85–110. For discussion of the "A" additions to *pa*, see Easting, 'The South English Legendary "St Patrick" as Translation'.

speculative and meditative material found in *T*, as mentioned above. But it extends even to the omission or simplification of the biblical metaphor of donning the armour of God (Eph. 6:11–17); the single line, *And Armede him with holie beden : aȝen þe deuelene to fiȝte* (136), replaces five sentences in *T* (W56:1–20). The translation de-emphasises the monastic text's presentation of Owein as *miles Christi*.

Conversely, explanatory, interpretive and didactic material is expanded, as in the addition of lines clarifying the progress of the soul via purgatory to the Earthly Paradise,[19] a place termed our *kuynde heritage* (550–60). This offsets the use of the same phrase earlier in the poem to designate hell as the proper abode of the fiends (450–53). Such expansions instruct the audience about the shape of the otherworld, and give hope in the possibility of salvation, to be achieved by spiritual steadfastness (25, 28, 117, 125, 132, 518, 520) and the intervening grace of God (51, 58, 72, 74, 86, 115, etc.). Owein is the model of penitence and fortitude, as emphasised in the expanded account of his sorrow and determination when he first enters St Patrick's Purgatory (lines 43–63, cf. W38:8–40:40). Narratorial intrusions directly call the audience to penance to avoid purgatory, as in lines 290–92:

> Alas, ȝwi nellez men beon i-war: are heo heonnes wende,
> ȝwane he miȝten here with a luytel pine : bete heore mis-ded
> And þare heo schullen so bitere a-bugge : alas, þe
> wrechhede!

I have dealt elsewhere with some of the ways in which *pa* enhances the concretization or dramatization of the narrative, by the expansion of exclamations, direct speech, and imaginative details, such as when it seems to souls that they

---

[19] See further Easting, 'Purgatory and the Earthly Paradise in the *Tractatus de Purgatorio Sancti Patricii*', *Cîteaux: Commentarii Cistercienses*, 37 (1986), 23–48.

will burst, so tightly are they squeezed by serpents (225–26). In terms of what Jankofsky calls acculturation or making the story immediately pertinent to an English audience, we may note that the translator had little difficulty, for the bulk of the poem deals with comparatively recent history: Owein's visit *bi-fel bi þe kingus daiʒe steuene ; þat novþe late was* (39). When dealing with the remote past of St Patrick, the translator reinforces links with the present by pointing out that the saint's Purgatory *ʒeot stant, i-wis*, and the canons whom Patrick (supposedly) established *ʒeot þare beoth al-so* (8–9). As the poem ends, the audience is exhorted to apply the lessons of Owein's past experience of future pains to their own lives in the immediate present:

> god leue us ovre sunnes here so biete : for is holie wounde,
> Þat we ne þoruen in purgatorie : bi-leue bote luyte stounde.
>
> (672–73)

Although only the first eighteen of the poem's 673 lines deal with St Patrick, *pa*'s place in the Legendary is secured by its forceful presentation for the laity of a pious adventure story aimed at inducing penance.

The interest in adventure itself is more prominent in the second translation.

II. Auchinleck version — *OM*1[20]

Of the forty-four extant items in the famous Auchinleck manuscript (A), half are unique copies;[21] one such is the second Middle English version of 'St Patrick's Purgatory'.

It has not previously been recognised that *OM*1 is not a direct translation from *T*, but is based on one of the five extant, mutually independent, Anglo-Norman verse versions, that contained in Cambridge University Library, MS Ee.6.11 (hereafter F), and a fragment in British Library, MS Lansdowne 383.[22] (Hereafter I call this version AN.)[23]

Brief examples must suffice here to demonstrate *OM*1's dependence on AN. When St Patrick prays for assistance in converting the Irish, *Sone he fell on slepeing/ Toforn his auter* (A7:5–6);[24] this follows *Il s'endormist devant l'auter* (F96). This detail is not found in *T*, or in any other English, French or Anglo-Norman version. Later Owein tells the bishop he will enter St Patrick's Purgatory if the bishop wishes him to: *Þei þou me wost comandy* (A35:4) follows *Si vus le volez comander* (F273). This line translates *β T te precipiente*

[20] For the text, see Kölbing in *Englische Studien*, 1 (1877), 98–112. For a brief discussion of the poem, see Easting, 'The English Tradition', in the volume edited by Haren and de Pontfarcy, cited above, note 3.

[21] See the facsimile, *The Auchinleck Manuscript*, with an Introduction by Derek Pearsall & I.C. Cunningham (London, 1977).

[22] This version is printed in C.M. van der Zanden, *Etude sur le Purgatoire de Saint Patrice, accompagnée du texte latin d'Utrecht et du texte anglo-norman de Cambridge* (Amsterdam, 1927), pp. 90–135.

[23] French texts close to those from which the English translators worked are extant for thirteen of the eighteen romances in A: see L.H. Loomis, 'The Auchinleck Manuscript and a possible London bookshop of 1330–1340', *PMLA*, 57 (1942), 595–627 (pp. 605–07).

[24] I cite A from my own forthcoming edition. References are to stanza and line, matching the text in Kölbing.

(W38:25–26), not found in α, and is one of a number of passages that clearly show that AN is itself translated closely from a *β* text of *T*, unlike *pa* which was translated directly from α.

Although the author of *OM*1 undoubtedly worked from a copy of AN he did not make a full translation but selected and condensed it, at the same time amplifying his poem by reference to another text, one of the Middle English translations of the *Visio Sancti Pauli*. The rest may be the author's own invention or he may have used another source for his expansion of the section dealing with the Earthly Paradise, but if so I have not identified it. In any case, *OM*1 is by far the most elaborately developed of the Middle English versions.

Whereas *pa* tends to emphasise Owein as an example of spiritual fortitude and presents the story very much as an encouragement to penance, *OM*1, while not discounting these claims, makes more of the tale's innate appeal as romance quest. The poem is in six-line tail-rhyme stanzas, a form much used for popular chivalric romance. Owein is a layman, not a monk or hermit, the more usual recipients of medieval otherworld visions. He is moreover a knight and his adventure starts from a real place. His story is presented not as spiritual vision but as physical otherworld journey, a motif which of course forms one of the most ancient and richest strands in all narrative. The underworld descent is the ultimate quest; as Mircea Eliade says, '*The descensus ad inferos* constitutes the initiatory ordeal *par excellence*.'[25] For medieval pilgrims,

---

[25] See *The Quest: History and Meaning in Religion* (Chicago and London, 1969), p. 123. On the relationship of St Patrick's Purgatory to the 'descent' motif, see Easting, 'An Edition of *Owayne Miles*', pp. clxxiv–cxciv.

entering the Purgatory was a personal re-enactment of Christ's harrowing of hell.

Accordingly *OM*1 lays much stress on the marvellous aspects of St Patrick's founding the Purgatory and of Owein's undertaking and journey. At the same time the poem seeks to make the marvellous real. This is the key to the appeal of the whole St Patrick's Purgatory cult, that the otherworld is made accessible to everyone, or at least to anyone faithful and daring enough to attempt it. Owein certainly is. For an English audience he is made a Northumbrian, and he is a great sinner and fighter: *Wel michel he coupe of batayle* (30:4) — a no-nonsense translation of the more refined *Mult ert de grant chivalerie* (F241). Though the plot encourages the frissons of romance, it is as if the very act of translating a romance vocabulary into Middle English tends to shift the poem towards realism.

The otherworld is most definitely concrete. A representative passage of the narrative depicts the punishment of the usurers in one of the boiling pits in the great hall of torment (101–104):

101   Ich man after his misgilt
       In þat pein was ypilt,
       To haue þat strong hete;
       And sum bere bagges about her swere
       Of pens gloweand al of fer,
       And swiche mete þer þai ete:

102   Þat were gauelers in her liif.
       Be war þerbi, boþe man and wiif,
       Swiche sinne þat 3e lete.
       And mani soules þer 3ede vpri3tes,
       Wiþ fals misours and fals wi3tes,
       Þat fendes opon sete.

103   Þe fendes to þe kni3t sede,

"Þou most baþi in þis lede
Ar þan þou hennes go;
For þine okering and for þi sinne
A parti þou most be wasche herinne,
O cours or to."

104   Owain drad þat turment,
And cleped to God omnipotent,
And his moder Marie.
Yborn he was out of þe halle,
Fram þe paines and þe fendes alle,
Þo he so loude gan crie.

Here the first three lines and their rhymes are indebted to the description of the pit in *Vision of St Paul* (17:1–3), the matching of the degree of punishment to the sin being prompted by AN *Checun home sulunc sa fesance/ Peine i aveit u aliance* (F895–96). This demonstrates neatly the way in which the *OM*1 translator used both AN and the *Vision of St Paul*; he must have had both poems before him as he worked. *T* and F do not list the sins punished and he evidently used the *Vision of St Paul* as a model by which to rectify what he felt to be a deficiency in the story's moral force. 101:4–102:1 are not found in *T* or F either, but draw on widespread iconography and tales of the punishment of usury, in which the sinner is usually fed with his burning coins or molten gold; the neck pouch is familiar from the famous wall painting at Chaldon in Surrey, for instance. The remainder of 102 is also new in *OM*1, the warning to the audience (102:2) being voiced in the same terms earlier in the poem (81:5). The punishment of these sinners is precisely visualized as they lie on their backs (*vpriȝtes*) on the molten metal with fiends sitting on them. The fiends' direct speech (103) is an elaboration of three lines of indirect speech in AN, and the mention of *okering* is prompted again by the *Vision of St Paul* (15:1). The reference to Owein's bathing and washing (103) is typical of the fiends' ironic trickery throughout. In 104 *OM*1 substitutes the cry to God omnipotent and his mother Mary for the invocation to Christ in F; elsewhere *OM*1 follows F by including prayers to Mary; she is not mentioned at all in *T*. The last three lines in the passage are again a narrative addition.

This brief section, taken at random from the account of purgatory, shows many of the translator's concerns: didactic clarity and moral exhortation, visual specificity and dramatic liveliness.

When Owein has crossed what the fiends call *þe brigge of paradis* (117:5), we find that the translator's amplification is at its greatest. Of the three Middle English versions, *OM*1 devotes the largest proportion of its length to the treatment of the Earthly Paradise,[26] and no other text of 'St Patrick's Purgatory' is as elaborate. This bespeaks a refreshing

[26] The following percentages are approximate.

		Introduction	Purgatory	E. Paradise	Ending
pa		Ld1–94	95–455	456–648	649–73
		14%	53%	24%	3%
*OM*1		1–43 (+5)	43–127	128–88	189–98
stanzas		23%	42%	30%	5%
*OM*2	C	1–202	203–460	461–656	657–84
		29%	37%	28%	4%
	Y	1–195	196–507	508–661	662–85
		28%	45%	22%	3%

The C copy of *OM*2 omits a 100-line section of purgatory found in Y, so its account of the Earthly Paradise forms a disproportionately greater percentage, but it is the proportions in the versions rather than in the surviving copies that I am concerned with here.

difference in sensibility in *OM*1. The additions include, for instance, an eleven-stanza section (141:4–152) detailing the dance of the souls accompanied by angels' music, and the names of flowers and the four rivers of paradise. The romance appeal is prominent also in the richness of the gates of paradise adorned with precious stones:

132   In tabernacles þai wer ywrou3t,
       Richer mi3t it be nou3t,
       Wiþ pilers gent and smal,
       Arches ybent wiþ charbukelston,
       Knottes of rede gold þeropon,
       And pinacles of cristal.

As with the musical terminology used to describe the elaborate birdsong (145), the vocabulary here is both technically specific and up-to-date.[27]

*OM*1 may well have been produced in the Auchinleck 'bookshop'. In the manuscript it is placed appropriately after the legends of *Seynt Mergrete* and *Seynt Katerine* and before *Þe desputisoun bitven þe bodi & þe soule* and *The Harrowing of Hell*. By its combination of saintly and knightly prowess, and the vigour of its presentation of the marvels of otherworld adventure, *OM*1 is well suited for its inclusion in the Auchinleck collection of romances and religious tales. Moreover, as the brief excerpts here may suggest, Gerould was not far wrong when he said that *OM*1 was 'made by a poet of real imaginative attainment'.[28]

---

[27] See Easting, 'Some Antedatings and Early Usages from the Auchinleck *Owayne Miles*', in *Sentences for Alan Ward*, ed. D.M. Reeks (Southampton, 1988), pp. 167–74. Cf. Loomis (see note 23 above), pp. 626–27 on the up-to-date newness of the Auchinleck contents and the stress on newness in romance.

[28] G.H. Gerould, *Saints' Legends* (Boston and New York, 1916), p. 218.

III. Couplet version — *OM2*

Maybe a century later than *OM*1, and seemingly working directly from *T*, another translator produced a more workaday version in octosyllabic couplets. In its original form it was probably less than two-thirds the length of *OM*1. The two surviving copies are both incomplete, but in different ways. Cotton (C) omits a one-hundred-line section from the depiction of purgatory but otherwise preserves a reasonably good text. The omission is very likely a conscious decision on the part of the copyist, who also omits the description of Lucifer from the *Vision of Tundale*, which follows *OM*2 in the manuscript. It has been plausibly suggested that the eschatological pieces in this section of the manuscript have been pruned for a particular reader(-ship) or client.[29] In contrast, Yale (Y) preserves a scrappier text with a large number of smaller omissions: couplets, small groups of couplets, and single lines are missing and the nature of the numerous verbal changes suggests this copy or one of its antecedents was written down from memory.

Whereas in the Cotton manuscript *OM*2 is followed by *Tundale*, both edifying and exciting otherworld adventure stories, in the Brome commonplace book (Y) *OM*2 is followed by a saint's life (St Margaret), and it is worth noting that over a quarter of *OM*2 deals with St Patrick and the Purgatory revealed to him; as the figures in column 1 of note 26 show, this is the largest proportion in the three Middle English translations, more than twice the allotment given to St Patrick in the original "Z" version of *pa*, albeit that text is part of a Legendary. Like A, C also contains a large number of romances and a smaller body of religious tales, amongst which

---

[29] See Rodney Mearns, *The Vision of Tundale* (Heidelberg, 1985), pp. 46–47.

*OM*2 may be counted. In both C and Y, *OM*2 fittingly follows the interest in the Last Things discussed in the *Fifteen Signs before Doomsday*.

Unlike *pa*, *OM*2 is based on a *ß T* text, as one example here may serve to show: compare

> *pa*   Ake þet weder nas nouȝt cler, : bote ase it were *neiȝ*
>   *eue* (Ld103)

and

> α   Lux ibi non habebatur nisi qualis hic *uespertinis horis*
>   in hieme habetur (W48:15–17)

with

> *OM*2   Such was hys lyȝth whan hyt was beste,
>   As in þe wynter *when þe sonne goth to reste*
>   (C213–14)[30]

and

> *ß*   Lux autem ibi non apparuit nisi qualis
>   hic in hyeme solet apparere *post solis occasum.*

*OM*2 opens with a new 28-line section locating St Patrick in a sequence of wise men via whom God continually reveals *the ryghte way to heuen-blysse* (C4): the prophets, Christ, the apostles, bishops, preachers, and in Ireland St Patrick, preaching of heaven, hell and purgatory. This interest in the chronology of God's revelation is matched towards the end of *OM*2 by the addition to the bishops' explanatory speech in the Earthly Paradise, of details about Adam (Eve is also included in C though she is not mentioned in *T*): his life is computed at 915 years, and his stay *yn helle wyth Lucyfere* at 4,604

---

[30] As with A, I cite C and Y from my own edition. For previous printed texts, see Kölbing, *Englische Studien*, 1 (1877), 113–21 (C), and Lucy Toulmin Smith, *A Common-place Book of the Fifteenth Century* (London and Norwich, 1886), pp. 82–106 (Y).

years (C581–84) — the same figure as is used in, for example, the *Ludus Coventriae.*

But it is less history than *aventure* (C622) that interests the author of *OM*2, albeit this aspect of the story is not as heightened as in *OM*1. Christ tells St Patrick that whosoever completes the pilgrimage, be he *sqwyer or knave* (C79), will be able to tell of *Mony a mervayle*, and this is certainly the case. Even before Owein enters the Purgatory the bishop of the diocese has told him that *all hys lyf he moste faste* (C132), and *ryche relykes* (C190) accompany Owein's procession to the entrance (in Y183 Owein even carries them himself). But again, the emphasis on the marvellous is not so prominent in *OM*2 as in *OM*1. *OM*2 stresses the trials and triumph of a fearful yet repentant sinner. Owein gropes his way in a dark (C208) and barren world (C218); he discovers that the fields of purgatory are not like the battlefields on which he has previously borne his shield (C365–66); and his adversaries, as in *OM*1, are fiendishly ironic. Indeed, all three versions increase the participation and visualization of the demons. As in *pa*, the drama of Owein's quest is enhanced by the space given to direct speech, either changed from indirect speech and expanded or newly introduced in translation: *OM*2 has the highest proportion of direct speech in the three versions, some 10% more than in *OM*1.[31]

* * *

Like the *Vision of Tundale*, Owein's story had a powerful attraction for a lay audience because the protagonist is not a

---

[31] Percentage of direct speech in each version: *pa* 27.9%, *OM*1 20%, *OM*2 — C 30.6%, Y 27.4%, reconstruction 29.7%.

cleric but a knight.[32] The English translations all capitalise on Owein's chivalry; in both speeches and narrative *OM2* repeatedly reminds the audience that the hero is 'Sir Owein'.[33]

Vision literature, the cult of St Patrick's Purgatory, and the Latin and vernacular transmission of Owein's story in particular, offer valuable material for studying the relationships between learned and 'popular' modes of thought, feeling and outlook. Owein's own account was probably first influenced by the Saints' Island community of Augustinian canons who introduced him into St Patrick's Purgatory.[34] According to *T*, Owein subsequently recounted his *aventure* to Gilbert on

---

[32] Compare Eileen Gardiner on the *Visio Tnugdali* and the Middle English *Vision of Tundale*, which follows *OM2* in C: 'Originally written in prose for monastic reading and found in manuscripts with theological works, it eventually, after discernible steps in its progression, was translated into vernacular poetry, found in manuscripts with romances, and transformed to appeal to the more secular tastes of a pious audience.' See résumé of a paper entitled 'The *Visio Tundalis*: The Altered Perception of a Literary Work as seen through Its Manuscript Tradition', presented to The Seventh Saint Louis Conference on Manuscript Studies, reported in *Manuscripta*, 25 (1981), 3–13 (p. 6).

[33] Fourteen times in C, sixteen in Y; cf. twice only in *OM1*. In *pa* his name is given only when he is first introduced (Ld40, Co90, 91), and he is usually referred to as *þis (seli* or *guode) kniȝt*. Yolande de Pontfarcy, 'Le *Tractatus de Purgatorio Sancti Patricii* de H. de Saltrey: sa date et ses sources', *Peritia*, 3 (1984), 460–80, has proposed the possibility that the name Owein was given by Gilbert of Basingwerk to 'l'aventureux pèlerin irlandais' in homage to the memory of the Welsh prince Owein Gwynedd. (See also her introduction to *Saint Patrick's Purgatory* (1985), p. 16.) This can be neither proved nor disproved, but seems to me superfluous. I prefer Dr Pontfarcy's alternative: 'A moins que ce nom n'ait été la transcription galloise d'un nom irlandais qui phonétiquement lui ressemblait' (p. 471).

[34] There are no compelling reasons for doubting the historicity of Owein; see Easting, 'Owein at St Patrick's Purgatory', *Medium Ævum*, 55 (1986), 159–75.

many occasions. Owein was bilingual, presumably in Irish and French (or Irish and English or even Latin?), and he served as Gilbert's interpreter in Ireland. He was also external provider in the Cistercian monastery Gilbert founded, most likely Baltinglas, and thus lived in close contact with the monastic community. Here again there was the possibility of influence by the learned, monastic tradition of vision literature. Gilbert subsequently retold the tale many times in England, and defended Owein's veracity against sceptics. Thereafter Henry of Sawtry recounted the story orally to the monks at his mother house, Wardon in Bedfordshire, and only subsequently wrote it down at the request of abbot Hugh of Wardon.[35] At this point Owein's story was doubtless embellished, ordered, and bolstered by references to and extracts from the works of Augustine, Bede, Gregory the Great, Hugh of St Victor, Jean of Fécamp, Anselm and others. *T* thus grew out of a long process of oral narration both secular and clerical, but was compiled in a Cistercian milieu for monastic consumption in a manner designed to prompt meditation on sin and the

---

[35] See Easting, 'The Date and Dedication of the *Tractatus de Purgatorio Sancti Patricii*', *Speculum*, 53 (1978), 778–83. H.E. Shields, 'An Old French Book of Legends and its Apocalyptic Background' (unpublished Ph.D. dissertation, Trinity College, Dublin, 1967), has raised the interesting speculation that Henry of Sawtry may have been supplied by Gilbert with a written text of the main narrative composed by himself or even another. There seems, however, no adequate justification in stylistic terms for distinguishing the prologue and narrative of *T* as the work of separate authors. Shields also says that Henry 'may have heard' the story 'told without recording it from memory' (p. 345), but this is to countermand the last sentence of the prologue, *Quam quidem narrationem, si bene memini ita exorsus est* (W14:150–52). I see no grounds for regarding this as spurious, or for saying that Henry 'may have mentioned hearing it simply in order to provide another authenticating fact'. A written text, if he had had one, would surely have been regarded as lending much greater authority.

rewards of the monastic life.[36] Though learned, it transmits attitudes to the otherworld which are decidedly 'popular' when compared to the pronouncements of scholastic theologians and Church councils.[37] Indeed, Bakhtin spoke of *T* as part of popular culture in opposition to 'official' culture, but the text itself really exhibits an amalgamation of these divergent tendencies.[38] Historians are now alert to the interrelationships rather than the opposition between *lered and lewed*. Jacques Le Goff, writing on otherworld vision literature, has well said:

> Il ne faut pas oublier dans cette histoire complexe d'acculturation à l'époque médiévale que la réalité culturelle a été rarement celle d'une opposition tranchée entre le populaire et le savant, l'oral et l'écrit (ce qui n'est en outre pas la même chose), mais celle d'interaction entre des acteurs et des actes culturels plus ou moins savants ou plus ou moins populaires.[39]

The Middle English versions of 'St Patrick's Purgatory' all variously modify the story in the interests of lay audiences.

[36] On the relationship between oral and written elements in the transmission of the visions of Owein, Tnugdal and Gottschalk, see also Hedwig Röckelein, *Otloh, Gottschalk, Tnugdal: Individuelle und kollektive Visionsmuster des Hochmittelalters* (Europäische Hochschulschriften, III, 319, Frankfurt, 1987), pp. 121–71.

[37] See Easting, 'Purgatory and the Earthly Paradise'.

[38] Mikhail Bakhtin, *Rabelais and His World*, translated by Helene Iswolsky (Cambridge, Mass., 1968), chapter 6, esp. pp. 386–96.

[39] From the essay 'Aspects savants et populaires des voyages dans l'au-delà au Moyen Age', in *L'imaginaire médiéval* (Paris, 1985), p. 114. For the most recent discussion on the relationship between learned and popular opinion as evidenced by vision literature, see Aron Gurevich, *Medieval Popular Culture: Problems of Belief and Perception*, Cambridge Studies in Oral and Literate Culture 14 (Cambridge and Paris, 1988), pp. 104–52.

pa, translated as part of a Legendary, retains and emphasises *T*'s stress on the need for penance, while simplifying and clarifying the didactic, and heightening the dramatic.

*OM*1 and *OM*2, as the manuscripts containing them suggest, were designed more explicitly for the reader of romances.

*OM*1 strengthens the case for penance by categorising sins and their punishments and by direct warnings to the audience, but offsets moral exhortation by the appeal of the tangibly exotic and sensuously marvellous delights of paradise.

*OM*2 is more concerned to depict the depravity, penitence and bravery of Owein, *a dou3ty man and bolde* (C119), who ends his days as *a mon of good deuocyoun* (C676). Here the rewards of the aristocratic laity are highlighted by the inclusion of emperors, dukes, earls and barons, alongside friars and hermits in the company of the purged in the Earthly Paradise.

All three Middle English versions, by their excisions and additions, allow us to trace some of the tendencies in late medieval translation from Latin to the vernacular, from the monastic to the secular, from the potentially meditative to the more purely narrative, from an interest in theoretical eschatology to the immediate romance and drama of personal heroism. (It is not surprising that Owein was later destined for the stage.[40]) And this translation of attitude and manner in the vernacular texts was made the more readily precisely because Owein was a knight, and St Patrick's Purgatory was

---

[40] In the guise of Ludovico Enio, hero of Juan Perez de Montalban's prose *Vida y Purgatorio de San Patricio* [1627], edited by M. G. Profeti (Pisa, 1972), Owein becomes the subject of later plays in Spanish (by ?Lope de Vega and Calderon) and Breton (see G. Dottin, *Louis Eunius ou Le Purgatoire de Saint Patrice* in *La Bretagne et les pays celtiques*, vol. 2 (Paris, 1911)).

a real location, where it was believed any sufficiently pious and penitent pilgrim might be 'translated' into the otherworld.

Brigittine Tracts of Spiritual Guidance in Fifteenth-Century England: a Study in Translation

DOMENICO PEZZINI

I

IN A RECENT study on 'The English Cult of St Bridget of Sweden' F. R. Johnston comes to the conclusion that this 'widespread' cult was 'mainly a literary one based on her writings'.[1] Probably Bridget herself would have welcomed this development, given the remarkable editorial care and firm theological control with which the *Liber Revelationum Celestium* was produced. We cannot wonder at the success of a book which Bishop Alphonse of Pecha, an enthusiastic disciple of the Saint and the final organizer of her writings, presented as a 'Librum Gloriosum, scriptum in corde predicte Domine digito Dei vivi'.[2] The wide reception of the *Liber*

---

[1] F. R. Johnston, 'The English Cult of St Bridget of Sweden', *Analecta Bollandiana*, tome 103 (1985), pp. 75–93 (p. 93).

[2] In his *Epistola Solitarii ad Reges*. Latin quotations of the work are taken from *Revelationes Sancte Birgitte*, imp. B. Gothan (Lübeck, 1492), except for Book VII for which I use the modern critical edition by B.

shows that this conviction came to be shared by a growing number of people.

When the *Revelations* arrived in England, probably no earlier than the 1380s, they aroused the interest of Oxford theologians such as the Carmelite Richard Lavynham and the Dominican Thomas Stubbes, but in the course of the fifteenth century they became favourite reading for a steadily increasing audience, religious as well as secular, looking for books of meditation and spiritual instruction. Margery Kempe was by no means alone in choosing 'Seynt Brydys boke' to foster her spiritual life. Cecily of York, mother of Edward IV and Richard III, had the book read to her during dinner time,[3] and wills from the end of the century show that the *Revelations* were among the belongings of other pious lay women.[4]

To a modern eye the popularity of the *Liber* appears as surprising as the work itself seems disappointing. It is not a work with a clear structure: it has no centre, it seems to sprawl everywhere, and is best described as a huge storehouse where spiritual food can be picked up according to one's own personal needs. Despite considerable attempts by the first editors to organize the collection, the *Revelations* retain, in

Bergh, *Den Heliga Birgittas Bok VII* (Uppsala, 1967). On Alphonse of Pecha see further E. Colledge, '*Epistola Solitarii ad Reges*: Alphonse of Pecha as Organizer of Birgittine and Urbanist Propaganda', *Mediaeval Studies*, 18 (1956), 19–49.

[3] See W. A. Pantin, *The English Church in the Fourteenth Century* (Cambridge, 1955), p. 254.

[4] See F. R. Johnston, p. 86. The author of a treatise on the Passion which opens the compilation of spiritual tracts in ms. BL Arundel 286, where a translation of *Rev.* VII,5 appears as the second item, says that he was asked to write his treatise by 'a worschipful lady hauynge a symple spirit ful of heuenly desires', so that she 'in hir honourable age of elde my3t haue som comfort in contemplacion of þat blessed and profitable passion þat is þe welle of lyf' (f. 1r).

order and content, the occasional character of their delivery over thirty years of Bridget's life, and the book offers side by side meditations on the life of Christ and the Virgin, prophecies mixed with pastoral advice, miniature treatises of spiritual guidance, and even letters and debates in the form of questions and answers. Still, if the overall appearance is discouragingly uneven, the smaller units offer a solid sense of order. This is particularly evident in those chapters which contain teaching on the spiritual life: here the subjects are nicely developed around a numerical organizing principle, with the theme divided and subdivided into different parts, and the final result is a tightly structured network of ideas. This was extremely useful, especially in the case of spiritual instructions orally delivered and needing to be memorized.

The wide circulation of the *Revelations* is proved by a remarkable number of English versions different in kind and quality. This is clear evidence of the varied and continuous interest in the book itself. And, since they are independent of one another, they present us with a rare opportunity of studying different techniques of translation applied to the same Latin text. This will be particularly rewarding in the case of the Brigittine writings, since little has been edited so far, and even less study has been done on them.

The leading authority in this field was, until quite recently, W. P. Cumming, who published *The Revelations of Saint Birgitta* in 1929. This is the edition of the Garrett manuscript, and in his introduction Cumming gives what still remains the most detailed description of seven manuscripts which form the corpus of Brigittine translations in fifteenth century England. This corpus may be organized in three groups:

1. Translation of the full text: BL Cotton Julius F.II and Cotton Claudius B.I;
2. Partial translations (BL Harley 4800: Book IV and beginning of Book V), or selections in which a few

chapters, or parts of chapters, are   translated and
reorganized in new compilations (Garrett, Oxford
Bodleian Rawlinson C.41, and Lambeth Palace
Library 432);
3.   Single chapters existing as independent tracts, like
those in BL Arundel 197 (VI,65 and II,16).

J. P. Jolliffe drew the attention of the scholars to these last
when he published his *Check-List of Middle English Prose
Writings of Spiritual Guidance* in 1974;[5] F. R. Johnston
ignores them. Only Roger Ellis, to whom we owe the best and
most informative study to appear so far on the circulation of
Brigittine writings in England, mentions them and comments
briefly about the process of adaptation in the translation of
VII,5.[6] I edited this chapter in 1986 from the two manuscripts
in which it is extant,[7] and was favourably impressed by the
originality and the high quality of the translation. I have
formed the same impression of the other two chapters, II,16

[5] J. P. Jolliffe, *A Check-List of Middle English Prose Writings of
Spiritual Guidance* (Toronto, 1974). From this *List* we learn that the
translation of VI,65 appears in three other manuscripts (Oxford Bodley 423,
C.U.L. Ii.6.40, and Magdalene Coll., Cambridge, Pepys 2125); the same is
true of II,16 (BL Additional 37790, Oxford Bodley 131, and Taunton
Horae); and finally there is also a translation of VII,5 extant in two
manuscripts (BL Arundel 286 and Harley 6615). For full reference to these
manuscripts see the *Check-List*, respectively: Item I.13 for II,16; Item H.13
and O.23 for VI,65; Item D.10 for VII,5. Jolliffe prints VII,65 instead of
VI,65, and VII,7 instead of VII,5.

[6] R. Ellis, '*Flores ad fabricandam ... coronam*: an investigation into the
uses of the Revelations of St. Bridget of Sweden in fifteenth-century
England', *Medium Aevum*, 51 (1982), 163–86 (note 31, and pp. 175–76).

[7] D. Pezzini, '*How resoun schal be keper of þe soule*: una traduzione del
Quattrocento inglese dalle *Rivelazioni* (VII,5) di S. Brigida di Svezia',
Aevum, 60 (1986), 253–81.

and VI,65, which I also intend to edit.[8] What emerges from the detailed study of these translations in the following pages of this paper obliges us to revise the rather harsh opinion expressed by Cumming about the Brigittine translations:

> The Garrett MS. has passages of excellent prose and gives evidence of care in the selection of the revelations; the other manuscripts vary from businesslike translations to mere rough jottings which show the general content of the work... The translators of most of the manuscripts, when they follow the Latin at all, hold as nearly as possible to the Latin order in the sentence, and frequently use the Latin word in translation.[9]

None of these statements is applicable to the texts of the third group, which for practical reasons I shall call 'independent tracts'. As for the 'passages of excellent prose' in the Garrett manuscript, this hardly seems adequate. Comparison with the Bodley translation of VI,65 does not work in Garrett's favour. Cumming is more convincing, in fact, when he writes that 'The translation (in the Garrett MS.) follows the Latin closely. Occasional passages which are awkward and unidiomatic are so because of the strict adherence to the Latin order. The sentences are sometimes long and involved'.[10] Literalness seems to be the most regular feature of these Brigittine translations. Literal is Garrett, and so is Harley 4800, which shares also with the two Cotton manuscripts 'a tendency ... to

---

[8] Since the presentation of this paper I have also edited the versions of II,16 from the four manuscritps in which they are extant, adding the translation of the whole chapter from BL Cotton Julius F.II.: see D. Pezzini, 'The Twelf Poyntes: versioni di un trattato brigidino (*Rev.* II,16) nel Quattrocento inglese', *Aevum*, 62 (1988), 286–301.

[9] *The Revelations of Saint Birgitta*, edited from the Garrett MS. by W.P. Cumming, EETS OS 178 (London, 1929), p. xx.

[10] Cumming, p. xxii.

abbreviate by the excision of words and phrases', a method more pronounced in Claudius B.I. Cumming's remarks fail to consider Arundel 197 and Lambeth 432 as translations.

Cumming's opinions went into S. K. Workman's much quoted and highly influential book, *Fifteenth-Century Translation as an Influence on English Prose*. Workman analyzes some passages in Lambeth 432 and in Garrett, where two scribes were at work, and concludes:

> All three translators have worked in a similar way. They did not try to 'augment'; and they rephrased only enough to Anglicize the language. The inevitable consequence was that the structural characteristics of their English prose, down to considerable detail, were derived from the foreign original.[11]

Workman's words, though true as far as they go, do not apply to the texts I am going to analyze, which adopt a technique of translation based on a highly original rephrasing and restructuring of the Latin. At the end of his general survey Workman says that the prevailing method in the fifteenth century was 'to keep as close as the syntax and grammar of English permitted ... to the sentence structure of the composition under translation', but adds that 'there were ... several interesting exceptions'.[12] The 'independent tracts' are just such interesting exceptions in the panorama of Brigittine writings in English.

[11] S. K. Workman, *Fifteenth Century Translation as an Influence on English Prose* (Princeton, 1940). I have just edited the Brigittine portion of MS Lambeth 432 with an analysis of the translational style, particularly of the conflation techniques, here used. The paper will shortly appear in the *Saint Bridget's Festschrift*, edited by J. Hogg and V. Lagorio, under the title '*The meditacioun of oure lordis passyon* and other Bridgettine texts in MS Lambeth 432'.

[12] Workman, p. 84.

II

Rev. VI,65 is a treatise on contemplative and active life likened to Mary and Martha. It was probably the most popular of these independent tracts, since it is now extant in four manuscripts as such; this same chapter was chosen by the compiler of the Garrett manuscript, and is present, of course, in the full text translation of Cotton Julius F.II: surprisingly it does not appear in the other full text translation in Cotton Claudius B.I. The reason for this success is probably due to the subject itself and to its traditional link with the two sisters of Lazarus.[13] To this we should add the skill and vivacity with which the *Revelations* develop the images of hospitality as metaphors of different important attitudes in the spiritual life: the result is a compendium where nothing essential is lacking. The three versions are sufficiently different to enable us to compare their techniques of translation: one (Julius Ms., hereafter J) is a sort of skilful summary, literal but with many omissions; another (Garrett Ms., hereafter G) is also literal and strictly faithful to the Latin; the third, the independent tract, is also faithful, with a few omissions and additions mostly due to the adaptation to a new audience, but surpasses the others in its clever use of rhetorical devices. If we also note that one of the four manuscripts, Arundel 197, has been heavily corrected by a later hand, we may say that we have also a fourth 'revised' version of this chapter, one worth an analysis of its own. I shall take my examples from the Bodley 423 version of the tract and compare them with the other

---

[13] So, for example, in the *Epistle on Mixed Life*, 'a deuout boke compyled by mayster Walter Hylton to a deuout man in temporal estate', where the two lives are linked with Mary and Martha, in the second chapter: 'þat þe lyf of Marie and Martha menged to-gedere is acordyng to hem þat are in hiȝ degre' (C. Horstmann, *Yorkshire Writers* (London, 1895), I, pp. 264–92).

translations to show the difference in technique and response to the Latin text.[14] The quality and originality of the former can be shown not only in wording, but above all in the large use of parallelism and inversion, and in the restructuring of the periods in harmonic units: these figures, although ultimately derived from Latin, are not found at the corresponding points of the Latin text of the *Revelations*.

The most striking feature of the Bodley translation is probably the constant love for musical parallelism which the author often obtains by slightly modifying the Latin: the idea remains the same, the addition or omission of a word in English creates a different and more visible balance. For example we have cases where an adjective is added or repeated:

> Non debet gaudere de mundi honore et eius prosperitate
> He... shal not ioye of no worldly worship ne bodily prosperite
> (cf G: not to Ioye of the wyrship of the werlde ne of the prosperyte þer-of).

Repetition can be used to form a perfect antithetical *isocolon*:

> Maria non debet esse ociosa sicut nec Martha
> As Martha was euere besy / so shal Mary neuer be ydel
> (G: Marie oweth not to be idelle no more then Martha)

> Quando opera bona reputantur multa, et mala sunt in obliuione
> Whan he holdith moche by his good werkes / and foryetith lightly alle his euel dedes.

Here the sequence verb-adverb-adjective-noun is exactly repeated so that the two clauses maintain the same rhythm and

---

[14] The translation of VI,65 in Bodley is on ff. 150r–156v; Cotton Julius F.II, ff. 216r–217v; Garrett MS., ff. 14r–21r (text printed in Cumming, pp. 25–36). Fuller discussion of the Bodley translation is reserved for the projected critical edition.

cadence, and the result is quite different from Garrett's: 'when goode dedes ar counted money, and evyll few and foryett'.

A similar technique can be found in another case, where a noun is added to keep the balance between two clauses derived from the resolution of a hypotactic order:

> ut tolerando opprobria temporalia fugiam sempiterna
> þat I mowe haue grace to suffre temporal blame /
> þe raþer to escape euerlastyng peyne
> (G: that by suffraunce of temporall repreues I may escape euerlastyng).

In other cases the parallelism is obtained at the expense of the Latin by ruling out one or more words to have a better balanced series of clauses; greater precision and clarity results:

> tunc excitat eum ad facilitatem magne ire, aut ad dissolucionem vane leticie, aut ad verba dissoluta et iocosa
> he wil þan lightly excite him to be wrothe / or elles to veyn glory / or elles to dissolute wordes.

I am not contending that the English text is here superior to the Latin: some words giving a more refined articulation to the sentence in the original have disappeared, like 'magne', 'dissolucionem', and 'iocosa', and one might ask whether 'veyn glory' is the exact correspondent of 'vane leticie'. The English translator has worked very freely on his text: the noun 'facilitatem' becomes the adverb 'lightly', 'ire' is turned into 'to be wrothe', 'dissolucionem' is eliminated as a quality repeated, and faithfully translated, in the following 'dissoluta'; as a result, the stress falls rightly on the two nouns at the end of each clause, 'glory' and 'wordes', with their negative qualifications. What is lost by the excision is outweighed by the clarity and precision that results.

Other examples confirm the impression that our translator is fond of figures of parallelism. In a three-sentence period, where the Latin has only two verbs, the English text restores the balance by the addition of a third one:

> cohibere linguam ..., et manum ..., et animum debet continere
> ... to wiþholde þe tonge .../ and wiþdrawe his hondes .../ and
> refreyne his hert ..
> (G: kepe his tonge ... and his honde ... and hys herte).

The expansion can be considerable, as in the case of a
metaphor developed into a perfectly balanced comparison:

> et sicut mater diligebat universos
> and as a good moder loueth alle hir children / so loueth she
> alle men and wymmen
> (G: and loved all as a moder).

In some cases, to be sure, the parallelism may seem
exaggerated and even pedantic, as in a connecting passage
between the two parts of the chapter:

> Ideo dicam tibi nunc quomodo Martha institui debet. Ipsa
> quippe debet habere sicut et Maria eciam quinque bona.
> I saide before that V thinges be nedful to eche man and
> woman that wil folewe Mary. And in the same manere V
> thinges be nedful to eche man and woman that wil folewe
> Martha.

This is the fullest possible realisation of the implications of
the Latin 'sicut'. The first sentence has almost no
correspondence in the Latin, but this distinctive resolution is
much favoured in the Bodley tract and in the following text,
the translation of VII,5, and is obviously a useful mnemonic
to the reader and listener alike.[15]

   A well-known figure of repetition is the doublet, on
which much has already been said. Our translator has, not

---

[15] The manuscript Arundel 286, which contains the translation of VII,5
examined here, appears to have been used for public reading: from f. 82 to
f. 99 there are catch-words written by a later hand on every recto folio, a
device absolutely unnecessary for the binder, but very useful for the reader.

surprisingly, a good many examples of this very widespread practice, like 'vocat' rendered by 'clepith him and drawith him', or more complex forms like 'qui conturbat cor eius' translated as 'they whiche trouble his hert, and brynge hym out of rest'. At times the doubling of an adjective is further elaborated on by the use of *hyperbaton*, a figure which occurs when a noun is put between two adjectives:

omnis infirmus	eche febil man or sike
eos letificare verbis bonis	to say gode wordes and holy to comforte
damnabile est	a foule thing it is and a dampnable

But the trend is not always one way:

immo laudabilis et beneplacens deo	but muche to goddis plesynge
ab omni inhonesta et illicita operacione	from dedes þat ben vnleful

And this is a further indication of the freedom of our translator.

The other figure often used in this translation is inversion in its various forms. Frequently a sentence begins with an adverb or an adjective: 'strongly he must arise', 'bisely he must take hede', etc. Perhaps the best example of this procedure, where we have parallelism and inversion combined to a fine effect, is:

recurrat statim ad mentem suam cogitando quomodo ...
spedful it is to haue in mynde / and ofte theron thenke / ho
(G: renne he then anon to hys mynde, thinkyng how ...)

The front-shifting of an infinitive or a participle is also frequent (arise she most, born he was of a mayde, blesse he shal his enemys), and so is the inversion object/verb (clothes he must haue, greuous gestes he resceiueth, his owne wille

vtterly to forsake), or even the combination of two inversions
(litel hede wil I tak).[16]

   A more complex case, where the object is inserted
between the auxiliary and the infinitive, and the verb between
its two objects (*hyperbaton*) can be seen in:

> quibus proximo et sibi ipsi prodesse posset
> by þe whiche he might himself profite, and oþer of his
> neighbours

Nothing of the kind is found in Garrett.[17]

   Our text has very few examples of chiasmus. The best
instance is probably:

> cuius bonitate anima creata est, et sanguine benedicto
> redempta
> by whos godenes he is made, and bought wiþ his blode

The elimination of 'benedicto' creates a better balance in the
English clauses and results in a distich with the stresses on the
essential words: godenes-made / bought-blode. Another

---

[16] These patterns of inversion, and the more complex splitting of
auxiliary and infinitive by dependent object, are also found, for example, in
Chaucer's *Melibee* and Usk's *Testament of Love*: see R. Ellis, *Patterns of
Religious Narrative in the Canterbury Tales* (London, 1986), pp. 109–11.
They reveal, as in the more famous writers, a translator consciously aiming
at a 'high style', a feature we do not find in the other Brigittine translations,
except, of course, the versions of VII,5 and II,16 here examined.

[17] We may notice in the last case given that the sequence 'proximo/sibi'
of the Latin has simply been inverted in the translation. This is not a single
case, but would seem rather a habit of our translator, a sort of stylistic tic.
I have collected eight other instances, for a total of nine, of this curious
procedure: dicunt et cogitant : thenke or say; tacuit/locutus est : preched and
taughte/helde his pees; leuioribus verbis/seuerioribus : harde wordes/light;
vincuntur/tolerantur : suffre/ouercome; potentibus/parentibus : kinnes-
men/grete or riche; exemplis/verbis : wordes/ensamples; Maria/Martha :
Martha/Mary; honores et prelaciones : prelacies and gret worldly worshipes.
The frequency of this choice might indicate a very distinctive personal style.

example where the chiasmus is combined with *paronomasia*
is this:

> ne (...) oraciones et predicaciones diminuat, seu alia bona ex
> hoc omittat
> wherby his praiers or other gostly workes shul be amenused
> / or ellis þat he leue oþir gode werkes

This independent translation of *Rev.* VI,65, then, is highly
original, especially where the structure of the period is
concerned, and far from literalism on the one hand, and
paraphrase on the other. The author knows very well how to
use other rhetorical devices too. One of these is *prolepsis*; for
example:

> Sic erit e contra de illis qui ambiunt honores et prelaciones
> The contrary mede shal thoo prelates haue, whiche taken
> prelacies and gret worldly worshipes;
> cogitando quomodo ego deus contemptus et despectus
> pacienter tolerabam
> he shal also thenke hou stille he stode, þat good lorde, while
> he was demed

The change of subject in the second example is due to the fact
that, while in the original Christ is imagined as speaking
directly to Bridget, in the translation his words become general
spiritual doctrine addressed to any Christian soul.

This rhetorical ability is seen at its best in the reworking
of longer sentences:

et apponet omnem diligenciam	he shal also besy hym with ful wille
ut opera pietatis	to fulfille alle dedes of mercy
et oraciones deuote augeantur	and gladlye occupye him wiþ deuout praiers
quibus	for where they be vsed
spiritus sanctus delectatur	þe holygost wil bliþely abyde

The three Latin clauses have become five in English, and many modifications occur: 'apponet ... diligenciam' has been translated by two equivalent verbs (besy/occupye), which, together with the elimination of 'augeantur', create a new parallelism; 'omnem' is interpreted as 'with ful wille' and 'gladlye', and the result is again a parallelism absent in the Latin; the sequence verb/adverbial phrase (besy hym with ful wille) is repeated but in inverted order (gladlye occupye); 'augeantur', which in the Latin refers both to 'opera pietatis' and 'oraciones deuote', goes only with the first of these two things, and, rendered by 'fulfille', creates a sort of internal rhyme with 'ful wille'; the relative clause is turned into an explicative one plus a dependent relative clause which introduces the new image of the indwelling of the Holy Ghost, while the Latin main verb, 'delectatur', is turned into the adverb 'bliþely'.

The originality of the translator can also be seen in smaller units, such as the individual words:

sapienter respondere
yeue a wyse aunswer (G: aunswer wysely)
ascendere ad gradus Marie
come to the hye degre of contemplatif lyf (G: ascende up to
                               the degre of Marie)
ex nullis se in cogitacione preferat
he shal not holde hymself moor worthy than other in thoughte ne in dede
(G: that he ne prefer notte ne exalte him-selfe in his owen conceyte).

We must consider now additions to the text of the original, and omissions from it. Some of these, as has already been shown, are used to readjust a sentence. In other cases the result is a modification of the Latin text, where perhaps the translator attempts to make his original more specific:

> castitatem sine vlla delectacione praua
> chastite of body wiþoute al maner shrewde delit of flesshe

A more substantial addition with a clarifying intent appears in:

> sic Maria debet distribuere spiritualia sua
> so must he parte aboute his gostly godes in praieng and in techyng

Again:

> Si Maria non valet predicare
> If it so be þat... he is lette þat he may not, or elles it longith not to his degre (to teche and preche)

Elsewhere amplification produces a stronger emphasis:

> nec consentire viciis, nec in eis delectari
> neither to assente to her false suggestions, ne haue delyte ne likyng in her wicked sterynges

The possessive adjective 'her' (=their) refers to the 'wicked thoughtes' which in the preceding sentence have been compared to mischievous guests who cannot be kept out when they come to the house of the soul, 'as an hostiler suffrith bothe good and badde come in', but must be strongly opposed once they are in; 'viciis' has not been translated because the word had occurred in the preceding sentence, and was translated there.

A particular and noteworthy kind of expansion occurs when the translator repeats what has already been said or adds a short summary as a sort of *aide-mémoire*. So, for example:

> Sic Maria faciat In the same manere he that wil be in charite must haue compassion of al other man

This addition glosses the Latin 'faciat' by resuming the whole content of the preceding paragraph. This feature occurs seven times in all in the tract, and shows a translator clearly conscious of what he is doing, and revealing a purpose and a deliberate choice. There is also a short summary at the end of the two parts of the treatise, and one, already noted, which serves as a link between the two.

This translation, contrary to its usual choices, has two considerable expansions towards the end: one is a tirade against bad prelates, the other is a warning and an invitation to widows 'to take gode hede and folewe Martha in liuyng'.

As part of a long *exemplum* of a ship led to the port where she was bound notwithstanding storms and strong winds, we find a comparison of prelates to helmsmen: the good ones will receive a double reward, the bad a double punishment. While, following the Latin closely, the translator deals quickly with the reward, he describes the punishment at much greater length:

Sic erit contra de illis qui	The contrary mede shal thoo prelates haue,
ambiunt honores et prelaciones:	whiche taken prelacies and gret worldly worshipes noþing for helpe and comfort of oþer mennes soules, but for foule couetise and pompe of þe worlde. Alle suche prelates
erunt quippe participes	shul parte wiþ her peynes,
omnium penarum et peccatorum	and also wiþ her synnes, whos soules they shuld haue kepte,
eorum quos susceperunt regere,	and presheden for mysgouernaunce, or for defaute of teching, and for her owne pride, and oþer wicked vyces,
secundo quod confusio eorum erit sine fine.	þey shul haue by goddis rightwesnesse confusion wiþouten ende.

Such an expansion is unique in the text, but the negative attitude revealed towards authority is confirmed by a consideration of other changes to the original. The invitation to Mary to intercede for her ill treated neighbour 'eciam apud potentes seculi' has not been translated, neither has what follows: 'Si vero Maria talis est quod non exauditur apud principes nec proficit egressus eius de cella ...'. This same dismissive attitude is found again at the beginning of the second long addition, which serves as an introduction to the second part of the treatise, where instruction is being offered on active life:

> Therfor, hou euere it be of soueraynes, and prelates, whiche
> shuld haue contemplatyf lyf and actif, as in outwarde besynes
> of preching and techinge openly, I counceyle netheles wyues
> and widowes, maydens, and other peple to folewe Martha, as
> muche as they may, in wille, and in dede, and namely
> widowes ...

It seems clear that our translator had a feminine audience, probably secular, in mind. Other additions and omissions reinforce this conclusion. For instance, the author has not translated the exhortation to fast reasonably in order to keep strong 'ad puniendos rebelles et ad subijciendos iugo fidei infideles'; he thus appears to have excluded clergy from his readership: the addition concerning the impossibility of preaching already quoted (p. 189 above) follows the same line, since preaching 'longith not to his degre'. Professed religious also are probably not included by our translator, who omits the phrase 'consilia euangelice veritatis', the well-known monastic expression for the religious vows, and leaves only the practice of the commandments; moreover, he translates 'opus dei', probably a reference to the monastic choral office, by 'praiers and deuocioun'.[18] It seems safe to say that a lay audience, if not specifically intended, is certainly allowed for as users of the tract.

Other omissions are not so easy to explain. Our author, for example, seems not to like metaphors: he eliminates the nice image of a fox examining the ground in order to find a good resting place, used to say that, if Mary cannot preach, although she wants to and knows how, she should explore the hearts of the people she meets, and when she finds someone more capable of receiving the word of God, there she should stay and rest, and give her spiritual advice and exhortations. The translator also cuts the long *exemplum* of the ship led astray by storms and contrary winds, and steered to the port to which she was directed by a good mariner faithful to his lord's orders. Even the biblical reference to Paul's flight from Damascus down the city walls has been cut. Other sentences have been omitted for no apparent reason, like 'et de aliis sicut de seipsa curabat. Ideo semper cogitabat caritatem meam et passionem meam'. This last omission is particularly surprising if we consider that in much devotional literature any slight hint at the Passion was regularly emphasized. But even when he omits part of a sentence, our translator is always careful and attentive to make sense of what he keeps.

So far the comparison has been between Bodley and Garrett. A quick look at the Julius manuscript will show that, although this translation is literal with substantial cuttings, it is not insensitive to the demands of style and structure. In the following passage, for example, the clauses are nicely

---

[18] Whereas Garrett renders 'opus dei' by 'the seruyce of god', and Julius 'the werke of god', the translator of Bodley 423 catches more clearly the specific reference of 'opus dei' to prayer. It is thus the more significant that by translating it 'praiers and deuocioun' he does not confine the meaning of the expression to the liturgical office, but includes also the private devotions, which were the daily practice of ordinary people.

constructed and finely organized:

Tercio Maria non debet	Also Mary shuld nat be
esse ociosa sicut nec	ydil no more þan
Martha, sed peracto	Martha, but aftir his
somno suo necessario,	nessessary slepp shuld
surgat et regracietur deo	arise and thanke god
ex cordis attencione, quia	with intent of herte, for
omnia ex bonitate sua	þat he has creat all
creauit, et ex caritate sua	thingis of his goodness,
assumendo carnem	and he has takyn
omnia recreauit,	mankende of his cherite,
ostendens per passionem	shewing his loue to man
et mortem suam	be his passion and his
dileccionem suam ad	deth.
hominem qua maior esse	
non posset.	

Only two elements have disappeared: the 'recreation' of mankind, and the excellence of God's love shown in Christ's passion and death. This is a very good example of literal translation.

Julius is not always so respectful of the text. For a single example:

Maria quoque sit discreta in oracione	
et laudibus dei ordinata. Nam si habet	Yf he haue
necessaria vite sine sollicitudine	nessessary
	thingis to leve,
debet facere oraciones prolixiores.	he shuld make
	lenger prayoris.
Si vero in orando attediatur	Yf he be yrke
	of prayours,
et accrescunt temptaciones,	
potest quidem laborare manibus	than to werke
aliquid honestum opus et vtile,	sum honest and
	profitable
	werke

vel ad vtilitatem propriam si	to put awey temptacions.
indiget, aut ad commodum aliorum.	
Si vero attediatur in utroque,	And yf he be wery of bothe,
scilicet in oracione et labore,	
tunc quidem potest habere	þan he may haue
aliquam occupacionem honestam	sum honest occupacioun,
vel verba audire edificatoria	
cum omni grauitate,	
omni scurrilitate remota,	
donec corpus et anima	til þe body and þe soule be
habiliora ad opus dei efficiantur.	moore abill to the werke of god.

III

Rev. VII,5 appears in the Latin text as a spiritual instruction delivered in the form of a letter addressed to a young man, Elziarius, son of the countess of Ariano, in answer to his request for prayers; the revelation was given to St Bridget by our Lady when she was in Naples. The translation of this chapter as an independent tract exists in two manuscripts: BL Arundel 286 (ff. 15v–19v), and BL Harley 6615 (ff. 104r–109v). My earlier edition of the text included a detailed analysis of the translation. I would like to supplement that discussion by consideration of sentence-structure, following the same lines of analysis as in the preceding section: in both tracts the translators' choices in respect of sentence-structure are strikingly similar.[19]

The subject of *Rev.* VII,5 belongs to the well-known genre of 'remedies against temptations',[20] and is developed in an elaborate allegory of a mighty king (God): this king has built a house (the body), and put in it his daughter (the soul), and assigned her a keeper (reason) as a defence against a host of menacing enemies (temptations). The author of our translation has given a title to the tract taking what is strictly essential for his purpose from the short Latin summary at the head of the chapter: 'How resoun schal be keper of þe soule to putt out and to wiþstande temptaciouns, þat þei entre not into þe soule', and omitting its references to where and why Bridget wrote to Elziarius.[21] This is a normal procedure with these independent tracts, which suppress any historical or other context the original might have so as to generalize its message as widely as possible. But in this case our translator was unable for long to keep the Saint and her disciple out of his text, and was soon obliged to insert a gloss to tell his reader

[19] For the English and the Latin text of this chapter I refer to my edition of the tract: see note 7. For the analysis I use the Arundel text, unless otherwise noted.

[20] In Harley 6615 our tract is inserted between *The Chastising of God's Children* and two versions of William Flete's *De Remediis contra Temptaciones*.

[21] Compare the Latin heading: 'Domina Birgitta habuit istam reuelacionem in Neapoli ad requisicionem domini Elziarii filii comitisse de Ariano, qui iuuenis tunc et scolaris bone indolis erat. Et tunc ipse rogauit dominam Birgittam, quod oraret Deum pro eo. Ipsa vero in oracione existente apparuit virgo Maria ei, que dedit ei istam reuelacionem, per quam informat eum de modis tenendis in vita sua, valde pulchre dicens, quod racio debet esse hostiarius et custos anime ad expellendum omnes temptaciones et resistendum eis viriliter, ne intrent domum interiorem hominis.'

about the 'ȝonge scoler ... to whom þis holy lady seynt Bride
wrote in a pistel þese wordes before, and þis informacioun þat
folewiþ'. In fact some knowledge of these biographical
circumstances, of a man who was 'iuuenis tunc et scolaris
bone indolis', is necessary to understand the kind of
temptations he underwent.[22]

The translation itself immediately reveals an impressive
fondness for parallelism. At the very beginning we have a real
triumph of *isocolon*. Reason, the keeper of the house, is
instructed about the dangers he must beware of:

> Primum est, quod nullus fundamentum domus suffodiat;
> secundum est, quod nullus murorum altitudinem transcendat;
> tercium est, quod parietes domus nemo frangat;
> quartum est, quod nullus inimicorum per portas introeat.

The parallelism, already present in the Latin, is strongly
emphasized in the English translation.

> Þe firste is þat noon enemy vndermyne þat hous;
> þe seconde is þat noon enemy clymbe ouer þe heyȝ walles
> wiþout;
> þe þridde is þat noon enemy breke þe foure wowes wiþinne;
> þe ferþe is þat noon enemy entre by þe gates of þat hous.

The effect is brilliant, the stress appropriately on the two
crucial terms of the problem: the enemy, repeated four times
using the same phrase (compare the Latin 'nullus', 'nemo',
'nullus inimicorum'), and the house, which must be watched
over and kept safe by reason, the keeper. In fact, the four last
words of the cola are 'hous / wiþout / wiþinne / hous', and
one is left with the impression that the walls are the point
where the battle between the soul and the temptations is
fought, and they receive the proper emphasis in the English
text, replacing in an original way the emphasis of the Latin on

[22] R. Ellis (pp. 175–76) had already noted this adaptation.

the four verbs meaning danger and destruction. By this subtle
solution the rules of a different syntax are obeyed, but the
force of the original text is retained, although translated into
a new image.

To obtain perfect parallel phrases our translator uses the
same techniques as noted in the previous section. He may
repeat a word which is not in the Latin:

> Prima est via auditus, secunda visus.
> Þe firste weye is heerynge, þe secunde weye is si3t.

Or he may modify the Latin:

> corpore et bonis totisque tuis viribus
> wiþ al his body and wiþ alle hise wittes

He maintains this choice even when using the doublet:

> omnes proximos tuos
> alle myn euencristen and alle my nei3bores[23]

The text of this translation is almost identical in Arundel
and Harley, but it is interesting to note that some of the few
differences are due to the attempts of the Arundel scribe to
restore a clearer parallelism. For instance, in the first example
above 'weye' is not repeated in Harley, which has 'þe firste
weye is herynge, þe secunde is sy3t'. In the second case, too,
Harley has a different word-order: 'wiþ alle hys body and alle
with hise wittys'. The same may be said of two more complex
examples. Where Harley has 'lerne þan lyberal scyence ... and
be preyer and be 3iftys procure to þe ...', Arundel puts the two
verbs at the beginning of the clause, and writes 'lerne þan
liberal sciencis ... and procure to þee by prayer and by 3iftes

---

[23] The changes from 2 p.sg. to 1 or 3 p.sg. in these as in other examples
of this section are due to the new destination of the text: originally a letter
addressed to a specific person, it has been transformed into a tract meant for
the general reader.

...'. The second example occurs in a passage where the Latin itself is nicely balanced:

> humilitatem ... quam Spiritus Sanctus inspirat
> superbiam ... quam malignus spiritus cordibus infundit

Harley's translation runs:

> mekenesse, whiche is inspiryd to mennys hertys be þe Holy Goste
> pryde of þe worlde, wiche þe wickyd spiriȝt puttiþ into mennys hertys

By choosing a passive and an active construction Harley destroys the perfect parallelism of the Latin. The Arundel scribe restores the balance by resolving the two active verbs as passives, and reinforces the effect of radical opposition within a pattern of similarity by the repetition of the verb 'inspire':

> mekenesse, which is inspired to mennes hertes by þe Holy Gost
> pride of þe worlde, which is inspired to mennes hertes by his venimous stirynge

'His' refers to the devil, who is the subject of the first clause of the period.[24]

---

[24] As I have shown in my edition and analysis of this tract (Pezzini 1986, p. 267), the Arundel scribe has a much stronger sense of 'regularity' than Harley. My view is that Ar works on the translation found in H, or in a copy from which H has been derived, trying to 'tidy it up', while keeping at the same time an eye on the Latin original. This is certain at least in one instance: 'delectaciones internas', translated 'gostely meditacions' in H, is rendered in Ar by 'inwarde delectaciouns'. This may be supposed in another case: the Latin 'quandoque eciam turbari et letari' appears in H 'and somtyme be glad, and somtyme be sory, and somtyme be trobelyd'; Ar restores the double opposition, and writes 'and somtyme be glad, and somtyme be sory and troublide', using a sort of half-way solution in that he keeps the doublet for 'turbari', but eliminates the third 'somtyme'.

This pattern of repetition is maintained even in longer and more articulated periods. In the following example, the translator links three Latin cola employing a mixture of passive and active constructions: he makes the first verb active and so generates a formal similarity between the three clauses:

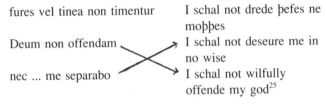

fures vel tinea non timentur	I schal not drede þefes ne moþþes
Deum non offendam	I schal not deseure me in no wise
nec ... me separabo	I schal not wilfully offende my god[25]

Elsewhere, too, the sequence of the elements of the Latin text is rearranged in order to create a perfect parallelism:

Sicut in sumpcione cibi et potus cauendum est / ne inimicus per superfluitatem introeat / que corpus ad seruiendum Deo accidiosum reddit // ita eciam cauendum est ne per abstinencie nimietatem / que corpus ad omnia facienda defectuosum reddit / hostis ingressum habeat.

Ri3t as it is nedeful to be war in takynge of mete and drinke / þat þe enemy haue noon entre by excesse and superfluite / whiche li3tly wole make þe body slowe and heuy to þe seruyse of god // in þe same maner it is nedeful to be war / þat þe enemy haue noon entre by to mych abstinence / which li3tly may feble þe body þat he mowe not do his dewte.

The Latin sequence 1-2-3 // 1-3-2 has been regularized and turned into a perfect parallel 1-2-3 // 1-2-3, with the central clauses verbally identical, except for the contrast 'excesse / abstinence'.

Another feature of the figure of repetition appears at times as the use of a sort of verbal echo:

[25] For this tendency to invert the order in a sequence, which can also be observed in the last example given in the preceding note (turbari/letari), see note 17.

> per quem altitudinem murorum intelligo caritatem,
> que omnibus virtutibus est sublimior
> by þe whiche hei3te I vnderstande þe vertue of charite, which
> in hei3te passeþ alle vertues

Here the brilliant idea is to translate 'sublimior est' by 'in hei3te passeþ', which, together with the repetition of 'vertue', builds up a parallel totally absent from the Latin.

An even better example of this technique is the figure of *anadiplosis*, or *gradatio*, skilfully used by our translator:

> Per fundamentum (intelligo) bonam et firmam seu stabilem voluntatem; super ipsam namque omnia bona opera construenda sunt, quibus anima optime defenditur.
> By þe fundament is vnderstonde a good and a stable wille; vp þis stable wille alle goode werkes schul be sett, and wiþ siche werkes þe soule schal be strengþed and defended from enemyes.

We find in this tract all the types of inversion already seen in the translation of VI,65. Chiasmus is also intelligently employed, as can be seen in the following instance:

> vt soli Deo possis totaliter complacere, ipsumque in omnibus honorare
> so þat fully I mowe plese only god / and hym worschipe in alle þinges

Here a perfect inversion can be observed, and the new order is:

> 1 fully, 2 plese, 3 god / 3 hym, 2 worschipe, 1 in alle þinges.

The same tripartite inversion occurs in another case:

> (diuicias) que numquam illi, qui eas adeptus fuerit, auferuntur
> who so may ones gete hem / þei schul neuer be take awey fro hym.

Again we have 1 who so, 2 gete, 3 hem, reversed into 3 þei, 2 be take awey, 1 hym, with the opposition stressed by the contrast 'ones/neuer'. The Latin has none of these choices, and the originality of our translator is once again confirmed.

In this text, as in the previous one, the attention of the translator to his reader/listener is shown in the addition of explicative passages resuming what has just been said. So 'sic' becomes 'þus, wiþ siche answeres', 'predictos parietes' is turned into 'þese foure wowes of heuenly delyte', and 'si forte tibi aliquis talia persuaserit' is expanded into 'whan eny siche enemyes comeþ wiþ queynte and flaterynge wordes to vndermyne þi good wille and torne þi holy purpos', where anyone can see how generic words like 'aliquis' and 'talia' have become definite expressions, and the action suggested by the verb 'persuaserit' has been, so to speak, visualized. The same attention to the reader appears in the addition of two short summaries in the middle and at the end of the tract, where the reader is reminded that 'þus schal resoun be keper of þe soule, and putt out enemyes, and wiþstande temptaciouns of þe deuel, of þe world, and of þe flesch, wiþ clepynge of god and askyng of grace.'

Occasional alliterations are found in this text, like 'delectaciouns of *s*eculere *s*onges or of oþere *s*wete *s*ownynge instrumentes', '*m*any *d*isches or *m*esses of *d*iuerse *d*eynte *m*etes for *w*orldly *w*orschipe and fauour of men', and finally '*sl*ugrye of *sl*eep or of *sl*umbre'. These are a further, final sign of our translator's interest in matters of style, and a fair indicator of his achievement.

IV

Little needs to be said about the translation of the third independent tract taken from *Rev*. II,16. Its popularity was widespread, since we have it in three different versions in four manuscripts: the writer of the chapter heading called it 'optimum documentum', which proved to be a good advertisement.[26]

I shall mainly consider the first of these three versions (Jolliffe's Item I,13a) which is found in two British Library manuscripts: Additional 37790 (f. 236v), and Arundel 197 (ff. 46v–47v), the other two being very literal. For various reasons this tract is less interesting the two previously examined, and its study adds almost nothing to what previous analysis has shown. First it is too small a sample. Only the second half of an already short chapter has been translated; the first part, giving the occasion of a teaching on humility and an *exemplum* explaining God's behaviour towards Bridget, has been left out in all three versions. This, as earlier noted, is a rule with these tracts, directed as they are to the general reader. Secondly, the text in Add. 37790 is further reduced by one third, since 13 lines out of a total of 40 have disappeared with the excision of the last folio of the manuscript. Thirdly, and most important for our purpose, the Latin text itself did not allow any significant reworking except for the expansion by means of the doublet. Apart from the opening period, which in the Latin original serves as a bridge between the two parts of the chapter, we have twelve short sentences, linked by three in four groups, and reduced to bare essentials: the verb and its object, and sometimes the object only. The subject is God, who gives this series of three positive and three negative orders, three concessions and three counsels.

---

[26] For the texts, full description of the manuscripts, and a detailed analysis of the translations, the reader may refer to my edition of this tract (see note 8), where I have also published the version of the chapter from Cotton Julius F.II. For comparison with Cotton Claudius B.I the reader may refer to the edition of this manuscript by R. Ellis, *The Liber Celestis of St Bridget of Sweden*, vol. I — Text, EETS OS 291 (London, 1987).

The basic choice of the translator is then amplification. See what becomes of a very simple Latin sentence in Add. 37790:

> Dilige omnes eciam qui te odire videntur et tibi detrahere.
> Luf alle in me / and them that hate the / and detracte the /
> and scorne the / or any iuel do to the / luf them for the luf of
> me.

This is a good and balanced use of rhetorical devices such as *anaphora*, *epistrophe*, and *epanalepsis*, which gracefully encloses the whole passage in two repeated parallel clauses. One may argue if this can still be called a translation, since it goes a long way from the original. But this is not the end of the road. The second scribe of ms. Arundel 197, who corrects the original version by erasing, rewriting and adding words and phrases over the line and on the margins, expands even more:

> Love al maner of pepul for mi sake / and þem þat þou
> knowiste dothe hate / and wille bacbyte þe / and speke eville
> of þe / sclaunder or scorne þe / or any oþer wronge or harme
> do vnto þe / yet love þem for þe loue of me.

Other expansions are more reasonable. We have the doublet, like 'fugere' rendered by 'fle and forsake'; explanatory additions, such as 'superbiam et arroganciam' which Ar. translates 'alle maner of pride and hiȝ berynge, boþe in herte and in countenance'; or a combination of the two, as with 'carnis luxuriam' which becomes in Add. 'the vices of thy flesch, þat is to vndyrstonde the syn of lechery'. In this translation, then, and given the peculiar character of the Latin, the translator treats the original like a naked pattern on which he embroiders freely without ever losing the main thread of his argument.

The other two independent versions of II,16 do not show any particular reworking of the Latin text, and have no close link with the previous version. They both omit the opening sentence containing the teaching on humility, and concentrate on the 'twelf poyntes', as Bodley 131 calls this summary of Christian practice, revealing once again how fascinating was the numerical organizing principle in medieval times. The versions in ms. Taunton Horae (f. i r-v) covers the first folio of a Book of Hours and is written in a different hand, most probably from the second half of the fifteenth century; the bottom of the first folio has been partly torn off so that now the text of the translation is incomplete. The translation itself is literal, except in two cases, where an explanatory sentence is added. The difficulty of making much of a text so reduced to essentials can be further demonstrated by brief consideration of the two full-text translations, in the Julius and Claudius mss. Generally the two texts cut the Latin in a substantial way; they are not so free here, although, as soon as they can, they eliminate a rare Latin doublet, or conflate two similar sentences into one. Claudius is more ruthless than Julius: he substitutes all the cardinal numbers of the sequence with a colourless 'also', for example. But when he rules out an entire sentence, 'hec cogitacio excitat caritatem ad deum', which refers to the meditation on the Passion, the result is a positive blunder, since the thought of the Passion becomes one with the meditation on Doomsday, and 'þese two sall engendir drede and fere in þi herte'. This is wrong and one-sided: the delicate balance between love and fear, which is the fruit of the double meditation, and a corner-stone of a sound Christian life, is thus destroyed.

V

A few closing remarks are in order.

1. These tracts show further evidence of a widespread practice of taking smaller parts out of longer works, which were translated for and adapted to what we may call the

general reader,[27] meaning by this a growing literate audience increasingly composed of lay people, mostly women.

2. The style of these translations, rich in figures of parallelism and inversion, points towards the use of these tracts for private meditation and spiritual instruction. I agree with Lois K. Smedick that 'Parallelism has a special suitability for meditative texts ... Memory is aided, attention focussed, and the effect of incantation produced through the reiterative style'.[28] But the same suitability can be found in the figures of inversion, which stimulate the mind with the effect of surprise induced by the frustrated expectation of parallelism. This is to say that the rhetorical devices were not primarily used for their own sake, but as a help to meditation.[29] The same principle applies to the use of these tracts as spiritual instructions orally delivered, for which parallel sentences, explanatory additions and summary passages were particularly

---

[27] In this process of generalization the tract may at times lose its link with the work from which it has been taken. This happens with the translation of VI,65 which appears as an anonymous treatise in ms. Pepys 2125, while in C.U.L. Ii.6.40 it has not got even a title, coming immediately after the *Fervor Amoris* so that it was taken, until quite recently, as the last two chapters of this work. Also in Bodley 423 and Arundel 197 this tract comes after the *Fervor Amoris*, whose author seems quite familiar with the *Revelations* (see Ellis 1982, p. 175), but in these two manuscripts the short title of the tract says that it is 'drawe oute of the Reuelacion of seint Bride'.

[28] L. K. Smedick, 'Parallelism and Pointing in Rolle's Rhythmical Style', *Mediaeval Studies*, 41 (1979), 404–67 (p. 405).

[29] E. Salter has rightly suggested that 'An account of the development of highly-wrought English devotional prose might well ... lay great stress upon the development of certain kinds of religious sensibility, and the varied needs of a teaching Church, interpreted in varied literary ways: the 'rhetorical tradition' is established and corroborated by religious demand and only secondarily determined by literary taste', in *Nicholas Love's 'Myrrour of The Blessed Lyf of Jesu Crist'*, Analecta Cartusiana no. 10 (Salzburg, 1974), pp. 212–13.

useful. The technique of reducing or expanding the Latin for the sake of better precision and clarification follows the same line.

3. Given the remarkable similarity of certain stylistic habits, it is tempting to suggest that the translations examined here as 'independent tracts' are the work of the same hand. But this is only a supposition at present. The evidence of the manuscripts, although not decisive, does not particularly favour a common origin: the tracts appear singly, except in Arundel 197, which contains VI,65 and II,16 in sequence. Moreover, the study of late medieval devotional prose in English is still in its infancy, and a good deal of analysis, like the one I offer here, is needed in order to draw a clear and articulate pattern of translational techniques[30] and, more generally, define the map of medieval prose in England as a tradition comprising both continuity and variation.[31] Only

[30] The need of 'a much larger study of intertextuality in Middle English devotional writing' is aptly stressed by B. Nolan in her chapter on 'Nicholas Love', in *Middle English Prose: A Critical Guide to Major Authors and Genres*, edited by A. S. G. Edwards (New Brunswick, 1984), pp. 83–95. 'Such a study would necessarily include medieval Latin as well as English texts; and it would involve discussion not only on themes, imagery, and meditative structures, but also of rhetorical techniques adapted from Latin into English and then transformed to become part of the native literary idiom.' (p. 90) This is exactly what we may observe in our three Brigittine tracts. Also relevant in this respect is the chapter by A. Barratt, 'Works of Religious Instruction', *Middle English Prose*, pp. 413–32, particularly the remarks and suggestions made on p. 427.

[31] A first draft of this map is N. F. Blake, 'Varieties of Middle English Religious Prose', in *Chaucer and Middle English Studies in Honour of Rossell Hope Robbins*, edited by B. Rowland (London, 1974), pp. 348–56. The criterion adopted by Blake is 'the purpose for which a particular text was written, since the purpose will often determine the form and approach, as its most important feature' (p. 349). To this may be added Jolliffe's *Check-List*, which, although more limited in scope, is far more articulate in

against such a background could the value and meaning of single texts be assessed.

its sections. I would also like to indicate as a good example of detailed analysis, although not applied to a translation, R. K. Stone, *Middle English Prose Style: Margery Kempe and Julian of Norwich* (The Hague, 1970). The merit of this book is that the texts are really analyzed in full detail, and not just superficially skimmed through and described with random inconclusive impressions.

Techniques of Translation in the Middle English Versions of *Guy of Warwick*

MALDWYN MILLS

AS HAS LONG been recognized, no less than four distinct Middle English versions of the Anglo-Norman *Gui de Warewic* have survived; three of these, like their originals, are in short rhymed couplets; a fourth — which covers only the later stages of Guy's story — is in tail-rhyme stanzas. Considered as a translation, this last version is the most interesting of them all, and is bound to dominate the pages that follow, but the couplet-versions must not be entirely neglected. The closeness with which each, in its own way, renders *Gui* into Middle English makes possible some precise definition of the range of procedures used in such work; some of these, at least, may also be discerned behind the more free-wheeling tail-rhyme version of *Guy* (TGW).[1]

Of these couplet translations, the earliest (*c.* 1300–1325) is the very fragmentary text preserved in binding fragments

---

[1] In *The Romance of Guy of Warwick*, ed. J. Zupitza, Early English Text Society, Extra Series, 42, 49, 59 (Oxford, 1883–91), pp. 384–490, 502–628. This also contains texts of the couplet versions of the Auchinleck and Caius MSS, mentioned below.

that were originally contained in National Library of Wales NLW 572 and British Library MS Additional 14408 (F);[2] only a very little later (*c*. 1327–1340) is that represented by lines 123–7306 of the Auchinleck copy (National Library of Scotland MS 19.2.1 (A)), lines 1–7444, 8219–8807 and 10232–11095 of that contained in Cambridge Caius College MS 107 (C), and the fragment of 216 lines in British Library MS Sloane 1044 (S). By contrast, the text of the third couplet version that is found in Cambridge University Library MS ff.ii.38 (c)[3] has most recently been assigned to the very late fifteenth or early sixteenth century.[4] The range of material is thus very considerable, but before any detailed comparative study is attempted, one seriously complicating factor must be taken into account.

This is that there was in existence not one version of the Anglo-Norman *Gui*, but two. Ewert noted that the first of these was best represented by the text contained in the Edwardes MS (British Library MS Additional 38662 (E)),[5] while the second appears in its most respectable form in Cambridge Corpus Christi College MS 50 (C), and its most extreme and reworked form in Wolfenbüttel Herzog August Bibliothek MS Aug. 87.4 (G). On the whole, the earlier M.E. couplet versions are more often to be related to this second

---

[2] For which, see *Fragments of an Early Fourteenth-Century Guy of Warwick*, ed. M. Mills and D. Huws, Medium Ævum Monographs, New Series, IV (Oxford, 1974).

[3] *The Romance of Guy of Warwick: the Second or 15th-century Version*, ed. J. Zupitza, Early English Text Society, Extra Series, 25, 26 (Oxford, 1875–6).

[4] See P. R. Robinson's discussion in the Scolar Press facsimile *Cambridge University Library MS Ff.2.38* (London, 1979), pp. xii and xiv.

[5] Which he used as the basis of his own edition, *Gui de Warewic: Roman du XIIIe Siècle*, Les Classiques Français du Moyen Age, 74, 75 (Paris, 1932–3).

redaction than to the first, but their detailed affiliation is often complicated by eclectic tendencies in their translators. The text of F becomes much more obviously dependent upon the second French redaction in its later parts than in the earlier ones, while those of A and C, although close to this redaction for much of their length, draw upon a text of the first version for quite substantial passages.

Together, all of these considerations very severely restrict the number of places where all three of the M.E. couplet versions offer significant variants that are quite certainly from the same Anglo-Norman original. All the same, one such place can be found at a relatively early point in Guy's story; when, after discovering that all his triumphs in foreign parts have not been sufficient to break down Felice's reserve, he has once again to set out on his travels. Here the only difference between the M.E. versions that seems inherited, relates to the country-names of lines 5 and 6, since while F and A follow C, c, getting the best of both worlds, follows E in its own lines 7–8, and superimposes the reading of C on its lines 11–12.

E

A la mer s'en est alé,
Bon vent ad, si est passé,
Venuz est en Normendie;
Mult i fait grant chevalerie.
5   D'iloeques s'en va en Bretaigne (Espaine C);
N'ert turneiement desqu'en Espaigne (Almaine C),
Qu'il n'i voist pur turneier;
Mult se fait par tut preiser.
En Espaigne ad tant demoré
10   Que d'armes i est mult preisé.
D'iloeques s'en va en Lumbardie,
U dunques ert la chevalerie;
Iloeques se fait mult preiser:
Le Lumbarz l'aiment e tienent cher,
(1167–1180)

F

Gy went tu the see,
   thay dwelle
     behende;
Wen he com thar he
   had gud wend.
Nou hys he cumen tu
   Normunydy
Thar he did gret
   chiualry
5 Sithen he yed
   vntu Spayn
Tu tournay, and tu
   Halmayne:
To ilkay tournement he
   was dethe
[To] get [lo]s with gret
   mythe.
Ar he out hof Spayn
   yed,
10 He was halden
   the best of ded.
Fra thethen he went tu
   Lumbardy
Fortu kyid his mastry;

Thar was nouther
   baroun ne knyth
That thay ne luf[e]d
   hym tu thar myth.
   (590–603)

A

To þe se he is
   y-come

Gode winde he haþ
   atte frome.
Y-comen he is into
   Normundye,
Kni3tschip he
   schewed on hye.
5 Þennes he went into
   Speyne;
Nis turnament non
   into Almeyne
Þat Gij no haþ þerat
   y-be,
And michel
   y-preised so is he.

Þennes to
   Lombardye he went
10 Þer ben þe iustes
   and þe turnament.
Þer he dede him
   preyse miche:
Þe Lombardes him
   loued inliche.
   (1253–1264)

c

To þe see he is goon:
A gode schyppe there he nome.
He passyd the see in hye,

Comen he ys to Normandye.
5   Thorowe the londe vtturly
He dud grete cheualry.
Forthe he went to Bretayne —
There were justyngys in Spayne,
That he went to turnaye,
10   Whyll he was there, every day.
Now wendyth he fro Spayne,
Comen he ys to Almayne.
Fro þens he went to Lumbardye,
There was grete cheualrye.
15   Thorowe hys strenkyth þere he wanne
Grete looueyng of many a man.
(901–916)

In this passage, the proper names at once provide a handful of ready-made rhymes, and somewhat limit the translator's freedom of movement in the rest of the lines which contain them. And indeed, even in the great majority of cases where the rhyme-words of the original cannot be retained, there is a strong tendency to keep more-or-less intact the actual semantic range of the original couplets. Only at the beginning of c do we find a more expansive approach, with the total scope of **E** 1–2 retained at the expense of spilling over into a third line, and the dislocated sequence of couplets set right by the insertion of a completely new line between **E** 3 and 4. And where the translators worked strictly within the limits of the original couplets, the problems of reproducing the sense of the original in a largely different language and with largely different rhymes made them resort to a variety of translation strategies.

(a) The most simple of these was to keep the first line of the Anglo-Norman couplet virtually intact, but radically alter, or wholly replace, the second one (c 9–10, where the praise received by Guy gives place to a comment on his non-stop jousting). (b) More flexibly, the beginnings of both of the lines in the couplet might be kept, with quite new rhymes provided for them (A 1–2, 11–12). (c) A crucial word, whether in or out of rhyme-position, might be moved into a different position in its line, together with a good deal of supplementary alteration to the rest of the couplet. The most spectacular example here is the shifting of A.N. *vent* (as M.E. *wend*) into rhyme-position in F 2; also noteworthy are the moving back in the line of **E** 4 *chevalerie* (as *kniʒtschip*) in A 4, and of *Lombardye* in A 9 — possibly to avoid what was felt as tedious repetition in the original version. (d) Most freely of all, the general sense of the whole couplet might be given, but with very few — if any — of the original words retained (F 9–10, 13–14). And, inevitably, the choice of any one of these procedures might be suggested or supplemented by sequences of rhyme-words of general usefulness to romances of this kind; see for example, A 1–2 *y-come:frome*, A 9–10 *went:turnament*, F 7–8 *dethe* (**diʒt*): *mythe* (**miʒt*), F 13–14 *knyth* (**kniʒt*):*myth* (**miʒt*).

*　*　*

The Auchinleck couplet text of *Guy* breaks off about two-thirds of the way down f. 146vb (at the point at which the hero returns to Warwick to present his king with the head of the dragon slain in Northumberland). The tail-rhyme version (TGW) then follows. The change, while not marked by any gap in the text, or by any title or initial miniature, is still made unmistakable by a marked change in the appearance of the hand (with the letter forms significantly larger than in the couplet text), and by the more frequent use of tinted paraphs to indicate the limits of the individual stanzas. There must certainly have been a break in the copying at this point,[6] whether because the exemplar was so defective that work could not proceed until a supplementary version of this part of the story was found,[7] or because the scribe had to wait for a wholly new version of it to be composed, as a self-contained romance, and in a different metrical form.[8] What is not in doubt, however, is that this new tail-rhyme version went back to a French source that was more akin to **E** or **C** than to **G**. This rules out the possibility, once tentatively put forward by Zupitza,[9] that TGW was a redaction of the M.E. (couplet) archetype of the Sloane and Caius texts.

It should be noted at the outset that TGW is not composed in exactly the same stanza-form throughout its length. At first, the translator uses only the 'four-rhyme' variety of the tail-rhyme stanza (*aabaabccbddb*), a minority form in the corpus of tail-rhyme romances as a whole, but one that is very well represented in MS Auchinleck. Here, indeed, no less than three of the other five texts of this kind make use

---

[6] For the likely sequence of copying in MS Auchinleck as a whole, see J. C. Mordkoff, 'The Making of the Auchinleck Manuscript: The Scribes at Work' (unpublished Ph.D. dissertation, University of Connecticut, 1981), passim.

[7] This is suggested by the fact that C, the other derivative copy, not only has many lacunae in its version of the later part of the story, but supplements its basic text by borrowing, on the largest scale, from a M.E. version in the same tradition as c. See Zupitza's Preface to E.E.T.S., E.S. 25 and 26, p. viii.

[8] Given the amount of copying that appears to have been done by the principal scribe between the couplet and the tail-rhyme *Guy*, it seems most unlikely that he could have undertaken to produce the original of the latter himself.

[9] 'Zur Literaturgeschichte des Guy von Warwick', *Sitzungsberichte der kaiserlichen Akademie der Wissenschaften* (Vienna, 1873), 631.

of it, either consistently (*The King of Tars*[10] and *Amis and Amiloun*[11]), or with only the rarest of exceptions (*Horn Childe and Maiden Rimnild*[12]). Its densely asymmetrical rhyme-structure encourages some distinctive narrative procedures and produces some particular dramatic effects; its first half tends to be relatively self-contained, involuted, static; its second, both more varied in content and more dynamic in impetus.[13] To the translator of TGW, however, it was probably seen only as a strain upon his limited versifying skills, and after oscillating briefly between it and the 'five-rhyme' pattern (aabccbddbeeb) in stanzas 48–52, he abandoned it more or less completely in favour of the latter (in which, of course, the great majority of all the twelve-line tail-rhyme romances found outside MS Auchinleck are composed).

As might have been expected, it is in this much more extensive five-rhyme part of TGW that we find the most extensive of the close parallels with the Anglo-Norman text, and, therefore, the most use of the procedures identified in the couplet-translations. Once again, we find entire lines, or the openings of successive couplet-lines that exactly reproduce their Anglo-Norman counterparts; once again, whole couplets that reproduce the general sense of their originals. But at the same time, the presence of four tail-lines in every stanza makes impossible as long-sustained an equivalence of sense with the original as can be found in the couplet versions.

---

[10] Ed. J. Perryman, Middle English Texts, 12 (Heidelberg, 1980).

[11] Ed. E. Kölbing, Altenglische Bibliothek, 2 (Heilbronn, 1884).

[12] Ed. M. Mills, Middle English Texts, 20 (Heidelberg, 1988).

[13] For all the importance that he attached to these Auchinleck romances, Trounce did not take note of these particular possibilities in his pioneering study 'The English Tail-Rhyme Romances' (*Medium Ævum*, I (1932), 87–108, 168–82; 2 (1933), 34–57, 189–98; 3 (1934), 30–50).

What is more, the distribution within the stanza of the lines of the original that are precisely rendered will vary considerably from one stanza to the next. Two especially clear-cut and representative patterns are exemplified below:

(a)

Li reis Triamor puis i
ala,
Sun fiz Fabur od lui
mena.

Cum devant le soldan
erent venu,
De la mort grant pour
unt eu.

Li soldan forment les
encolpa,
De la mort sun fiz les
reta;

Se defendre ne se
poeient,
A grant peril livré
serreient.
(**E** 8041–8)

King Triamour com to
court þo,
And Fabour, his sone,
dede also,
To þe Soudans
parlement.
When þai biforn him
comen beþ
Þai were adouted of her
deþ:
Her liues þai wende
haue spent;
For þe Soudan cleped
hem fot hot,
And his sones deþ hem
atwot,
And seyd þai were
alle schent.
Bot þai hem þerof were
miȝt
In strong perile he schuld
hem diȝt
And to her iugement.
(TGW <u>61</u>)

(b)

Quant li pelerin oi aveit

K'il la bataille prendre
          voleit,
Al vis le regarde e as
          pez,
Mult le veit povrement
          conreiez,
Mais grant le vit e corsu,

Ben sembla hume de
          grant vertu;
La barbe out encrue e le
          vis covert,
Ben semble home qui ait
          mis en desert.
     (E 8201–8)

When þerl herd him
          speke so,
Þat he wald batayl fong
          for him þo,
He biheld fot and
          heued:
Michel he was of bodi
          piȝt,
A man he semed of
          michel miȝt,
Ac pouerliche he
          was biweued;
Wiþ a long berd his neb
          was growe.
Miche wo him þouȝt he
          hadde y-drowe:
He wende his wit
          were reued.
For he seyd he wald as
          ȝern
Fiȝt wiþ þat geaunt stern,
Bot ȝif he hadde
          him preued.
     (TGW 75)

In TGW 61 the translator has exactly preserved the division of the action into four stages that he found in the couplets of his original (together with the close grammatical link between the third and fourth of these); he has also allowed almost nothing found in the couplets of his original to spill over into the tail-lines (the only exception is the transposed allusion to the sultan in his third line, which conveniently lightens the couplet-line that follows); in consequence, these tail-lines are largely new in content, though none is strictly a tag; even the second, which broadly repeats the couplet-line that immediately precedes it, has its own force. In (b), on the other hand, the splitting of *E* 8203-4 to give the first and second tail-lines makes it possible for every one of the first eight lines of the passage in *E* to be taken over into TGW. The needful tail-lines could thus be created by the rearrangement of material from the source, as well as by invention of a rather simple-minded kind.[14]

At the same time the absence from *E* of anything that at all resembles the last four lines of TGW 75 shows that the translator did not simply plod through his original at a pace as even as the conversion of couplets into stanzas would permit. The stanza-form brought with it a very definite need to shape the story-material, whether by abbreviation or by amplification, and what had been acceptable as the final couplet in a run of four or five such might not be appropriate as the core of the final three-line unit in a stanza. In the present instance, the couplet that immediately follows line 8208 in E would have seemed very awkward at the end of TGW 75, since it forms the beginning of a new speech that is made by the pilgrim to Guy. Instead, it is kept for the beginning of TGW 76, and the resulting gap in TGW 75 made good by writing in an additional passage that refers back to the second half of TGW 74, where Guy had expressed his resolution to fight *oʒain þe geaunt þat is so strong.* Interestingly, this earlier passage was itself largely novel (**E** 8199 refers only to the battle that is to come, with no specific mention of the giant at all).

The translator's concern to rearrange and re-proportion his material in ways appropriate to the new metrical form is apparent throughout TGW, and sometimes the same kind of

---

[14] In his edition of Thomas Chestre's *Sir Launfal* (London, 1960), pp. 34–5, A. J. Bliss gives a detailed account of these two major patterns. Here however the main direct source was the M.E. couplet version of *Sir Landevale.*

material will be found to have been reworked in the same kind of way, whether the stanza is of four or of five rhymes. This is particularly apparent in the translator's amplification of two very short catalogues of geographical names in his source; first in the four-rhyme stanza <u>40</u>, later in the five-rhyme stanza <u>70</u>. Both of these describe elaborate — and unsuccessful — searches made for the elusive Guy.

(a)

Puis unt lur messages
         pris,
Par tote la terre l'unt il
         quis.

Menssangers anon þai
         sende
Ouer al þis lond fer and
         hende
Fram Londen into
         Louþe,
Ouer al biȝonde
         Humber and Trent,
And est and west
         þurchout al Kent
To þe hauen of
         Portesmouthe.
þai souȝt him ouer al
         vp and doun
Ouer alle þe lond in
         euerich toun
Bi costes þat wer
         couþe.

Mais quant pas trové ne
         l'unt,
Arere repairé se sunt.
        (E 7815–18)

And seþþen to Warwike
         þai gan wende,
And seyd þai miȝt him
         nowhar fende
Bi norþ no bi souþe,
        (TGW <u>40</u>)

(b)

'Dreit m'en alai en
    Alemaigne,

En Loheregne e en
    Espaigne,
E en Puille e en
    Sessoigne,

E en France e en
    Burgoigne'
    (E 8135–8)

'Y souȝt hem into þe
    lond of Coyne,
Into Calaber and into
    Sessoigne,
And fro þennes into
    Almayne,
In Tuskan and in
    Lombardye,
In Fraunce and in
    Normondye,
Into þe lond of
    Speyne,
In Braban, in Poil and in
    Bars,
And into kinges lond of
    Tars,
And þurch al
    Aquitayne,
In Cisil, in Hungri and in
    Ragoun,
In Romayne, Borgoine
    and Gascoine
And þurchout al
    Breteyne.'
    (TGW 70)

Taken together, these suggest that, before proceeding to any detailed rendering of the words of the Anglo-Norman, the translator would first have broken down that source into passages, each sufficiently coherent in its subject-matter to serve as the basis for an effective tail-rhyme stanza. Where the original material was of very limited extent, and could not convincingly be expanded by his unaided powers of invention, it was supplemented by material from cognate texts already in Middle English, whether consulted or remembered. In TGW 40, the two couplets of E 7815–18 were prised apart to let in a cluster of extra topographical detail (as well as some further generalization in the third stanza-unit); some of this, at least, could have proceeded from first-hand knowledge on the part of the translator. In TGW <u>70</u>, by contrast, the first couplet of **E** 8135-8 was opened out to provide the first two tail-lines of the stanza, but the second couplet was more radically broken up, and its material diffused through four separate lines of the stanza, amongst a mass of new detail derived from other parts of *Gui*,[15] as well as from other literary texts. At least one of these (the *King of Tars*, whose eponymous hero is mentioned in TGW <u>70</u>) was already in English, copied into the Auchinleck MS by the same scribe as TGW.[16]

But altogether more important than *Tars* as a secondary source of TGW is *Amis and Amiloun* (AA), also composed in the four-rhyme version of the tail-rhyme stanza, also copied into MS Auchinleck by its principal scribe.[17] Its pervasive emotionalism and emphasis upon suffering, together with some of its narrative themes,[18] gave it particular relevance to TGW, while its redactor's ubiquitous (and — this time — skilful) use of the four-rhyme stanza provided a repertoire of extended rhyme-sequences of words or phrases that would have been most useful to one who was finding the demands of the form increasingly irksome. These sequences in AA may sometimes be used to expand short-winded passages in *Gui* to stanza-length (as in the description of feasting in TGW <u>16</u>;

---

[15] Seven of the fifteen additional names of countries provided in TGW are to be found at other points in **E**.

[16] On ff. 7ra–13vb. It is held by Mordkoff to have been copied by the principal scribe after the couplet *Guy*, but before TGW (op. cit., pp. 97–8 and Table 4).

[17] On ff. 48vb–61ara.

[18] The central episode of TGW places much stress on the theme of sworn brotherhood that dominates the whole of AA.

compare **E** 7539–42 and **AA** 433–7), sometimes to give greater intensity to passages that were originally of much the same length (as in the description of Guy's self-reproaching in TGW <u>22</u>; compare **E** 7583–94 and **AA** 2137–42). Most interesting of all, however, are instances where they help the translator decisively to cut his original down to size.

These are best exemplified by TGW <u>34</u>, which is less than half of the length of the corresponding part of *Gui*:

Puis s'en avala del dungun	Now is Gij fram Warwike fare
De la cité s'en va a larrun;	
Unques a home ne parla,	
Neis a Heralt qu'il mult ama;	
Mais a la mer dreit s'en ala,	Vnto þe se he went ful 3are,
En Jerusalem puis aler voldra.	And passed ouer þe flod.
Desore d'errer ne finera,	
En Jerusalem si vendra	
E en meinte estrange terre	
U les sainz Deu purra requere.	
La dame est remise en la tur,	Þe leuedy bileft at hom in care
Qui mult i meine grant dolur:	Wiþ sorwe and wo and sikeing sare:
	Wel drery was hir mode.
'Deu!' fait ele, 'que ferai,	'Allas, allas!' it was hir song:
Quant mun seignur perderai,	
La ren del mund que plus amai?	
E jo coment vivre purrai?'	

Atant chet pasmé a la
tere,
Tel duel ne veistes femme
faire:
Ses dras depecer, ses
crins detraire,
De sa vie ert grant
arveire;
Ses mains detort, qui
blanches erent,
Que les anels des deiz
depecerent,
Par sum des deiz le sanc
parut,
Dure vie demena la nuit;
De pasmer e plurer ne
fina,
Sun bon seignur tutdis
regretta.
(E 7727–52)

Hir here sche drouȝ, hir
hond sche wrong,

Hir fingres brast o
blode.
Al þat niȝt til it was day
Hir song it was
wayleway:
For sorwe sche ȝede
ner wode.
(TGW 34)

As can be seen, a wide variety of explanatory and linking detail has been omitted here: Guy's concern with keeping his intentions secret; his journey to the Holy Land (together with a statement of his purpose in doing so); the actual words of Felice's lament. And the proportions of the original have also been changed, with the journeying of the hero now more clearly subordinated to the lamentations of the heroine. Given the translator's weakness for producing whole stanzas that described wanderings over the face of England, Europe, or the Near East, it is at first surprising that he should not here have produced another wholly given up to Guy's pilgrimage (following it with another concerned only with Felice), but this becomes easier to understand once we have noted that the rhyme-words in the first two couplets in TGW 34 correspond exactly to those found, in the same position in the stanza, in AA 253–7. This passage also tells how a journey to be made

by one character is deeply unwelcome to a second (who will
be staying put), and the emotional voltage — generated in the
first instance by the common sequence of rhyme-words — is
high:

> When þat sir Amiloun was al ȝare,
> He tok his leue forto fare,
>   To wende in his iorné.
> Sir Amis was so ful of care,
> For sorwe and wo and sikeing sare
>   Almest swoned þat fre.
> To þe douke he went wiþ dreri mode
> And praid him fair, þer he stode
>   And seyd, 'Sir, par charité:
> ȝif me leue to wende þe fro;
> Bot ȝif Y may wiþ mi broþer go,
>   Mine hert it brekeþ of þre!'
>   (AA 253–64)

Here the 'paragraphing' of the source-text, that was an
indispensable preliminary to turning it into tail-rhyme stanzas,
has been controlled, both in respect of form and of content, by
familiarity with an already existing tail-rhyme romance of trial
and tribulation. At other points in TGW the influence of AA
upon the actual phrasing may be confined to the first two
couplets of the stanza; that is, the 'mould' which AA provided
for our translator was very much an open-ended one.[19] And
in at least one of the half-stanzas produced in this way, the
compression of the narrative by the AA rhyme-sequence
creates an intriguing discontinuity in the narrative. The lines
involved are AA 121–6, in which the fathers of the two heroes
reply to the duke's request that they should leave their sons in

---

[19] AA seems also to have provided 'moulds' for half- and whole stanzas
in *Horn Childe*: see M. Mills, op. cit., p. 73, and the notes to lines 817–22
and 961–72.

his charge:

> Þe riche barouns answerd ogain,
> And her leuedis gan to sain
>   To þat douke ful ȝare
> Þat þai were boþe glad and fain
> Þat her leuely children tvain
>   In seruise wiþ him ware.

This sequence of rhyme-words was carried over into the TGW
version of **E** 7461–70, in which a different duke receives an
answer to a different question: when will his daughter (Felice)
stop prevaricating and choose a husband for herself at last?

'Sire,' fait ele, 'jo en
          penserai,
De ci al tierz jur le vus
          dirrai.'

Felice answerd oȝain:

'Fader,' quaþ hye, 'ichil
          þe sain
Wiþ wordes fre and
          hende.'

Cum il vint al tierz jur,
Li quons apele par grant
          amur
Felice sa fille qui tant ert
          sage:
'Fille, di mei tun corage.'
'Sire,' fait ele, 'ben vus
          mustrai
Cum en mun corage
          proposé l'ai;
Ne vus en peist si jol vus
          di,
Bel dulz sire, ço vus en
          pri.'
   (**E** 7461–70)

'Fader,' quaþ sche, 'ichil
          ful fayn
Tel þe at wordes tvain,

Bi him þat schop
          mankende.'
          (TGW 9)

This time, it will be noted, the material taken over has compressed what were originally two distinct occasions in **E** into one (as in AA), with **E** 7464–6 completely squeezed out as a result. In consequence, the heroine now seems to be clearing her throat at somewhat excessive length, giving a (nervous?) hiccough in the middle of doing so, and starting again from the beginning. None of which is really like her at all.

*   *   *

If we bring together all that the individual comparative passages have suggested about way in which TGW was put together, and arrange these inferences in their most plausible chronological sequence, we shall arrive at the following:

> The romance of AA, broadly cognate in tone and in some of its material, first suggested that the final stages in Guy's story should be told as a self-contained romance, and told in tail-rhyme stanzas instead of in couplets. Like AA too, this new 'pious' romance of Guy was originally to have been cast in the four-rhyme stanza throughout, but this proved too difficult for the M.E. translator, even with the help of a number of sequences of rhyming lines, phrases, and words drawn from AA itself, and some very free handling of the source material at certain points. After stanza 52 he gave up the struggle, and adopted the less demanding five-rhyme form of the stanza, which, with only rare and perhaps accidental exceptions, he stayed with to the end of the story.[20]

Apart from its intrinsic interest, a scenario of this kind would also have its relevance to the long-continued debate

---

[20] The only stanzas in the rest of TGW that are certainly four-rhyme are 88, 92, 98, 135, 184, 210 and 252.

about the origins of MS Auchinleck as a whole; whether it
was, as L. H. Loomis first suggested, the product of a London
'Bookshop', in which vernacular texts were not only copied,
but sometimes created for the first time — presumably in a
small back room on the same premises — out of native or
foreign originals.[21] Of course, TGW has been of central
importance to this theory from the very beginning, though for
aspects of it that have not usually been of central importance
to the present study. Particular stress has been laid on the fact
that only in the Auchinleck texts are the stories of Guy and
his son Reinbrun disentangled one from the other, to become
separate, homogeneous romances. This radical rearrangement,
together with the (equally unique) narration of both stories in
tail-rhyme stanzas, and their assigning to different scribes, has
been taken to imply a collaborative exercise in bookmaking,
that was very consciously 'directed' by someone concerned to
produce a commercially viable collection of texts with
maximum speed.

To suppose that the form and narrative range of a new
translation would have been determined by a person quite
distinct from the one who did the actual translating, would, in
itself, be quite consistent with what has been noted of TGW.
It would certainly explain why the translator here adopted, and
for some time persisted with, a metrical form that seemed to
put so great a strain upon his powers. Equally, the period of
time needed to produce his 'new' version would be one way
of accounting for the gap in the copying that is so clearly
apparent on f. 146vb. It must, however, be noted that the view
that has been taken of the relationship of TGW to AA is the

---

[21] L. H. Loomis, 'The Auchinleck Manuscript and a possible London
Bookshop of 1330–1340', *PMLA*, 57 (1942), 595–627. Recent scholarly
opinion has been much divided over the plausibility of this theory; see M.
Mills, op. cit., pp. 79–80.

exact opposite of Loomis's own,[22] as it is of W. Möller's[23] before her, and C. Fewster's[24] after her, since all of these scholars have supposed or accepted that AA, and not TGW, was the derivative text. The present study is clearly not the place to consider in detail the arguments put forward for this opposing view of the matter; it would in any case seem premature at this stage to attempt either to demolish them, or to reinterpret any part of the evidence put forward in their support.[25] Such developments must wait upon the production of a detailed study of all three Auchinleck texts of *Guy*, both in relation to their principal sources, and to *Amis*; an updating, and extension, of Möller's own, that would take some time to complete, but which would certainly justify the time and effort involved.

---

[22] Op. cit., 612.

[23] See his *Untersuchungen über Dialekt und Stil des mittelenglischen Guy of Warwick in der Fassung der Auchinleck-Handschrift und über das Verhältnis des strophischen Teiles des Guy zu der mittelenglischen Romanze Amis und Amiloun*, diss. (Königsberg, 1917), 47–105.

[24] *Traditionality and Genre in Middle English Romance* (D. S. Brewer, 1987), pp. 60–66.

[25] It may still be noted, however, that the seventeen parallels between AA and TGW that are given by Möller in fact give very variable support to his case; a number of them could imply the dependence as well of TGW as of AA, and one of the most striking — as he himself concedes (op. cit., 94) — quite positively supports the precedence of AA. Even the descriptions of feasting in TGW 15–18 / AA 97–132, 409–44, 1505–24, which are conveniently set out by Fewster (op. cit., p. 61) are not quite conclusive, since although a description of feasting is to be found at the relevant place in the Anglo-Norman *Gui* (E 7533–54), but not in any of the surviving texts of the Anglo-Norman *Amis e Amilun*, none of these texts can actually have been the direct source of AA.

Partonopeu de Blois and its Fifteenth-Century English Translation: a Medieval Translator at Work

BRENDA HOSINGTON

THE Old French *Partonopeu de Blois*, probably written around 1180, was translated into seven languages and has been preserved in seven more or less complete manuscripts, the oldest of which is the Paris Arsenal. There are two English versions of the poem, both entitled *Partonope of Blois*. One has survived only as a fragment and is based on a now-lost French source. The other, which is the subject of the present paper, is a 12,000-line translation of a no-longer extant French manuscript. It follows the Arsenal manuscript in parts but ends differently. The most complete of the five fifteenth-century manuscripts of this longer version is the British Museum Add. MS 35288 dating from between 1470 and 1500 and written by three scribes of varying ability and different dialects. This is the manuscript that Bödtker used as the base text for his edition and that has mainly served for the present study.[1] Like most of the Middle English romances, *Partonope of Blois* reflects the changes in literary and social conventions one would expect in a poem composed much later than its French source and for a very different audience. Although probably fairly sophisticated, the Partonope audience nevertheless would have been a bourgeois one, not as familiar with courtly literature conventions as most of their French aristocratic predecessors. This must be kept in mind when discussing the nature of some of the changes that the translator made. As to the number and importance of these changes, they are not the subject of the present study. Rather than making an overall evaluation of the translation's fidelity, I shall focus on two aspects: the translator's comments on his source and declarations about his translating methods, and his handling of the complex Narrator figure.

Partonopeu de Blois, a reworking of the Cupid and Psyche story combined with strong elements of Celtic myth, tells how Melior, the queen of Byzantium, falls in love with Partonopeu, the young nephew of the King of France, and brings him by magic to her palace in Chief d'Oire in order to wed him when he is old enough. Although they become lovers, he is forbidden to see her. One day he breaks the taboo and is banished. He resolves to die but is saved by Urraque, Melior's sister, and Persowis, her favourite lady in waiting. Returning incognito to Chief d'Oire, Partonopeu wins Melior's hand in a three-day tournament.

---

[1] All quotations will be from the following editions and line references will be indicated in parentheses in the text. *The Middle English Versions of Partonope of Blois*, edited by A. Trampe Bödtker, EETS ES 109 (London, 1912). *Partonopeu de Blois: A French Romance of the Twelfth Century*, edited by Joseph Gildea, O.S.A., 2 vols (Villanova, Penn., 1967–68).

The narrative is preceded by a 134-line Prologue, which falls into two parts. The first deals with personal matters (1–76). It is spring and the birds' songs call one to love, but this brings the Narrator both the joy of remembering his own love and the pain of being denied it. His youth and energy, together with his lord's generosity, will enable him 'par envoiseüre/En escrit metre une aventure/Et bele et bone et mervellouse' (70–72) (for amusement's sake to write a fine, beautiful and marvellous adventure story), but devoid of either 'vilonie' or 'folie'. The promise constitutes a link with the second part of the Prologue, which defends the moral worth of literature (77–134). All written works, the Narrator states, contain examples of good and evil and teach how, by extracting the 'miel' from the 'amertume' (123), to choose between wisdom and folly. Moreover, he contends, stories told in the vernacular are as useful as those told in Latin, despite clerks' claims to the contrary.

The translator omits the first part of the Prologue, presumably because the Narrator's description of himself as poet and lover did not pertain to him, a point which will be dealt with in some detail in the final part of this paper. The second part, on the contrary, is translated quite closely, some changes notwithstanding. One of these, the omission of the defence of the vernacular, is wholly appropriate. Firstly, the English poet is translating from one vernacular to another so that the question of using Latin does not arise. Secondly, the defence was a poetic convention recognizable to many in the French poet's twelfth-century audience but probably not to the translator's.[2] The statement that books teach good and bad by example is on the other hand expanded: old stories also inform

---

[2] In *From Memory to Written Record: England 1066–1307* (London, 1979), M. T. Clanchy discusses medieval authors' statements concerning their sources and their use of the vernacular topos, pp. 250–51.

us of 'thynge that was be-fore/Wroghte or don' (8–9), making
old things seem new. They also teach us a more specific moral
lesson: 'How we moste gouerned be/To worshyppe Gode in
trinite' (16–17). 'Governing' and 'governance' are terms that
will reappear many times in the English poem.

Another amplification in the Prologue is of particular
interest for what it tells us about the audience and presentation
of the Middle English romances. While the French poet only
alludes in passing to the two types of audience for whom he
is writing, 'cil qui l'oront et veront' (92) (those who will hear
and those who will see it), the translator devotes ten lines to
pointing out the usefulness of books to both the 'letteryd' and
the 'lewed', those who please 'Stories for to rede' and 'for to
here'. Adding to his source, he defends the worth of all
genres, 'bokes ben wryten in prose,/And eke in ryme' (5–6),
and all modes of presentation, 'in gestes songe,/Or els in prose
tolde wyth tonge' (26–27).

Although explicit about the genre and presentation of
'olde stories', the translator nowhere suggests in the Prologue
that the one he is about to tell is a translation. We have to
wait for over 2000 lines before we learn that:

> Y am comawndyt of my souereyne
> Thys story to drawe, fulle and playne,
> Be-cawse yt was ful vnknowthe and lytel knowe,
> From frenche ynne-to yngelysche, that beter nowe
> Hyt my3th be to euer-y wy3hthte.
>   (2335–39)

The doublet 'fulle' and 'playne' emphasizes the fact that the
translation is not an abridgement (many of the romances
were), but a faithful rendering, at least in terms of length.

While this reference to the work as a translation appears
rather late in the romance, there is no attempt to conceal the
fact that the author is working from a French source. It is
preceded by no fewer than fifteen references to 'my auctour',

'the ffrenshe boke', 'thys cronycle which I rede', and so on. The translator even compliments his source on being 'full well I-wryted/In ffrenshe also, and fayre endyted' (500–01). In all, there are thirty such references, and they fall into three distinct categories.

The majority are of a general nature and do actually refer to a specific line in the French that conveys the same information. Most are simply source tags, functioning as line-fillers or rhyme-providers, 'boke/toke' being a favourite example. Some are used for emphasis, or to give credence to a statement, in much the same way as 'auctoritees' are invoked in medieval poetry. When Persowis' amatory sufferings are being foretold, for example, the translator states that her present disinterest in love stems not from chastity but from youth, adding 'as seith myn auctour' (7626–29), and then concluding, 'Wherfore myn auctour seith truly' she will one day feel love's dart (7630–32).

The second and third categories of source reference concern instances in which the translator has actually changed his source in some way, despite his claims to the contrary. There are only two cases where he adds materials that he pretends can be found in his source (685–87 and 2050–52). Both are simply small details included in descriptions. The last category of inaccurate references however is more complex, with some of the examples contributing significantly to the, at times, independent nature of the English poem. In one case, the translator turns a 'pucelle' into a man but immediately adds 'hys name telleth not [t]hys boke' (265). In another, he makes an appropriate cultural shift: 'Gaule ... nostre ancissor' (346) becomes 'Galles, as myne auctor seyes' (317). Other such source references are used to comic effect. The French Narrator describes Melior's fear of losing her reputation in 18 lines; his English counterpart takes 111, then follows this with a brevity *topos* that takes another five and concludes: 'Therfore fully I me purpose/After myn auctor to make an ende'

(1295–96). A similar technique is used at lines 5143–46 in the portrait of the King of France's niece. The Narrator wants to describe her beauty, 'Affter þe sentence off myne auctowre', but begs to be excused from performing such a 'grette labowre'; he nevertheless reproduces the portrait feature for feature in twenty-one lines rather than thirteen. In the portrait of Urake he uses a dismissal topic to similar effect. After asking why he should bother to describe the 'Idell mater' of her clothes, which can be found in the French — how could a fine lady be anything but finely dressed? — he gives a rapid catalogue of the parts of her body, while asking why it should be necessary; eschewing description, he will not repeat his author's 'grette tale' (6160–87). A final reference that also produces a comic effect, but perhaps unintentionally this time, occurs when Melior stretches out her leg in bed and 'o son pie le tousel sent' (1144) (feels the young man with her foot): this becomes she 'happed to ffele,/Trewely the ffrenshe boke sayeth þe hele' (1299). Rhyme, as Pope said about translating Homer, can prove a hard task-master.

The translator's handling of the literary *topoi* used in the French is of interest. The French Narrator deals summarily with a whole section of Partonopeu's ancestors because their names have been lost in history (396–97); the English Narrator dismisses them as unnecessary too, but because the French 'cronycle' has not recorded them (389–11).[3] Two veracity *topoi* — the poet stops his description because he would be called a liar (859–60) but his audience will believe him later (867–72) — are merged into a dismissal *topos* that blames the

---

[3] A later refusal by the French Narrator to list all the King of France's ancestors except Priam, 'Ne vuel son linage conter' (9907), is replaced by a direction to the curious reader to find the names in 'the boke called þe seege of Troy' (11577–78). This is undoubtedly Lydgate's *Troy-Book* where, in Book II, 236ff., Priam's lineage is listed. John Lydgate, *Troy-Book*, edited by Henry Bergen, EETS ES 97, 103, 106, 126 (London, 1906–35).

French for being too detailed and concludes: 'Hyt were to longe as nowe for me/Alle þat to telle' (929–32). Finally, a distancing *topos* is borrowed in form but its message is changed:

Se Persowis a un pou d'ire	The hete of love hir herte did feynte;
Et s'asiet sovent et sospire,	With wise abydying þe fyre she queynte.
Ne m'en devroit gaires peser,	Thus seith myn auctour after whome I write.
Car si vuelt om de moi gaber.	Blame not me: I moste endite
(6325–28)	As nye after hym as euer I may,
	Be it soþe or less I can not say.
	(7740–45)

(If Persowis is a little distressed and often sits and sighs, I shouldn't be too concerned about it. Otherwise people will make fun of me).

The opening line of the English intensifies the French, the second one introduces a moral tone, while the third constitutes a claim that is frankly untrue. The imperative 'blame not me' is a stronger and more explicit formulation of the French Narrator's rather uncaring statement in which he distances himself from Persowis for fear of derision. In the English poem, moreover, the translator is distancing himself not from a character but from the *author*. All the while shielding behind a declaration that he is translating closely, which of course he is not in this instance, he injects a personal note that throws into question the 'truthfulness' of the French Narrator's account. This final source reference raises the question of the Narrator's role in both the French and English poems.

The Narrator of *Partonopeu de Blois* stands squarely in the line of romance clerkly narrator figures, although he is sharply characterized to an unusual degree.[4] He defends *clergie*, both in the Prologue and in later places in some versions of the poem which did not serve for the English translation; he comments on general matters of social or moral concern; he expounds his views on women and love; lastly and perhaps most interestingly, he relates his own unrequited love for his Lady, the dedicatee, to the events taking place in his narrative.

The frequent interruptions made by the Narrator in order to present his worldly-wise views on life are handled with much freedom by the translator. Some are attributed to other characters and put into direct speech, as in fact are many of the passages that are simply narrated in the original. For example, the Narrator's terse comment on the dangers of seafaring (745–48) is put into a prayer offered up by a terrified Partonope as he is cut adrift in Melior's magic boat (800–09). Other general comments are omitted entirely, even when the surrounding text is closely translated.[5] The majority however are translated, although in a variety of ways.

---

[4] For a discussion of the Narrator figure in Old French romance, see Karl Uitti, 'The Clerkely Narrator Figure in Old French Hagiography and Romance', *Medioevo Romanzo*, 11 (1975), 394–408. A wider-ranging study covering Old French, German and English romance is found in Chapter Seven of D. H. Green's *Irony in the Medieval Romance* (Cambridge, 1979), pp. 213–45. The Narrator in *Partonopeu de Blois* is discussed in some detail in John Grigsby, 'The Narrator in *Partonopeu de Blois, Le Bel Inconnu,* and *Joufroi de Poitiers*', *Romance Philology*, XXI (1968), 536–43, and Roberta L. Krueger, "The Author's Voice: Narrators, Audiences, and the Problem of Interpretation" in *The Legacy of Chrétien de Troyes*, edited by Norris J. Lacy, Douglas Kelly and Keith Busby. Vol. 1 (Amsterdam, 1987), pp. 115–140.

[5] For example at 1071–72, 4488, 5405–07.

The translator sometimes elaborates on a short comment, thus losing the pithy quality of the original. At other times he makes a general comment more specific. The good speak of good things, the evil of bad, says the French (9009–11), but the English specifies, 'And evill tonges lust but Iape and play', adding for good measure: 'Of þis false worlde þis is þe gouernunce/Good and Evill haue dyuers purvyance' (1066–70). The number of general comments made by the English Narrator are not many, but three in particular deserve mention because they all treat the same subject, the vagaries of Fortune, and two contain possible echoes of Lydgate's *Troy-Book*, a work with which the *Partonope* poet was familiar, as we have already seen.[6] Lastly, many of the French Narrator's comments are rendered word for word although embedded in an otherwise freely translated passage, as the following example demonstrates:

Parthonopeu la voit el vis;	Full hevy and thoughtfull is he,
N'est merveille s'il est pensis,	Be-holdyng þe beaute of his lady,
Qui voit dame tant desiree,	So fayre, so fresshe, and so semely,
Dont a fait si grant consieree,	Stondyng be-fore hym gay arrayed.
Ensorketot si bele rien,	No wonder þough he were dismayed
Et ki plaine est de si grant bien,	To þinke how lovyng to hym she had be,
Et dont il a ses bons eüs,	And þrow his deffaute all loste had he.
Qu'il a par son meffait perdus.	
(7444–51)	(8966–72)

[6] The references in *Partonope* are at 591–92, 4389–91, 9226–35 and in the *Troy-Book* at IV 2683 and II 2038.

(Parthonopeu sees her face. It's no wonder he's so pensive, seeing the Lady whom he had desired so much and longed for so greatly. Above all, she was so beautiful a creature and full of such great qualities, and he had enjoyed her love. Now through his misdeeds he had lost her).

Here, as elsewhere in the poem, the translator has reordered the lines and made a few changes but reproduced the Narrator's interjection in line 7445 closely both in form and content. Its placement after the description of the lady rather than before does not have a weakening effect; rather, it constitutes simply a different rhetorical technique. In fact, it is reinforced in the English by the addition of an introductory line that prepares the reader for the exclamation. The surrounding text demonstrates the co-existence of freedom and fidelity that characterizes the whole translation. The lady's beauty is emphasized at the expense of her renown, desirability and virtues but equal attention is given in the closely translated final lines to her love for the hero and his fault in bringing about his own downfall.

The Narrator's general comments least well rendered are the seven couched in proverbial form.[7] Three are omitted completely: two occur in long passages entirely omitted (F4339–41, F4353–4), one occurs in an otherwise carefully translated passage (F5775–78, E7082–5). Three proverbs are paraphrased with, as one might expect, a loss of emphasis and

---

[7] For the French proverbs see Elisabeth Schulze-Busacker, *Proverbes et expressions proverbiales dans la littérature narrative du Moyen-Age français: Recueil et analyse* (Paris, 1985). The proverbial material in the English *Partonope* has been discussed, although rather superficially and at times inaccurately, by B. J. Whiting in 'Proverbs in Certain Middle English Romances in Relation to their French Source', *Harvard Studies and Notes in Philology and Literature* 15 (Cambridge, Mass., 1933), pp. 75–126.

change of tone, as in the following example:[8]

Mais ce solt estre l'aventure	Lo! so gan fortune with- outen leace
Ke cil vit trop ki n'en a cure,	Gyde a man right as hir luste,
Ki vivre vuelt, mort demanois:	For his comyng into þe forest
Tels est el siecle li bellois.	Was amonge the serpentes to dey.
(5775–78)	(7082–85)

(But that's the way fortune is. He who's tired of life lives too long while he who wants to live long dies young. Such is the injustice our times).

The proverb in line 5776 and its proverbial-sounding reinforcing statement in the following line are replaced by a rather prosaic comment on man's helplessness in the hands of fate, while the complaint of the final line disappears completely, to be replaced by an explanation of the narrative. The translator adds two proverbs of his own, both in the references to fortune mentioned on page 239. Lastly, he substitutes an English proverb, 'þought to a man is euer ffre', for a French one stating that troubles come unannounced and suddenly (F9223–24), introduces it with the formula, 'Therefore þis proverbe is seide full truly!' and then elaborates, 'What euer he luste þinke may he' (10883–5). The seven proverbs spoken by the French Narrator, being comments on the human condition, contribute to his placement in the tradition of reflective and worldly-wise romance narrator figures. Although the translator omits six of the seven proverbs, he does add two of his own and makes one

---

[8] Also at F3647–50, E4727–28 and F7829, E9436–37.

substitution, also of general import. His changes therefore do not weaken this particular aspect of the Narrator's character. Other comments made by the Narrator express social concerns. One states that much is heard about rich knights but nothing about poor ones, 'Por tant sont li povre teü/Et li riche home amenteü' (8955–56), but this occurs in a passage omitted from the English. On the other hand, a similar comment is added by the translator later: 'For he þat is destyned to be a knave,/Lyveth more in suerte þen doþe a lorde' (9233–4). The object of the French Narrator's censure however is the upstart, or 'filz a vilain', who has been raised to the nobility, a figure criticised elsewhere in twelfth-century romance. There are three such substantial comments, all reduced in length in the English. Anchises' treachery at Troy is explained by his having been a 'serf', or 'knave', and his actual kinship with Aeneas is denied because the latter is too noble to have such a father. While the English text remains vague as to the 'kinship' (272), the French text makes Anchises the step-father. This prompts the Narrator to advise noblewomen married to men of 'put lin' (ignoble lineage) to seek fathers for their children elsewhere, for 'Maus fruit ist de male rais' (307–14) (bad fruit comes from a bad root), a counsel perhaps considered too osé by the translator, who omits the passage. The 17-line passage on Clodon, who caused social upheaval by ennobling many a 'filz a vilain' (416 ff.), is reduced to seven lines, and the angry social comments to one: 'Chorles he cheresede, and no-þynge Ientyle' (420). Clovis' redressment of the social-class situation (445 ff.) is not given any emphasis in the English; only his overall ability to govern is stressed (422 ff). Since other passages describing the ennoblement of 'vilains' are also extremely reduced in length, although conveying the same ideas, it is probable that the fifteenth-century translator purposely shortened them; he might well have felt that criticism of the socially mobile would be less well received by his bourgeois audience than by their aristocratic predecessors.

The Narrator in *Partonopeu de Blois* plays an important role in commenting on love and women. He does so in over thirty places in the poem. Once again, the translator handles the comments in a variety of ways, rendering some closely, others less so, omitting a few but adding even fewer.

The opinions on love are varied, although admittedly none is very original. Love is a source of contention, as seen in both poems in the battle between Partonopeu and the Sultan: 'Molt duret entr'els li estris,/Bien semble qu'amors s'i est mis' (9557–58) (The quarrel between them lasted a long time. Apparently love was involved) becomes 'Love haþe hem sette in oo place boþe,/Wher-fore ofte they have be wroþe' (11104–05). Love brings great and inescapable cares: 'Ensi set amors fol cuer traire' (9780) (Thus love can make the foolish heart suffer) is rendered rather more poetically as 'Thei canne in no wise her care with-drawe,/Of loves servauntes suche is þe lawe' (11406–07). In another instance, the translator changes a metaphor from 'la riote' of love (9847) to 'Now hoppe if he can, he is come to þe ringe', and he adds to his source the motif of love-sick sleeplessness (11485–87). The translator also expands a one-line comment on jealousy into four; he had explored the theme in a fabliau-like exemplum that Partonope recounts to Melior, but which does not appear in any of the extant French manuscripts. Above all, love wields great power over people, says the French Narrator, a power that can drive one mad. This is played down in the English; only three out of the four comments are translated and even these are reduced in length.[9] On the other hand, both Narrators assure their audiences that once love has taken a hold, it can in no way be withstood (8235–46 and

---

[9] The proverb at 1814, 'Car bone amors ne set mesure', is ignored.

10150–60). Love does however have one positive quality, conveyed in both texts but with minor changes:

Ensi set amors engignier	Lowe, thys can love wyth-owte ffayle
Cascun home de son mestier :	Make eche man hys mastere vse:
Chevalier de chevalerie,	Knyghtes shame to refuse,
Et clerc d'amender sa clergie	Clerkes to love well clergye,
Vilonie tolt et pereche,	And ladyes to cheresse
Cortesie done et noblece.	curtesy.
(3425–30)	(4453–57)

(Thus love can make each man skilful in his trade: a knight in chivalry, a clerk in improving his learning. It removes shame and sloth and engenders courtesy and nobility).

The verb 'engignier' is rendered by the noun 'mastere'. In the English, the power of love to inspire chivalry is made more specific by moving the phrase 'shame to refuse' up from the penultimate line in the French and alongside 'Knyghtes'; clerks are made to 'love well' rather than to improve (*amender*) their learning; love's impact on sloth is omitted, while its effect on courtesy is directed specifically to ladies. This last change was perhaps intended to serve as a lead into the following lines describing women who cannot love.

The overall view of women presented by the Narrator is a complex one. His professed love and approval of them is a salient feature of *Partonopeu de Blois*. Yet a closer reading reveals undercurrents of irony that put into question his sincerity and prompt the reader to wonder if the 'defender of women' stance is not in fact a literary pose.[10] In discussing

---

[10] For a detailed comparison of the women in the French and English poems, see my forthcoming article, "Voices of Protest and Submission: Portraits of Women in *Partonopeu de Blois* and its Middle English Translation", in *Reading Medieval Studies*.

the women in the two poems, one critic has said that they are portrayed differently, and that the modification is due in part to the two Narrators' views.[11] Unfortunately, he bases his assumption on only four lines of verse dealing with a very specific subject: the lady's right to refuse a dishonest proposal, which only the English Narrator grants (4463–66). A more detailed and complete study of the pertinent passages is necessary before drawing conclusions as to the 'changed' narratorial stance.

Substantial comments on women are found in twelve different places in the poem, ten of which are translated fairly closely.[12] Early in the poem, the Narrator declares there is no creature as sweet as 'dame qui wet amer/Quant Dex le wet a bien torner' (1256–58) (a lady who wishes to love when God wishes to turn her mind to it), translated as 'so kynde/As be þys wymmen, ther as þey fynde/Here serwaundes trewe and stydfaste' (1513–15). Almost all his praise of women is directed only towards women in love or those who have

[11] Ronald M. Spensley, "The Courtly Lady in *Partonope of Blois*", *Neuphilologische Mitteilungen*, 74 (1973), 288–91.

[12] The two omissions are at 6755–66 and 10569–76 in the French text. The first counsels men to 'mount' (*contresaillir*) sleeping virgins rather than watchful older ladies, which like the advice to noblewomen quoted on page 242 was probably considered too daring by the translator; the second dismisses details about festivities as 'women's talk' and declares women are protected from the snares of the devil by their beauty. The translator adds two comments of his own. The first is in a passage ironically praising women for their fidelity (10492 ff): suitors should persist even when their ladies answer lightly, for women can change their minds (12105–13). The comment is in keeping with the tone of the French. The second is at 5281 and alludes to women's garrulousness: 'When wymmen be well they can not cese'.

granted favours to their suitors, not women in general.[13] Harsh words are reserved for those who are 'dangerose'. Nor is this accidental, as will become clear when we discuss his role as Narrator-Lover. Yet these passages expressing admiration or compassion for women in love are ironic. Thus Melior's acceptance of Partonopeu's pennant is condoned and gossips are upbraided (8435–54) because her action is normal for a woman in love. The English adds: 'For whome shuld a lady be glad to pleace/But hym on whome hir herte is sette?' (10150–51). The irony of course is that Melior does not know it is Partonope. Later, her fidelity is praised and offered as proof that women are 'trewe as stele' (10109–24 and 11744–55), while her slanderers are reproved. Again, the irony is that Melior will shortly change her mind and pretend to prefer the Sultan. In none of these instances is there any major shift in the translation.

Criticism of slanderers inspires two long passages but provides the Narrator with an opportunity to list all the faults traditionally attributed to women in medieval writings. In the first (8397–8424), the Narrator distinguishes between 'mesquines' and 'dames', and blames men for not doing so. The translator fails to render the strong distinction between good and bad women but emphasizes the fault of the slanderers by adding two highly colourful comments to describe those whose tongues run away with them. This concludes with a curse that they not be admitted to the company of women, which is not in the original (10121–40). There is thus a shift in placing the blame squarely on the slánderers' heads, and some of the ironical tone of the original

---

[13] The one exception is the paean at 7125–38 in which the Narrator says women are the most beautiful of God's creations; if they do not enter heaven, he adds ironically, he will willingly renounce his place there (7125–37). This is fairly closely translated, without any loss of tone, at 8675–89.

is lost. In the second passage, it is clerks who come in for the Narrator's harsh words: those who criticise women are 'vilains', for nice clerks would never write such things, and their experience is limited to 'meschines' and 'foles'. The Narrator of course is not of their company and one day when he has time will refute their claims, for he loves all women (5507–34). The English passage is twice the length, and the criticism of the clerks and of their women is more vehement: these 'lewed freres' and 'Ioly singers' are lecherous and cannot live without their 'strumpettes', 'lemans', 'queens' and 'paramours' (6759–96). The dismissal *topos* is omitted but the English Narrator's dissociation of himself from such clerks is as explicit as in the French.

Finally, the Narrator makes two long pronouncements on women and chastity. The first ironically suggests that the only women who are chaste are the ugly ones, *par la force des choses*, for beauty and chastity are not reconcilable (6261 ff.). The English follows closely but the order of the lines is reversed, as in many places in the poem, and the passage thus ends on a description of 'foule', not fair women, and on a stronger curse: not only should they have 'nul ami', but 'noþer knyght ne knave,/Gentilman ne yeman of no degree' (7667–68). The other passage criticising chastity is in strong satirical vein, looking back nostalgically to a time when women were won with courtly virtues and cared not a whit for chastity (F8009–68, E9664–705). The French Narrator blames the new chastity on a long list of church activities that the translator curtails; he criticises women for neglecting their appearance, again in more detail than in the translation; and he deplores their new-found inability to chatter and lie, a line that is omitted. Both passages end with the same exclamation: 'Car sordes sunt de chastee' (8068) and 'I trow chastite hath made hem defe' (9705). The tone is carefully preserved in the English version despite the one small omission and a heavier emphasis on the fruits of the new holiness, namely a disregard for 'worldly lustes'.

Undoubtedly, the Narrator's most original contribution in *Partonopeu de Blois* is the comparison of his own experience in love with that of his characters, and of his own Lady with the women in the poem. In this connexion, Krueger has rightly pointed out that the 'je' in the poem 'serves as a point of potential contact between the private world of the characters' emotions and the public sphere of the general audience'.[14] This potential is not however fully realised. Firstly, the fiction of the Narrator's love for his lady, unlike that of Partonopeu's and Melior's, remains incomplete; secondly, the Narrator's voice is heard too infrequently and inconsistently. Nevertheless, the Narrator's self-interjections comparing his own situation with that of his characters' number no fewer than sixteen and contribute to making him a strongly dramatized figure in the poem.[15] It remains to be seen whether the same can be said of his English counterpart.

It can be said straight away that the translator shows more independence in these passages than in his handling of the more general narratorial comments on women and love. Only seven of the sixteen self-interjections are translated; five are omitted completely, although they occur in passages otherwise carefully rendered; four undergo important changes. Inevitably, the effect of the English Narrator on the poem must be different.

The hint in the Prologue that the Narrator is suffering from unrequited love (omitted from the translation) is made

[14] Krueger, op. cit., p. 128.

[15] The sixteen passages describing the Narrator's own love or containing references to his lady are: 57–60, 1871–86, 3441–48, 4048–52, 4543–48, 6285–96, 7545–52, 7613–16, 8473–77, 8613–16, 9019–34, 9243–66, 10105–24, 10531–36, 10607–24, 10643–56.

explicit two thousand lines later when he contrasts his suffering with Partonopeu's joy (1871–86). The English is a close rendering and its final line echoes the French: 'J'en ai le mal, et il le bien' is '[I] Have the evyl and [he] the gode' (2323). But then the translator adds a disclaimer:

> Butte playnely excusyth me,
> I am no3th in thus in-firmyte.
> God schelde me ever fro that mischaunce
> To hoppe so ferre ynne loue-ys dawnce.
> He tellyth hys tale of sentament,
> I vnder-stonde no3th hys entent,
> Ne wolle ne besy me to lere.
> (2331–34, 2347–49)

In other words, he does not understand why his author is including a personal story in his narrative. Another disclaimer occurs at the end of both poems. The French Narrator cannot describe the lovers' wedding night because he is weeping too much at having lost everything (10607–10614). The English Narrator's inability arises from a different source: 'I was neuer yite in þat plite', he says in an echo of an earlier claim that he had never 'hopped' in the 'daunce of love' (12183). A wink from his Lady will enable the French Narrator to continue his story (10620–10624). Sensibly, the translator omits this, since there will be no continuation in English. The French Narrator is completely at his Lady's mercy, for 'Ne puis garir se n'est par li' (10648) (She is my sole means of recovery). This is omitted. He prays to god to give everlasting joy to all the women in the world 'Et il m'otroit qu'al derrain jor/Soit m'arme mise entre les lor' (10656–10658) (And may he grant me, on the last day, a place amongst them); his English counterpart invokes the God of love 'þat he/His seruaunte departe so of his grace,/That they may stonde in þe same case' as Partonope and Melior. By omitting the reference to the Lady and shifting from the first to the third person in the invocation, the English Narrator distances himself from his self-interjecting French model, without however disassociating himself completely from his source text.

Two other passages demonstrate similar distancing techniques. The French Narrator wonders how Persowis can be happy, for 'sai com els va malement' (8475) (I know how she is suffering). The first person is used only as a tag in the English: 'Ye may axe me, lorde, what chere/Was with Persewise' (10185–86). Moreover, the melancholic tone of the French is changed: it would be better to be 'a recluse or elles a frere/Or elles be dede and leide on bere' (10192–3). Later, the Narrator tells his audience few know what Melior's suffering is like, 'Mais je le sai tote par cuer' for 'Des biens d'amors ne sai je joie' (9019–30) (But I know all about it for I do not enjoy the benefits of love). The first person is put to a different use in the English. Melior is

> As I suppose, in grete troublenesse.
> Ye ladies þat have love, ye knowe, I gesse.
> For I deme and she hadde good leysere,
> With hym to speke.
>   (10679–82)

Of the French Narrator's other personal comments, some are translated closely while others are curtailed or omitted.[16] Rather than attempting to speculate on the criteria used, if any, for inclusion or omission — no consistent pattern emerges — I would suggest simply that the translator wished to reduce the overall number of personal interjections in order to de-emphasize the role of Narrator-Lover in the English poem and thereby discourage any confusion of himself with the 'je' of

---

[16] Passages closely translated are: F4048–52 and E5269–73, F6285ff and E7670fff, F7609–16 and E9141ff, F7613–16 and E9146–47, F10531–36 and E12139–43. One is curtailed: F9243–66 and E10908–21. Three are omitted: F4543–48 and 7545–52 and 8613–16.

his French source. Another factor however most certainly inspired the English Narrator's stance. The general influénce of Chaucer on the *Partonope* translator was convincingly demonstrated by Whiting, whose study was nevertheless restricted to pointing out verbal echoes.[17] I would suggest that Chaucer, and particularly *Troilus and Criseyde*, also greatly influenced the detached and seemingly uncomprehending Narrator figure of the English translation. Two of the disclaimers in *Partonope* even contain verbal echoes of the *Troilus*: the Narrator expresses the hope that, unlike his French model, he will never 'hoppe so ferre ynne loue-ys dawnce' (2334) and elsewhere pleads, 'Blame not me: I moste endite as nye after [myn auctour] as euer I may' (7742–5).[18] A second author who might well have exercised some influence is Lydgate, whose *Sege of Troy* is mentioned in line 11578. The *Troy-Book* Narrator also recoils at times from his original, disassociating himself from his author's opinions in what is probably more a literary stance than a genuine disclaimer.[19] Since the *Partonope* translator's passages on Fortune that he adds to his source text contain verbal parallels with similar

[17] B. J. Whiting, "A Fifteenth-Century English Chaucerian: The Translator of *Partonope of Blois*", *Medieval Studies*, 7 (1945), 40–54.

[18] Criseyde asks Pandarus, 'How ferforth be ye put in loves daunce?' to which he answers, 'I hoppe alwey byhynde' (TC II, 1106–7). Other references to the dance of love are found at TC, I, 517–8, II 1106 and CT A 475–6. The Narrator comments on Criseyde's feelings, 'And what she thoughte, somewhat shal I write/As to myn auctor listeth for t'endite' (TC II, 699–70). In the Prologue to the Miller's Tale, Chaucer's Narrator warns his readers: 'Blameth nat me if that ye chese amys' (CT, A 3181). All quotations are from *The Works of Geoffrey Chaucer*. Edited by F. N. Robinson. 2nd. edition (Boston, 1957).

[19] Such is the opinion of the *Troy-Book* editor in his notes to lines 2118–35 and 3555–68 of Book II. Lydgate, *op. cit.*, Part 4, pp. 105 and 213.

passages in the *Troy-Book*, Lydgate's influence is not to be discounted.[20]

Partonope of Blois is a translation in which unusually close renderings exist side by side with paraphrase. The author has mingled respect for his source text with a freedom that enabled him to produce a romance that is in fact a poem in its own right. These general statements certainly obtain as regards the Prologue and the comments made by the Narrator. The *clergie* which is a concern of the French Narrator is praised in equally strong terms in the English. The worldly-wise reflections of a social and moral nature are almost all translated, although with varying degrees of fidelity. The ironic comments on love and on women reflect similar opinions in both poems, although there are slight shifts of emphasis. The translator's most independent stance, however, is seen in his handling of the Narrator's personal interjections that parallel his own sentiments and those of his characters. By omitting over half — by far the highest proportion of omissions in any of the Narrator's passages — as well as by changing from first to third person in two places and adding three disclaimers, the translator introduces a sophisticated double perspective of the kind found in other medieval works. This, together with the other by no means negligible qualities of the work, ensures the English author a place not simply in the history of translation, but also in the literature of his time.

---

[20] Derek Pearsall claims that the 'whimsical, petulant and timorous' English Narrator is 'partly derived from Chaucer ... but is even more influenced by Gower's Amans'. *Partonope* is however 'quite uninfluenced by Lydgate'. 'The English Romance in the Fifteenth Century', *Essays and Studies*, n.s. 29 (1976), 56–83. The present close comparison of the Narrator in the English poem and its source, based on verbal echo as well as on his various stances, suggests a stronger influence by Chaucer and Lydgate than Pearsall allows.

Problems of Editing a Translation: Anglo-Norman to Middle English

C. W. MARX

THE OBJECT of this paper is to examine some of the practical and theoretical problems involved in editing a translation. Editorial work on a text of this type differs from that on original composition or original compilation. On one hand the editor of the translation has the source, or a reasonable approximation to the source, in front of him or her which should, one would think, make the task easier. On the other hand the presence of this source raises a whole series of problems which introduce uncertainties into editorial decisions. The presence of the source text raises problems precisely because one seldom if ever has access to the version of the text which the translator used, the exemplar. There are always therefore question marks over crucial variations between the witnesses to the source text and those to the translation: were these present in the exemplar of the translation; are they errors by the translator; are they conscious revisions by the translator, or are they the work of later scribes? These uncertainties cloud our understanding of the text as translation and the work of the translator, and they make the editor's task an unenviable one.

The text which is the focus of this paper is *The Complaint of Our Lady and Gospel of Nicodemus*. The ME text survives in three manuscripts, *P*, *Br* and *Hh*, and there are two witnesses to the original AN (*Rl* and *Eg*).[1] The text is a loose narrative sequence made up of an account of the passion of Christ given from the point of view of the Virgin Mary, and an account of the resurrection based on portions of the latter part of the *Gospel of Nicodemus*. These two texts survive together in five medieval manuscripts and were clearly thought by scribes and a translator to form a loose narrative sequence.[2] This paper will not go into the details of arguments for establishing the textual history of the sequence; a diagram given below shows the relationships among the manuscripts which are suggested by the textual evidence:[3]

---

[1] C. William Marx and Jeanne F. Drennan, eds., *The Middle English Prose Complaint of Our Lady and Gospel of Nicodemus*, Middle English Texts, 19 (Heidelberg, 1987). The ME and AN texts are here printed in parallel; references are given in the form: page, text (ME or AN), line. [*P*] Cambridge, Magdalene College, MS Pepys 2498, pp. 449a–463b; [*Br*] Leeds, University Library, MS Brotherton 501, fols 100r–v, 114r–v, 113r–v, 112r–v, 110r–v, 111r–v, 109r–v, 108r–v, 115r; [*Hh*] San Marino, Henry Huntington Library, MS HM 144, fols 21r–54v; [*Rl*] London, British Library, MS Royal 20. B. V, fols 147r–156r; [*Eg*] London, British Library, MS Egerton 2781, fols 131r–189v.

[2] J.F. Drennan, 'The Middle English *Gospel of Nicodemus*, Huntington Library MS HM 144', *Notes and Queries*, 225 (1980), 297–98; 'The *Complaint of Our Lady* and *Gospel of Nicodemus* of MS Pepys 2498', *Manuscripta*, 24 (1980), 164–70; C. W. Marx, 'Beginnings and Endings: narrative-linking in five manuscripts from the fourteenth and fifteenth centuries and the problem of textual integrity', in *Manuscripts and Readers in Fifteenth-Century England*, edited by D. Pearsall (Cambridge, 1983), pp.70–81.

[3] Marx and Drennan, pp. 16–25.

Figure 1

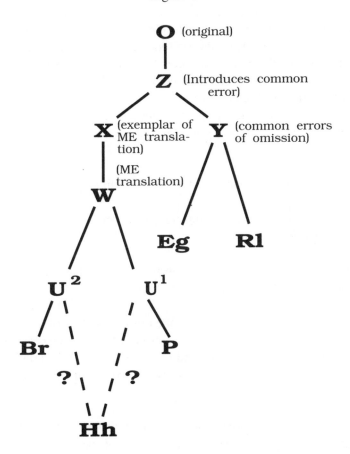

Certain hypothetical stages in the history of the sequence need to be posited to take account of variations and discrepancies, and these are the subject of this paper. The diagram illustrates the extent of our uncertainty and how far removed one from the other are the surviving witnesses in the textual history of the sequence. Although it is not immediately obvious from the diagram, *P* contains the text closest to the original of the ME translation although *Br* contains some useful readings not found in *P*. *Hh* has a much later version and can be left out of the present discussion. The two AN manuscripts, *Rl* and *Eg*, have equal claim on our attention and both are approximately the same distance from the exemplar of the ME translation.

Our main concern is with variation and discrepancy between the surviving AN and ME manuscript texts. These are of two types:

(i)   variations in readings of material common to the ME and AN, and
(ii) the presence of material unique to one of the surviving manuscripts or texts.

In dealing with this type of material the editor has a range of choices, but these come down to two:

(i)   to try to establish a text of the original ME translation, or
(ii) to compromise with the manuscript texts, to respect the integrity of each text, and to try to account for variation and discrepancy as part of a textual or manuscript history.

It is the latter approach which would probably find more favour in current thinking about the role of the editor.

Certain variations show the dependence of the ME on the AN; that is, they confirm that the ME text is a translation of the AN. For example, in the episode of the arrest of Christ the ME text reads:

hii fellen alle to þe erþe sodeynlich. (81 ME 11)

The AN reads:

ils chaieront toux a la tere souyn. (81 AN 9)

(they all fell to the ground flat on their backs.)

In the background is the biblical source, John 18. 6:

abierunt retrorsum, et ceciderunt in terram.
(they went backwards and fell to the ground.)

The Latin *retrorsum* ('backwards') and the AN *souyn* ('flat on the back') point to the ME *sodeynlich* as either a mistranslation of *souyn* at stage W in the diagram or the result of scribal error in the AN textual tradition at stage X. The ME variation, nevertheless, is derived from a problem with the AN. The second example is from the account of Judas negotiating with the high priests. The ME has:

& Iudas took þe þritti pens & seide to hem, 'I shal do ʒou to witen whan ʒe schull taken hym priuelich'. (76 ME 5–7)

The use of *schull* (*whan ʒe schull taken hym priuelich*) in this context is unexpected. In the AN text the passage reads:

Iudas prist les xxx deners & dist, 'Ieo vos fray asauoir quant vous ly prendretz'. (76 AN 2–3)
(Judas took the thirty pence and said, 'I will let you know when you may take him'.)

The form *prendretz* can be read as a *fut. 2 pl.* or as a *pres. subj. 2 pl.* The context suggests the latter interpretation in both texts ('when you may take him'). It is probable that the ME reflects a misunderstanding of the AN by the translator. A third example is taken from Mary's account of the death of Christ. The ME text reads:

And whan my susters comen to me I loked to my swete son
& seiʒ his heued bowʒeande, his cheke opon his schulder.
(107 ME 3–5)

The AN counterpart reads:

Et quant me sens reuyndrent, ieo regarday mon douz fitz &
vy sa teste encline, le menton sur le peitryn. (107 AN 2–4)

(And when I regained consciousness, I looked at my sweet
son and saw his head bowed down, his chin on his chest.)

The crucial variant is between *susters* (ME) and *sens* (AN).
The larger context of these passages points to the AN reading
as the original since Mary is said earlier in both versions to
have fainted; the return of her senses rather than her sisters is
a more plausible reading. A final example of variants of this
kind is the following from one of Mary's accounts of her
anguish at Christ's suffering:

> And whan ich had so bymened me, þan my swete son loked
> to me so pitouslich þat att his hert he feled myn anguisch þat
> he hadde of myne sorouȝes. (102 ME 10–12)

The AN text reads:

> Et quant me auoy ensi demene, mon douz fitz moy regarda
> tant pitousement qe a cuer senti les anguysses q'il auoyt de
> mes dolours. (102 AN 8–9)
> (And when I had lamented so much, my sweet son looked at
> me so piteously that in my heart I felt the pains that he had
> of my sorrows.)

The ME passage makes little sense and the AN reading shows
what was intended, '... that in (my) heart I felt the pains that
he had of my sorrows'. The awkwardness of the ME derives
from a misreading of *senti* as a *pa.t. 3 sg.* rather than a *pa.t.
1 sg.* The error is reinforced in the ME with the addition of
the possessive adjective *his, at his hert*. The misreading of
senti may reflect a scribal error or an error in translation.[4]

These four examples, and many more could be cited,
show variants in the ME text which are not independent of the
translation; that is, they are derived from the AN text in some

---

[4] *Br* (fol. 110r) shows scribal smoothing of the awkward reading: 'and
than y had so bemeinyd me that my swete sone lokyd on me so petously
that at hys hert he felt my anguysh'.

way, either as the result of scribal error in the AN text or mistranslation. These ME readings are also, in one sense, errors or misreadings or misrepresentations of the text, and in the fourth example the error has rendered the ME almost incomprehensible.[5] If we did not have access to manuscripts of the AN text and treated the ME as original prose, we would probably not suspect an error in the first two instances. In the third example we might eventually suspect a scribal error. The fourth instance would no doubt suggest corruption of some kind since the reading makes such poor sense. But, all these readings are in one sense errors, and in another sense they are integral features of the ME text; they are features of its composition as translation. The editor cannot interfere with these readings and must resist any temptation to emend. The translated text had errors in it and these are historical features of the text.

These examples suggest how the AN text can help to explain readings and problems in material common to the two texts. The second type of variation that can be isolated concerns passages unique to one manuscript or text. We find, for example, instances where the AN manuscripts contain readings for which there are no counterparts in the ME. In the

---

[5] It is possible that the ME reading reflects not so much an inadvertent error but the influence of devotional texts on the passion which allow for a multitude of almost simultaneous perspectives, for example in Bridget of Sweden's *Liber Celestis*, book I, chapter 36:

> Et cum ipse (i.e. Christ) me cerneret dolore confectam, in tantum amaricabatur de dolore meo, quod omnis dolor vulnerum suorum erat quasi sopitus sibi pre dolore meo, quem in me videbat. (Bridget of Sweden, *Sancta Birgitta Revelaciones Book I*, edited by C.-G. Undhagen, SSFS, ser. II, bd. VII: 1 (Uppsala, 1978), 344.
>
> (And when he perceived that I was consumed with grief, he was so troubled about my grief that all the pain of his own wounds was as nothing in the face of my pain which he saw in me.)

I am grateful to Roger Ellis for bringing this possibility to my attention.

episode of Christ's betrayal the AN treats the incident of the healing of Malchus's ear this way:

> & dist a ses desciples, 'Le me faitz venyr', & il tocha sa orayle & fuist tantost seyn. *& dist a felons Iues, 'Come a vn laron estes venuz od espes & bastons pur moy prendre?' Dont s'enfuyrent toux ses desciples.* Et les felons Iues lyerent mon douz fitz vilement. (82 AN 7–10; my italics)
> (And he said to his disciples, 'Have him come to me', and he touched his ear and it was immediately whole. And he said to the wicked Jews, 'Have you come with swords and staves to take me as if I were a thief?' Then all his disciples fled. And the wicked Jews despicably bound my sweet son.)

The ME reads:

> & þan he seide to his deciples, 'Doþe me come hym þat his ere was smyten of'. And he com & Ihesus took his ere & sette it on aȝein & it was als sone. And þan token þe wicked Iewes & bounden my suete son. (82 ME 8–12)

A substantial passage, that in italics, is unique to the AN. How do we account for this discrepancy? Has the ME text here lost a passage and should we therefore try to reconstruct the translation? Might the passage be a later scribal addition to the AN text and therefore not available to the translator? The case is not certain but it is probable that the unique AN passage is original. It follows the same biblical sources as the context in which it appears; it is an integral part of a larger passage of biblical paraphrase. It was probably omitted from the AN text by a scribe or the translator through eyeskip, *felons Iues* (AN 8) to *felons Iues* (AN 10). This is one way of accounting for the discrepancy and it suggests that either the AN exemplar contained errors not apparent in the surviving AN manuscripts, or the translator by a process of mechanical error failed to incorporate material into his text. Whatever the explanation, the absence of a counterpart for the italicized AN passage would seem to be a feature of the ME translation, not a later scribal error.

The next examples deal with material unique to the ME. In the *Gospel of Nicodemus* section Joseph of Arimathea describes his release from prison in this way:

> And I seide, '3if þou be Ihesus, schewe me þe beri3els þere I laide þe'. And he took me by þe honde & ledde me forþ, and lete adoun þe hous as it was toforn & lede me to þe monument. (130 ME 4–7)

The AN text reads:

> Et ieo ly dis, 'Si vous estes Ihesus, mostretz moy le monument ou ieo vous mys'. Et il par la mayn moy mena al monument. (130 AN 4–5)
> (And I said to him, 'If you are Jesus, show me the tomb in which I buried you'. And he led me by the hand to the tomb.)

The ME text has the unique phrase *& ledde me forþ, and lete adoun þe hous as it was toforn*. The repetition in the ME of *ledde me / lede me* suggests that the phrase unique to the ME was lost in its AN form from the textual tradition represented by the two surviving AN manuscripts through the simple mechanical process of eyeskip, *moy mena* to *moy mena*. So here the unique ME phrase can be accounted for not as a later scribal addition but more probably as witness to a lost AN passage. A second example is found in the episode of the judgement of Pilate. One AN manuscript reads:

> Et vous Dismas & Gestas q'estes atteint de homicide auerez la grace de graunt fest de Pasche si mes ne trespassez; ore, alez quites. (*Eg*, fol. 150r)
> (And you Dismas and Gestas who are convicted of murder, shall have the favour of the great feast of Easter as long as you commit no more crimes; now go free.)

The other AN manuscript, *Rl*, has this reading:

Et vous Barrabas q'estes ateynt de homicide, aueretz la grace de la feste de Pasche si qe mes ne trespasetz; ore, aletz ent. (94 AN 2–4)

(And you Barabbas who are convicted of murder, shall have the favour of the feast of Easter as long as you commit no more crimes; now go from here.)

The ME text reads:

And ȝee, Dismas and Gesmas, for it is founden þat ȝe ben þeues, schullen be done on þe roode, & þou Barabas þat art ateynt of mannesslauȝth schal haue þe grace of þe gret feste of Estre so þat þou trespas no more; goo now quite. (94 ME 3–7)

The variant here between the ME and the AN is the presence of material, the judgement on the two thieves, which is unique to the ME. The variant readings in the two AN manuscripts, *Dismas & Gestas* in *Eg* and *Barrabas* in *Rl* suggest that the textual deficiency is with the AN manuscripts. *Eg*'s error in assigning the condemnation of Barabbas to the two thieves resulted probably from eyeskip, *et vous* in the first to *et vous* in the second. *Eg*'s error, which it shared with *Y*, represents the first stage of corruption in which the original condemnation of the thieves was lost; *Rl*'s reading then is likely to be a scribal correction based on knowledge of the gospels. Here again the ME text is witness to material lost from the AN. A slightly more complicated example occurs in the description of the stretching of Christ on the cross. The ME text reads:

And after whan hii comen to his fete hii seiȝen þat his heles ne comen nouȝt to þe bore by a coute & more, þat is half a ȝerd. And wiþ a corde, as bifore is seide, *hii tiȝeden on his brest & anoþer opon his fete* & drowȝen euer til þat his heles comen ouer þe bore. (99 ME 14–18; my italics)

One AN manuscript reads:

Puys quant vindrent a ses piez trouerent qe ses talouns ne attendirent mye al trew d'un cout. Et en mesme la manere come desus est dist, treerent ses piez taunt qe les talouns des piez furent outre le treu. (*Eg*, fols 155v–156r)
(Then when they came to his feet they found that his heels did not reach the hole by a cubit. And in the same manner as is said above, they drew his feet until the heels of his feet were over the hole.)

The other AN manuscript, *Rl*, reads:

Puys quant vyndrent a ses pies trouerent qe ses talons ne attenderent mye al treu. D'une corde en mesme la manere, come deuant est dit, treherent ses pies tanqe les caues des pies feurent outre le treu. (99 AN 11–14)
(Then when they came to his feet they found that his heels did not reach the hole. With a rope, in the same manner as was said before, they drew his feet until the insteps of his feet were over the hole.)

There are two interesting variants in these passages. First, where *Rl* reads *d'une corde* (with a rope), *Eg* reads *d'un cout* (by a cubit). There are counterparts for both readings in the ME text, which suggests that neither AN manuscript has the correct or complete reading but that the two AN variants had a place in the original and the exemplar of the ME translation. The second variant is the phrase unique to the ME: *hii tiȝeden on his brest & anoþer opon his fete*. There is no obvious mechanical explanation to account for the absence of this phrase from the AN text, but it is integral to the description of the stretching of Christ on the cross and there is a possibility that here too the ME text is witness to a phrase lost from the AN.

These examples point to errors of omission in the surviving witnesses to the AN text. In these instances and others the ME text can be used to reconstruct features of the translator's exemplar and probably the original text as well. Also, in terms of constructing a textual or manuscript history of the sequence, these examples highlight the interdependence of the AN and ME texts. For the editor, the ME is not only dependent on the AN, but a fuller picture of the original AN emerges from a consideration of the evidence of the ME text.

The status of certain passages unique to the ME is frequently ambiguous. The last example discussed (*hii tiȝeden on his brest & anoþer opon his fete*) is a case in point. An even more problematic passage is the following. The ME text reads:

'And my swete son seide pitouslich, "For on of ȝou I schal ben bitrayed þat eteþ wiþ me at my boord". And vchone of hem hadde gret drede & seide, "Is it ouȝth ich?" And my swete son seide, "He þat eteþ wyþ me of my dische". *& ȝutt hii nysten nouȝth for soþe for all hii eten of þat mete þat he ete of. And seint Iohan þe Ewangelist lened hym to Ihesus breest and Peter loked opon hym for þat he schulde asken hym who þat it was. And seint Iohan asked hym who it was & Ihesus Crist seide hym, "He þat I wete þe bred in wyne & putte it in his mouþe, he it is". And he wett a morsel of bred & putt it in Iudas mouþe and þe deuel entred wiþ it & took þan so gret power ouer hym for he resceiued þe sacrement.'* And þat ilch resceyuynge made þat he fel into wanhope as summe of þise clerkes seien. And þerfore ich rede þat vche man bewar boþe lerde & lewed þat hym resceyueþ, and sorer owen þe lered to ben adradde þan þe lewed for he wot what he doþe. And Ihesus Crist whan he henge opon þe rode, he bisouȝt for hem þat ne wist nouȝth what hii duden. And þe lerde man wot what he doþe for he seeþ it toforn hym ywriten & þerfore he is þe more forto blame. Naþeles ich rede þat vche lewed man it doute & þe more whan he it wott. 'And þan Iudas seide onon, "Maister am I þi traytour?" And my swete son seide, "Þou þiself it haste yseide. Arise & goo fulfille þi wille." ' (76 ME 18 — 77 ME 21; my italics)

The AN counterpart to this passage is:

'Et mon douz fitz dist pitousement, "Par vn de vous serray
ieo trahis qi mayn est oue mei en ma table". Et chescun od
grand tristour demanda, "Sire su ieo celi?" Mon douz fitz
dist, "Celi qe touche oue moy en ma esquele est mesme celi".
Iudas dist, "Su ieo vostre trahitour, mestre?" & il respondi &
dist, "Vous mesmes l'auetz dit. Leuetz, parfetes tote vostre
pense." ' (76 AN 9 — 77 AN 4)[6]
('And my sweet son in sorrow said, "I will be betrayed by
one of you whose hand is with mine on the table". And each
one in great distress asked, "Master, am I the one?" My
sweet son said, "The one who reaches with me into my bowl,
he is the one". Judas said, "Am I your traitor, master?" And
he replied and said, "You yourself have said it. Arise and
fulfil your plan." ')

There is a large amount of ME text, that in italics, which is
not represented in the AN. What status does it have? The
unique material is of two types, biblical paraphrase and
commentary. The first, which describes how Peter and John
sought to know the identity of the traitor, is based on John 13.
22–27, and certainly a subjective impression would be that it
does not stand out as an addition; it continues the narrative,
the biblical paraphrase, quite smoothly and contains essential
detail. Without access to the AN text one would not suspect
it to be an addition. The second part, the commentary, the
warning against taking the sacrament in a state of sin, would
be very much out of place in the AN text, at least as it
survives in the two manuscripts *Rl* and *Eg*. Commentary of
this kind simply does not appear in this version of the
sequence, but it appears with some regularity in the ME text.
So the unique ME passage as a whole has an ambiguous
status. One part is characteristic of the AN text and might

---

[6] The phrase *qi mayn est oue mei en ma table* reads 'whose hand is with
mine [or 'with me'] on the table'; *qi* is a common AN form of *cui*. See
Luke 22.21.

therefore be witness to material lost from the surviving AN manuscripts; the other part is uncharacteristic of the AN and more typical of other passages unique to the ME. There is no easy or obvious solution to the question of this passage. Speculation over its status exposes a dilemma which is a central issue in the editorial matter of dealing with a translation.

At the beginning of this paper it was suggested that the editor of a translation might adopt one of two procedures; to reconstruct the translation using all available evidence, or to compromise with the manuscript texts and try to describe the textual history of the material. The current healthy scepticism towards the concept of the critical edition is useful in the present case, both on a practical and a theoretical level. As we have seen, it is possible in some instances to offer explanations for variations and discrepancies between texts, but all such solutions are provisional. The uncertainties which surround so many of the variant readings and unique passages would make the reconstructed text very tentative indeed in all its aspects. Such a text would require perhaps the reconstruction of ME material which we might judge on the basis of the AN text to have been present in the translation; it might involve the elimination of short phrases of scribal addition designed to make the sense more explicit, and larger passages, for example, in this case, of commentary, which on the basis of available evidence would seem to be uncharacteristic of the original. But, where can one draw the lines between translation, the work of the translator, and the work of scribes? Again, we would be involved in tentative judgements over which there could be little secure agreement. The prospect of the task of such a reconstruction is nightmarish. The other procedure, to compromise with the manuscript texts, is not an evasion of editorial responsibility but a healthy recognition of the very fluid nature of medieval texts, and that authors, translators and scribes were frequently one and the same. One might make the suggestion that our modern notions of translator and translation would be foreign to the Middle Ages and that what we call translation was simply one among many forms of textual revision.

Index

Abelard, Peter:
Correspondence with
Heloise, x, 100—122
passim; *Historia
Calamitatum*, 102 n. 4,
110
Abraham Bar Hiyya, 33
Abraham B.' Ezra, 33
Adelard of Bath, 33
Aelred of Rievaulx: *De
Spirituali Amicitia*, 100
Aiol, 27 n. 45
Alberic of Reims, 107
Alfaquin, Abraham, 38
Al Hakan, 29
Alphonse VI of Castile and
Leon, 29
Alphonse X of Castile and
Leon, xi, 32–3, 38–9, 41
Alphonse of Pecha 175:
*Epistola Solitarii ad
Reges*, 176 n. 2
Alvaro d'Oviedo, 38
Amis and Amiloun, 216, 222
Amis e Amilun, 229 n. 25
Anselm, St., 92, 171
Anselm of Laon, 107
Aristotle, 11, 31: *De
Interpretatione*, 10;
Nichomachean Ethics, 143
Auchinleck MS (Advocates
MS 19.2.1, National

Library of Scotland), 152,
161–6, 209–10, 214–16,
222, 228–9
Augustine, St., 1, 13, 90,
171: *De Civitate Dei*, 21;
De Doctrina Christiana, 3
n. 3

Bakhtin, Mikhail 172
Becket, St. Thomas, 59
Bede, 171
Beer, Jeanette, x
Benedict, St.: *Rule* 120–21
Benjamin Minor, x n. 4
Bernard the Arab, 38–9
Bernstein, Basil, 69
Bible, 90: Ephesians, 159;
Judges, 119; Luke, 119;
Matthew, 129
Blütezeit, 6
Boccaccio, Giovanni, 127,
130: *Il Filostrato*, 123–150
passim; *Teseida*, 126, 141
Bödtker, A. T., 232
Boethius, 1, 101–3: *De
Consolatione Philosophiae*,
99–100
Boitani, Piero, 124
Bola, Gruffudd, 55–6
Bonaventura of Siena, 38